Democracy and Custom in Sāmoa

Democracy and Custom in Sāmoa

An uneasy alliance

Asofou So'o

IPS Publications

University of the South Pacific

2008

USP Library Cataloguing-in-Publication Data

So'o, Asofou

Democracy and custom in Samoa : the uneasy alliance / Asofou So'o.
– Suva, Fiji : IPS Publications, The University of the South Pacific, 2008.

    256p. ; 21 cm.

    ISBN 978-982-02-0390-7

1. Samoa – Politics and government 2. Samoans – Politics and government
3. Democracy – Samoa 4. Samoans – Social life and customs I. The University of the
South Pacific. Institute of Pacific Studies Publications II. Title.

JQ6651.A38S66 2008   320.99613

Book design, layout
   and typesetting   Mark Garrett
Book production   Wendy Tubman
Cover design   Stanley Prasad
Printers   Oceania Printers Limited

IPS Publications, University of the South Pacific, Private Bag, Laucala Campus, Suva, Fiji.
Ph: +679 323 2248; Fax +679 323 1524; Email: editorips@usp.ac.fj

Online catalogue and book sales: www.ipsbooks.usp.ac.fj

This book is dedicated to my parents,
the late Le'apai Pua'i'aunofo So'o and Pa'uufilei So'o.

Fa'afetai tele i a oulua galuega lelei.

Contents

Acknowledgements

WITHOUT THE HELP of the following people (some of whom have since passed on) and organizations I would not have been able to complete this book. I would like to thank them sincerely for their help. *Fa'afetai tele lava.*

In Sāmoa, I had the privilege of interviewing some of the former and current members of parliament. Through these interviews, I gained insights into the views of Sāmoan politicians on various issues, including the nature and impact of traditional politics on Sāmoan society. Interviewees included the late Tauialo Lanu Palepoi, 'Ai'ono Dr Fanaafi Le Tagaloa, the late Salā Ulugia Suivai, To'alepai Toesulusulu Si'ueva, Leota Itu'au Ale, Fiamē Nāomi Matā'afa, the late Fuimaono Lotomau, the late Leleisi'uao Palemene, Le Tagaloa Pita, the late Polataivao Fosi, Pule Lameko, the late Sifuiva Sione, and Tupuola Sola Siaosi.

Heads of government departments willingly gave up their time for interviews, as well as providing documents I requested. I would like to thank Galumalemana Nētina Schmidt (then Registrar of the Land and Titles Court), the late Tupa'i Brown (then Director of Broadcasting), Maiava Iulai Toma (then Acting Ombudsman), Mase To'ia 'Ālama (Clerk of the Legislative Assembly), Fonoivasa Lolesio (then Secretary of the Public Service Commission), the late Galuvao Tanielu (then Commissioner of Police), Tuala Donald Kerslake (then Secretary for Justice), the late Māgele Musolini Crawley (then Government Statistician), Samuelu Sesega (then Deputy Director of the Land and Environment Department), Luagalau Fo'isaga Eteuati Shon (then Secretary of Women Affairs), Savea Fōma'i Sāpolu (then Secretary of Internal Affairs) and Levaopolo Tupae Esera (then Director of Education).

Others who provided information through interviews, informal discussions or in other ways included the late Tau'ialo Lanu Palepoi (who provided information on Palauli West constituency, for which he was a former member of parliament), the late Auva'a Faleto'ese (then Secretary of the Methodist Church in Sāmoa), Fata Meafou (Assistant Registrar, Land and Titles Court), Fui Silipa (*ali'i* of Sāvaia village), Isalei Sioa (history lecturer, National University of Sāmoa), the late Le'apai So'o (*tulafale* of Sāvaia village), the late Leatuāvao Fa'alata (*ali'i* of Faleāse'ela village),

Lepou Ropati (*tulafale* of Leulumoega village), Lilomaiava Fou (then a senior police officer), the late Māsinalupe Tautasi (*tulafale* of Sāfa'ato'a village), Moe'ono Penitito (then a senior police officer), Muā'ausa (General Secretary of HRPP), Pālagi Fa'asau (school teacher), Papāli'i Fitisemanu (then a lecturer at the National University of Sāmoa), Pepe Seiuli (senior officer, Office of the Ombudsman), Sifuiva Reupena Muāgututi'a (statistician), Suia Pētana (Congregational Christian Church of Sāmoa Office), the late Tau'ili'ili Uili (former Vice Chancellor of the National University of Sāmoa), the late Togia Siaosi (*ali'i* of Matāutu village), and Ugapō Pusi Urale (former General Secretary of HRPP).

Staff of the Land and Titles Court willingly provided information. I am grateful to the Registrar for allowing me access to department files. I would also like to acknowledge the help given by the staff of the Legislative Assembly of Sāmoa, in particular the library staff.

In American Sāmoa, I held interviews with Asora Misi'aita (then a Member of the House of Representatives), Faua'a (then an officer of the Internal Affairs Department), Leifi Fa'afetai (then a Senator), Te'o Fuavai (former Commissioner of Police and former Member of the House of Representatives) and Tuā'olo Lēmoe (then Adviser to the Governor).

I am greatly indebted to Penelope Meleiseā for her great work in shifting around sections of text of the original manuscript so that it reads more like a book than an academic thesis. You did a great job and thank you so much for all your time and patience. I would also like to thank Wendy Tubman, publications manager of IPS Publications at the University of the South Pacific, for her fine touch to ensure that the final product is of her normal high standards.

Last but not least, I would like to acknowledge the great support of my wife, Ainslie, and my sons Ainsof and Hilton. Without their understanding and patience 15 years ago I would not have been able to lay the foundation for this book.

Introduction

SĀMOA BECAME AN INDEPENDENT state on 1 January 1962 following two distinct periods of its political history: That before European contact in the 1830s, when Sāmoa's affairs were governed by its indigenous socio-political system, and that after the arrival of Europeans. Among the salient features of the country's constitution are provisions for both preserving custom and tradition and realizing democratic ideals. The fact that these two sets of provisions are incorporated into the constitution is of scholarly and practical interest because, despite the seemingly similar nature of the indigenous and democratic systems, most of the practices, values and ideals associated with them differ significantly.

The substantial majority of Sāmoans argued persistently in the 1954 and 1960 constitutional conventions that they wanted a future political structure for Sāmoa based on Sāmoan custom and tradition. In the latter convention, the two general arguments on this issue were that either custom or tradition should be left out of the constitution to ensure they were not adversely affected when it came into effect, or that they should be incorporated in it to ensure they were not abandoned following its enforcement. The final resolution, a compromise, is implicit in the constitution's eventual framework. The compromise was not important; what *was* important was the Sāmoans' determination not to abandon their custom and tradition.

The adoption of the draft constitution, following a plebiscite in 1961, implied that Sāmoans agreed with the incorporation of provisions for a democratic political system. It is doubtful, however, whether or not the majority of the Sāmoans at the 1960 constitutional convention who voted to adopt the constitution fully comprehended the long-term implications of these provisions. The post-independence period demonstrated the practical difficulty of reconciling provisions for both custom and democracy. Incremental changes towards the latter led to the distinct feeling that custom and tradition were being undermined; and the conservative section of the population reacted.

Ironically, this reaction against the realization of democratic ideals was countered by the promotion of democratic means, which saw the birth of the first parliamentary political party and the adoption of universal suffrage – both of which accelerated the realization of democratic ideals, and increasingly begged the question of the 'sister' aim of the constitution, the preservation of custom. The late prime minister, Tofilau 'Eti Alesana, was one of those instrumental in these democratic changes. 'Ai'ono (1992: 1320) wrote that 'changes forced by [Tofilau 'Eti Alesana] would have brought about a series of political coups in another culture and society', noting:

> Internally – at home, as it were – the Sāmoan culture expects Tofilau Eti to mend his ways himself by using the *tōfā fa'amatai* [cultural wisdom inherent in the *matai* system], and to reverse the damage that his ambition and short-sightedness has caused. If that does not happen, the *fa'amatai* [*matai* system] has other ways of redressing injustices and the violations of contracts, *feagaiga*, and the abuse of power and the rights of the Sāmoan heirs (*ibid.*).

Symbolically, the impact of these democratic changes on the *matai* system has been compared with 'the force of the tropical cyclones Ofa [1990] and Val [1991] combined' (*ibid.*).

The adoption of universal suffrage before the 1991 general election was contested in the Supreme Court and politicians spoke out against the establishment of political parties (Le Tagaloa 1991:76–83). Brothers, cousins, members of traditional families and villages, and so forth, have sat on opposite sides of the political divide following the adoption of political parties.

This study examines the extent to which the dual existence of an indigenous institution – broadly known as the *matai* system and centred around a system of chiefly titles – and the legalized democratic political system have affected each other in the period following independence. It seeks to answer such questions as: Has the existence of indigenous institutions hindered or aided the progress of democracy? To what extent has the progress of democracy impacted on indigenous institutions?

Issues of the contradiction between introduced Western and indigenous ideas have been discussed by Powles (1970, 1973, 1979) and Meleiseā (1987a). Powles examined the chiefly system from a legal perspective. As a constitutional lawyer and an advocate of human rights, he saw the persistence of chiefly authority as an impediment to the realization of Western notions of equality and individual rights. He concluded that Western ideas had not necessarily weakened the chiefly system, and argued that reform needed to come about through the establishment of Western-style political parties, which offer the electorate policy choices (1979: 351, 368).

Meleiseā agreed that modern Samoa had only a veneer of democracy. He provided an historical explanation of Sāmoa's dilemma in balancing the conflicts between two systems of legitimizing authority, illustrating his argument with cases brought to the Land and Titles Court in the colonial and post colonial period – and with more recent cases brought before the Supreme Court – that expose these conflicts. He argued that, although Sāmoan custom has changed tremendously since contact with the West, it has maintained its basic structures. The fundamental question, in Meleiseā's opinion, is the extent to which Sāmoan custom is compatible with the basic tenets of modern Western institutions (1987a).

This book re-examines the persistence of the chiefly system, though in the wider context of democratization in the period following independence. It builds upon and extends Powles's and Meleiseā's work, focusing on the working of the legally constituted democratic institutions of the state – among them representative institutions and political processes in general. It analyses the progress of Western values of liberal democracy, and notions of political equality and individual rights. It concludes that, although democratic institutions and practices have had both positive and negative impacts on indigenous institutions and their associated values and practices, democracy in the Western sense is still restricted by the persistence of customary ideals. Nevertheless, there has been significant progress towards the realization of democracy.

The focus of this book is on the citizens of Sāmoa in general (*demos*) rather than on the *matai* system – despite the fact that the predominant system historically controlling Sāmoa's socio-political affairs is the *matai* system. That system is an encompassing system inside which most, if not all, micro aspects of Sāmoan society operate, and under which all socio-political affairs are controlled. Among the ideals espoused in this system are appreciation and encouragement (even enforcement) of collectivist values, recognition of and respect for high-ranking titles, and adherence to traditional procedures and practices. Any change towards the realization of liberal democracy must, therefore, be examined against the existing *matai* system.

The constitution enshrines both democracy and Sāmoan custom – but the framers of the constitution appeared to be limiting its democratic provisions when they decided that only holders of *matai* titles could become candidates and voters in parliamentary elections. This confirmed the power, influence and authority that the *matai* system had had since time immemorial; a desirable outcome from the traditionalists' point of view, because it allowed the rights and traditionally defined roles and privileges associated with each *matai* title to be perpetuated. This system, however, adversely affected the level of political participation among the *demos*. Not only were non-*matai* disenfranchised but also village councils of *matai*, indirectly perpetuated through a number of clauses in the constitution, could use their powers to limit the number of candidates in elections, and to predetermine which ones village voters should support, thereby preventing voters from exercising their freedom to choose the candidates they prefer. The traditional preference for members of parliament to hold titles of high rank, effected by placing barriers to the holders of lower-ranking titles, also limited the realization of democratic principles.

Despite these limiting factors, there has been overall progress towards democracy since independence. Even though the general preference is still for high-ranking titleholders as members of parliament, an increasing number of low-ranking *matai* have not only contested parliamentary seats, but have done so successfully. Despite the general public distaste for political parties, the establishment of the Human Rights Protection Party (HRPP) in early 1979 has been followed by the establishment of other parties. Among other things, the acceptance of political parties as a necessary institution of democracy has helped organize and maintain the majority vote in parliament, thereby ensuring that the concept of majority decision-making prevails over traditional values of consensus. This concept of majority decision-making helps the government of the day govern effectively. Despite some public dislike of universal suffrage, especially among a substantial majority of *matai* and the conservative sectors of society generally, universal suffrage was eventually granted in late 1990. The granting of universal suffrage has greatly increased the level of participation by Sāmoan citizens in the conduct of their political affairs.

The constitutional recognition of substantial elements of indigenous institutions, combined with its provision for progress towards democracy, has resulted in a synthesis of tradition and democracy. Two examples illustrate this point. First, while political parties provide a means of organizing the voting public – in accordance with the political enterprise theory of political parties – in the case of Sāmoa they have been used as a means of soliciting support among families, villages and subdistricts, even though those solicited for political support do not necessarily share the political beliefs of the candidates who are asking for support. Second, even while refusing to grant universal suffrage, some politicians used what they considered to be their traditional rights in order to confer an unusually large number of *matai* titles, solely for the purpose of increasing their chances of winning parliamentary seats. This mixing of traditions has resulted in gradual changes. Some of the traditionally respected practices, ideals and values have been discarded as irrelevant to current political conditions, while others that are seen as more suitable have been adopted. In this way, Sāmoan custom and tradition continue to adapt to new circumstances – as has always been the case.

Democracy has developed over time everywhere it exists; the analysis here is primarily a historical one that aims to understand how that process has unfolded in Sāmoa. It is written from the perspective of an indigenous political scientist. The call for Pacific Islanders to write about their own affairs was made more than three decades ago. Referring to the problems of a European scholar attempting to understand a non-Western culture, Davidson (1966:10 11) wrote:

> He knows, when he is dealing with the history of his own culture, that the way in which men thought or acted is related to a tradition to which he is himself the heir. But when he is concerned with alien cultures this advantage is denied him... however far he may be able to go by applying the tests of logic and fact, the final acceptance or rejection of his conclusions is always against the image of truth in his own mind.

This study adds to the body of Sāmoan perspectives on Sāmoa's past and present.[1] Since the 1960s, a number of scholarly works by Sāmoans have been completed, among them Wendt (1965), Eteuati (1982), Meleiseā (1987a), Liuā'ana (1991,1993, 2001) and Va'ai (1999). These all claimed an insider perspective. For example, Meleiseā, in his analysis of modern political and administrative history, said that he was less concerned about presenting new evidence from primary sources by Europeans than with an attempt to present alternative interpretations or a different emphasis. Writing from an insider perspective can produce fresh insights and contribute to a deeper understanding of the motivations behind events that are not always evident to those without deep familiarity with the cultural settings (see Liuā'ana 1993:ix, Howe 1977:152). However, the differences between insider perspectives and outsider perspectives does not imply that differences do not exist among insider perspectives. Edward Said elaborates this point.

> No one has ever devised a method for detaching the scholar from the circumstances of life, from the fact of his involvement (conscious or unconscious) with a class, a set of beliefs, a social position, or from the mere activity of being a member of a society. These continue to bear on what he does professionally, even though naturally enough his research and its fruits do attempt to reach a level of relative freedom from the inhibitions and the restrictions of brute, everyday reality. For there is such a thing as knowledge that is less, rather than more, partial than the individual (with his entangling and distracting life circumstances) who produces it. (Said 1995:10)

This book represents the views of one Sāmoan, views which have been influenced by his particular family upbringing and its social context, his educational background, and so forth. The writer's starting point was the observation that political parties provided opportunities by which traditions and customs were undermined. This book aims to consider political change from both sides of the change process: Consideration of the impact of political parties on various aspects of the indigenous system is juxtaposed with analysis of how traditional values affect the democratic system.

Most of the data used in this study were collected during fieldwork in Sāmoa and American Sāmoa in the six months between June and November 1993, although some information was gathered in the period between 1989 and 1992, and between 1996 and 2008. The data fall into two main categories. The first includes materials from oral sources, such as informal discussions and formal interviews with members of the public, government employees, and former members of parliament. The second category includes information from written (primary and secondary) sources.

Note

1   In his book, *Sāmoa mo Samoa: The Emergence of the Independent State of Western Sāmoa*, J.W Davidson, one of the two European advisers to Sāmoa's constitu-

tional convention in 1960s, *tried* to write about Sāmoan affairs from a Sāmoan perspective because, at the time, Sāmoan scholars were only beginning to make a noticeable contribution to scholarly work. His aim was to present "the changes in the political structure, thought, and activity of Sāmoa resulting from its contact with the Western world....so far as possible from the point of view of the indigenous people"(1967:ix). Gilson (1970) and Powles (1979), among others, followed Davidson's approach in their studies of Sāmoan affairs.

Map 1. Sāmoa in the South Pacific.

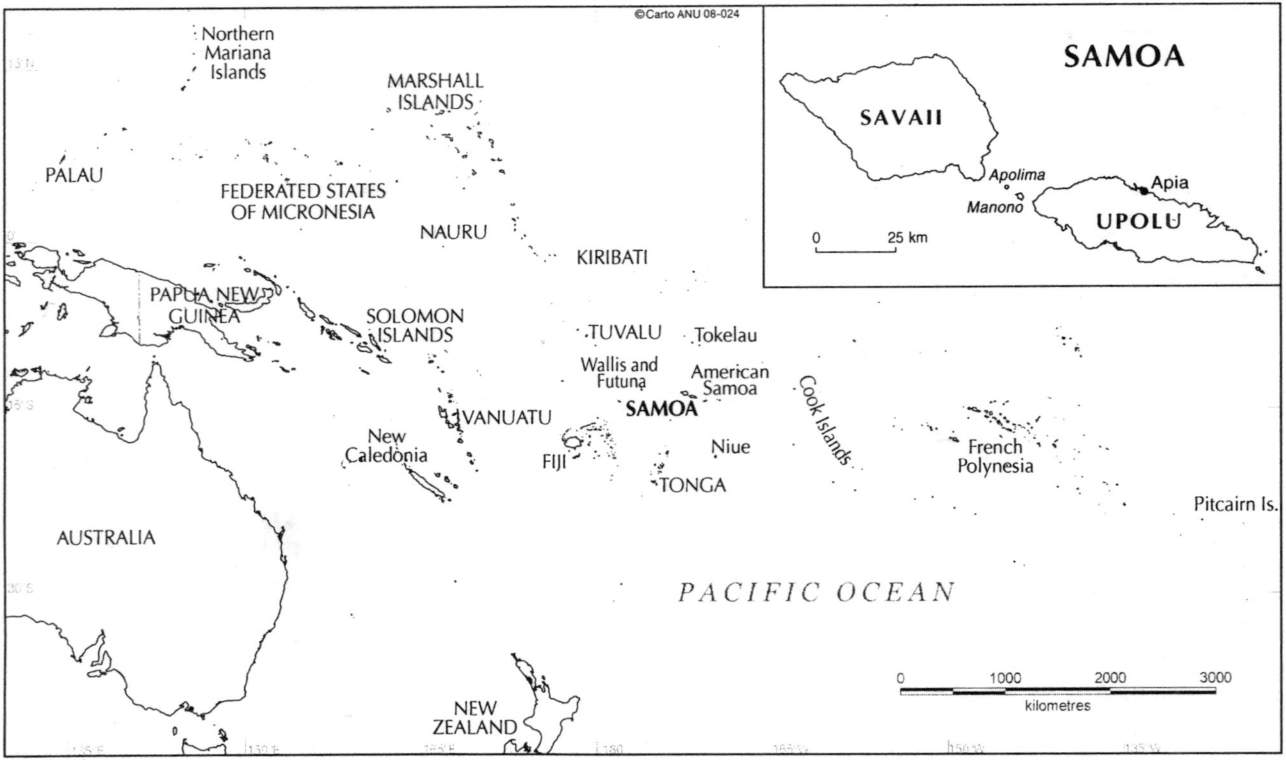

Map 2. Sāmoan traditional districts and parliamentary constituencies.

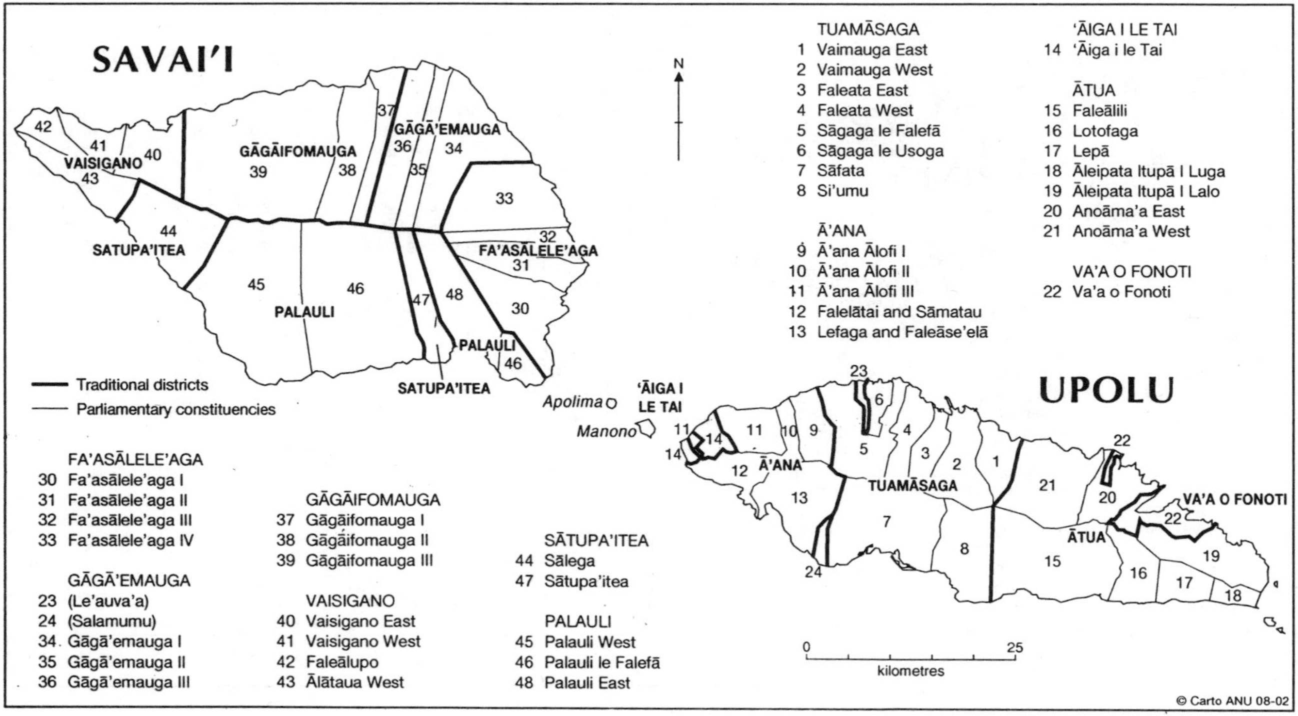
SAVAI'I
UPOLU
N
Traditional districts
Parliamentary constituencies
VAISIGANO
GĀGĀIFOMAUGA
GĀGĀ'EMAUGA
FA'ASĀLELE'AGA
SATUPA'ITEA
PALAULI
Apolima
Manono
'ĀIGA I LE TAI
Ā'ANA
TUAMĀSAGA
ĀTUA
VA'A O FONOTI
0
25
kilometres
TUAMĀSAGA
1 Vaimauga East
2 Vaimauga West
3 Faleata East
4 Faleata West
5 Sāgaga le Falefā
6 Sāgaga le Usoga
7 Sāfata
8 Si'umu
Ā'ANA
9 Ā'ana Ālofi I
10 Ā'ana Ālofi II
11 Ā'ana Ālofi III
12 Falelātai and Sāmatau
13 Lefaga and Faleāse'elā
'ĀIGA I LE TAI
14 'Āiga i le Tai
ĀTUA
15 Faleālili
16 Lotofaga
17 Lepā
18 Āleipata Itupā I Luga
19 Āleipata Itupā I Lalo
20 Anoāma'a East
21 Anoāma'a West
VA'A O FONOTI
22 Va'a o Fonoti
FA'ASĀLELE'AGA
30 Fa'asālele'aga I
31 Fa'asālele'aga II
32 Fa'asālele'aga III
33 Fa'asālele'aga IV
GĀGĀ'EMAUGA
23 (Le'auva'a)
24 (Salamumu)
34 Gāgā'emauga I
35 Gāgā'emauga II
36 Gāgā'emauga III
GĀGĀIFOMAUGA
37 Gāgāifomauga I
38 Gāgāifomauga II
39 Gāgāifomauga III
VAISIGANO
40 Vaisigano East
41 Vaisigano West
42 Faleālupo
43 Ālātaua West
SĀTUPA'ITEA
44 Sālega
47 Sātupa'itea
PALAULI
45 Palauli West
46 Palauli le Falefā
48 Palauli East
© Carto ANU 08-02

Map 3. Sāmoan villages.

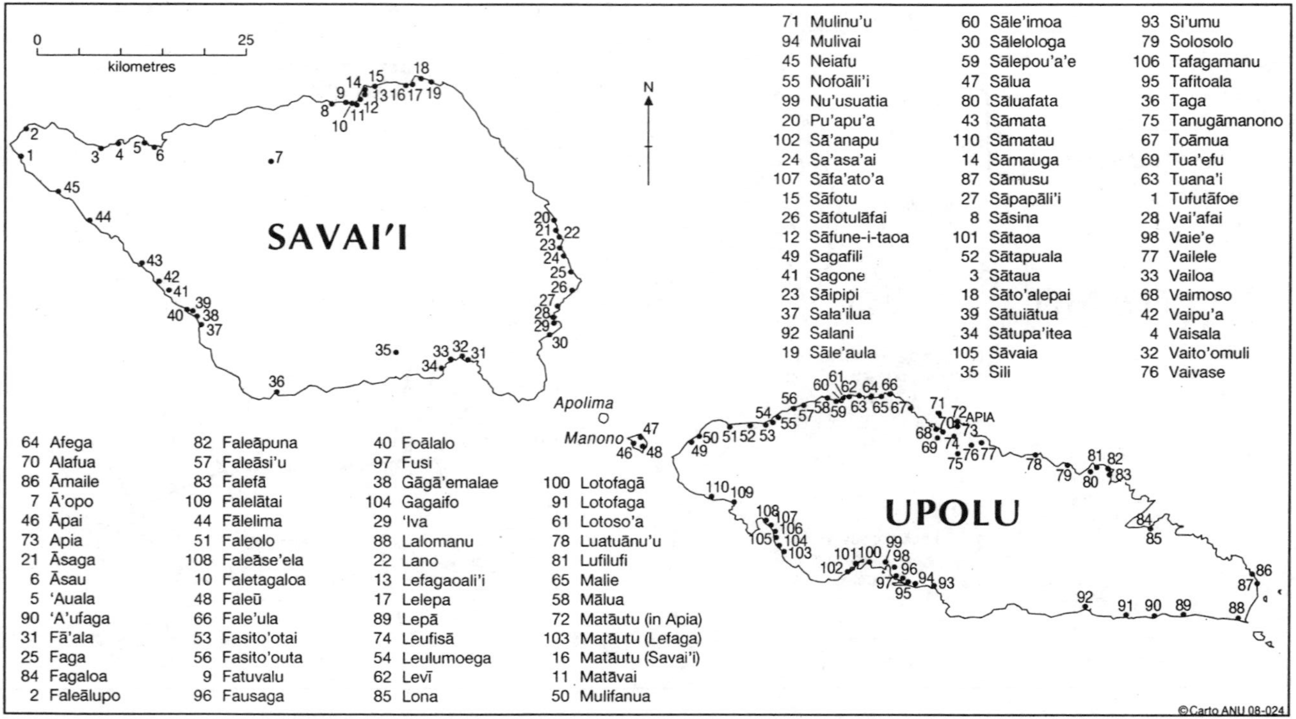

1 | Indigenous institutions

SĀMOA'S LONG HISTORY – remembered through oral traditions, which are now mainly recorded in writing – explains how the indigenous system of governance emerged and developed. This chapter sets out the way in which indigenous political institutions are perceived by Sāmoans, and describes the basis of Sāmoa's socio-political system until the time of contact with the non-Polynesian world, which commenced in the late 18th century. While some scholars[1] may argue that the system has changed greatly since the early 19th century, this is not the way that most Sāmoans see it. The *matai* system is believed to have been established since time immemorial, and to have been maintained and perpetuated as it was established, in a fixed order. For this reason, democratic innovations influenced by European contact and following independence were often not readily accepted by a substantial majority of the population.

Even European ideas and political influence have changed during the two centuries of Sāmoa's post-contact history: Hierarchical institutions prevailed throughout most of Europe's history – only in the 18th century did liberalist rejection of those institutions and values begin.

This chapter provides an historical and cultural reference point for subsequent chapters, which discuss the accommodation and rejection of democratic practices and institutions in the post-independence period. It traces the origin and development of Sāmoan indigenous institutions, and the practices and values associated with them in the period before European contact. The historical approach used in this chapter, and implicit in the whole book, is important because identifying the approximate centuries (based on genealogical calculations) in which events took place, and during which certain traditions and customs were established, shows the depth of time associated with them, and why Sāmoans attach such importance to their political traditions and customs, and gives some idea of the extent of change over time.

Major political divisions and paramount titles

The origins of indigenous institutions are associated with certain paramount titles and political centres, the origins of which can, in turn, be traced to the ancient gods.[2] Political centres developed in association with titles, or became associated with them.[3] Thus, the legendary political divisions of the island of Upolu are linked to Upolu's paramount titles and traditional political districts. One oral tradition relates that people from Fiji named the islands Upolu, Savai'i, Manono and Apolima (Turner 1884:222–23)[4] – suggesting that the Sāmoan islands were first settled by people from modern-day Fiji. Another, more widely accepted, version traces the political divisions of Upolu to Pili, a son of the god Tagaloa-a-lagi[5] (Meleiseā and Meleiseā 1987:29–30). Tagaloa-a-lagi is believed to have entered the Sāmoan islands (and Tonga) from the east, that is, from Manu'a Island (Meleiseā 1987b:11). Pili had three sons, after whom the political divisions of Upolu are named. Tua founded the political district of Ātua (that of Tua), which comprised the eastern third of Upolu. 'Ana founded Ā'ana ('of Ana'), a political district on the western third of the island. The third son was Saga. Because he was born after the twins, Tua and 'Ana, the district he founded was called Tuamāsaga ('after the twin'). This was the geographical region between Ātua and Ā'ana districts. Since then, the three political districts on Upolu island have been called Ātua, Ā'ana and Tuamāsaga (Meleiseā and Meleiseā 1987:29–30, Henry 1980:34–5, Kramer 1994: 26–3, Tupua 1995:3).

The paramount titles of Ātua and Ā'ana districts are prefixed Tui followed by the name of the district, thus, Tui Ātua and Tui Ā'ana for Ātua and Ā'ana districts respectively.[6] The original holders of these titles are traced to the god Tagaloa-a-lagi (Ella 1895:599; Kramer 1994:24).[7] From oral traditions, these titles appear to be among the oldest in Sāmoa. The first Tui Ātua, who was regarded as both *aitu* (god-like) and *tagata* (human-like), was Leutelele'i'ite[8] (Gurr papers).[9] He lived around 1170 AD. It is from his lifetime that the known pre-European history of Sāmoa associated with the Tui Ātua title and its holders began.[10]

The Mālietoa title was conferred for the first time upon Sāvea, who lived in approximately the 12th century.[11] The manner in which the Mālietoa title was first acquired is unclear and remains a matter for further research. For the purpose of this study, however, it is sufficient to know the approximate date it was established. Following its establishment, and for reasons such as intermarriage, the Mālietoa title became the paramount title of Tuamāsaga district. Descendants of various past holders of this title founded a number of villages in Tuamāsaga district. Others either founded or became members of existing villages – such as, Sāfotulāfai and Samalae'ulu – in districts outside Tuamāsaga.

Unlike the island of Upolu, where traditional divisions can be traced to one generally acknowledged tradition and associated legends, the political divisions on the island of Savai'i are attributed to several traditions, though generally in relation to certain prominent titles. The Le Tagaloa title is believed to have been first acquired in the 10th century by a man named Fune.[12] Fune is reputed to have been a great warrior who had established his court in a number of villages on the island of Savai'i, and was feared throughout the islands of the Sāmoa group. As such he earned the nickname Funefe'ai (literally, Fune the savage) (Kramer 1994:115; Henry 1980:30). Groups of *tulafale* (orator *matai*) associated with this title are known collectively as Sa Fune (the family of Fune).[13]

The Tonumaipe'a title[14] is said in a number of oral traditions to have been acquired through the connections between some Sāmoan families and the Tui Tonga, the paramount title of the Tongan group. The title was established in approximately the 12th century. The descendants of this title later became important in the history of Sāmoa (Lāfai 1988:25-35).

The Lilomaiava title is another ancient title of Savai'i; it was established in approximately the 15th century.[15]

Even though these three titles were established in Savai'i independently of any Upolu influence, they have over the years become closely associated with the Upolu titles by intermarriage and historical alliances.[16] Thus, when, in the 19th century, foreign settlers in Sāmoa pushed for the establishment of a monarchy as the basis of a newly created Sāmoan central government, the people of Savai'i supported one or other of the three Upolu titles – Mālietoa, Tui Ātua and Tui Ā'ana – for the position of king.

In pre-Christian times, Sāmoan aristocrats had a semi-divine status. Only the children of men and women of the highest rank were acknowledged as aristocrats and all were ancestrally connected to the gods. In several cases, titles were held by a single aristocratic individual; for example both the Tomumaipe'a and the Mālietoa titles and others were held by Talavou in the mid-19th century. All the *ali'i* (one of the two classes of *matai*) titles of Sāmoa can trace their descent to at least one of these Upolu and Savai'i titles, the origins of which can, in turn, be traced to divine ancestors (Meleiseā 1995: 19–35; 1987:8–9).

The *pāpā* titles

The paramount titles of Upolu and Savai'i are referred to as *ao* (head) titles of their respective political districts. Possibly because of the ceremony and pomp that is associated with the bestowal of these titles, they are also referred to as *pāpā* titles. Only four *pāpā* titles became important in the 19th century and the period thereafter and are remembered today. The importance of these four *pāpā* titles is associated with an aristocratic lineage originating in approximately the 16th century. The titles were conferred on Salamāsina, a female descendant of the Tui Tonga, the paramount title in Tonga. The political events that culminated in Salamāsina holding these *pāpā* titles legitimized the traditional authority of the political centres that continue to be directly involved in these events to the present day.

A series of wars in Upolu culminated in the Tonumaipe'a family acquiring four *pāpā* titles by the early 1500s.[17] The wars erupted following a series of disputes involving people associated with these titles. Because of the Tonumaipe'a family's assistance in these wars, the parties they sided with were victorious. In reward for their help, the Tonumaipe'a family returned to Savai'i with the titles. Two of the *pāpā* were the Tui Ātua and Tui Ā'ana titles. The other two were named after Salamāsina's grandmother, Vaetamasoāli'i (shortened to Vaetamasoa or Tamasoali'i), and Vaetamasoāli'i's aunt, Gato'aitele.

The Tui Ātua and Tui Ā'ana were by this time established paramount titles, but the titles Gato'aitele and Vaetamasoāli'i were created close to the time that they were conferred on Salamāsina. Vaetamasoāli'i and Gato'aitele were direct descendants of Mālietoa La'auli, who lived in approximately the 15th century. Mālietoa La'auli's two daughters were Gato'aitele and Gāsoloaiaoolelagi. Gato'aitele was barren, while Gāsoloaiaoolelagi bore three children (Henry 1980:62). One of her children was Vaetamasoāli'i. A dispute arising from the issue of a successor to the Mālietoa title, following the death of La'auli, resulted in an outbreak of violence in which the people who supported La'auli's children as successor to the title won. Following this event, the Gato'aitele name was elevated as a *pāpā* title and was taken to Savai'i by the Tonumaipe'a family.

Vaetamasoāli'i stayed at Sāfata, the place where her father, Manu'alesānalala, lived. A dispute had arisen between the people associated with Vaetamasoa's father and the nearby settlement of Vailu'u (which forms part of present day Lefaga, a subdistrict of Ā'ana district). The Vailu'u people had rejected the Sāfata people's pretence to superior authority, and this struggle culminated in the latter's defeat.[18] The Tonumaipe'a family came to the aid of Vaetamasoāli'i's supporters, as Vaetamasoāli'i's sister was then the wife of the incumbent holder of the Tonumaipe'a title. In reward for their assistance in the victory of the Sāfata people against Vailu'u, the Tonumaipe'a family returned to Savai'i with the name Vaetamasoāli'i as a newly created *pāpā* title. It is notable that the Gato'aitele and Vaetamasoāli'i *pāpā* were names of women; they are thus referred to as *pāpā fafine* (female *pāpā*), thereby differentiating them from the Tui Ātua and Tui Ā'ana *pāpā*. Moreover, they are closely associated with the Mālietoa title.

Although the Tui Ātua and Tui Ā'ana titles, in particular, seem to have been held by Salamāsina's descendants continuously to the present, in several generations the direct heirs disputed the right of succession. When the *pāpā* titles become vacant, each '*āiga* (network of families and kin) of the potential successors rallied in support of their preferred candidates to hold the *pāpā* titles. The term '*āiga*, as is the case of the English equivalent 'family', may refer to many levels of kinship, including all those descended from a common ancestor. Some '*āiga*, as will be shown, are represented by groups of important titles, all originating from the same ancestral lineage.

Each male holder and a few female holders of *pāpā* titles had many children by a succession of different spouses. Spouses from aristocratic families, with whole districts at their back, had considerable power to assert the claims of their children to succeed their father. Thus succession to paramount titles involved large-scale contests between allied districts through their kinship networks and senior and paramount titles. These alliances might be considered the traditional equivalent of modern-day political parties, in the sense that they had a degree of solidarity to pursue certain goals collectively, especially succession to the *pāpā* titles. These '*āiga* alliances exist to the present day and still influence Sāmoan political thinking and traditional attitudes to politics. All '*āiga* and their *matai* titles are historically connected to one or more of the maximal lineages associated with important titles and famous historical figures.

'Āiga Sa Levālasi

The 'Āiga Sa Levālasi (the family of Levālasi) is traced to Levālasi, who lived in approximately the 15th century.[19] Levālasi, also known as So'oa'emalelagi, was the first cousin of Tama-a-le-lagi, Salamāsina's father. Salamāsina's mother, Vaetōifaga, returned to her home in Tonga after Salamāsina's birth, and Levālasi brought her up (Henry 1980:101). Levālasi was one of the three children of the incumbent holder of the Tonumaipe'a title, who had possession of the four *pāpā*. Because of Levālasi's ancestry and rank, the Tonumaipe'a family wanted to confer the titles upon her, but Levālasi preferred that the titles be conferred on her adopted daughter, Salamāsina (Lāfai 1988:178, Henry 1980:103). Levālasi moved to Ā'ana to reside with her first cousin, Tama-a-le-lagi. She had been married to her other first cousin, Māta'utia, who at the time was the holder of the Tui Ātua title (Tupua 1995:5), but he was murdered by some Ātua rivals, also closely associated with the Tui Ātua title. Levālasi moved to Ā'ana where she could be with Salamāsina. Before she left Ātua, the Ātua relations of her murdered husband's family named their family after her (Henry 1980:94).[20]

'Āiga Sa Tuala

The 'Āiga Sa Tuala (family of Tuala) originated from Tuala who lived in approximately the 16th century; he was the eldest son of Tama-a-le-lagi and a half-brother of Salamāsina (Submission by Sa Tuala, LC 8384).[21] Although Tuala's descendants had been prominent in Sāmoan affairs, a war in the 17th century enhanced the political status of the descendants of Tuala. The conflict was the result of a dispute over succession to the titles held by Faumuinā, who held both the Tui Ā'ana and Tui Ātua titles. Faumuinā had two sons, Va'afusu'aga and Fonotī, and a daughter, Samalā'ulu, by different high-ranking mothers. Samalā'ulu favoured her younger brother Va'afusu'aga, but no agreement could be reached between the heirs and war ensued, with the maternal families and alliances of each of the children lending their support to the child of their own 'girl'. Fonotī and his supporters were victorious, and the supporters of

Va'afusu'aga and Samalae'ulu were defeated. Thereafter, Fonotī succeeded to both titles (Tupua 1995:6, Henry 1980:126–30, Kramer 1994:264–9). One of Fonotī's wives was Fuatino, a direct descendant of Tuala. Their son was Muāgututi'a, who succeeded Fonotī to both titles. Muāgututi'a was succeeded by his adopted son, Fuiāvailili, who was later known by the name Tupua.[22] Muāgututi'a, created the Sa Tuala as his lineal family. As an *'āiga*, Sa Tuala thereafter became associated with the Tupua title, the name of Muāgututi'a's adopted son, who succeeded to the Tui Ātua and Tui Ā'ana *pāpā*. In recognition of their status and historical right, Sa Tuala must be consulted on all issues associated with the conferral of the Tupua title.[23] 'Ai'ono, another direct descendant of Tuala, probably because of his bravery and vital contribution to ending the war in Fonotī's favour, was designated the spokesperson of Sa Tuala in all matters to do with the Tupua title. Taimālieutu was given the responsibility of summoning all members of Sa Tuala when a meeting of the family was required.[24] These traditions and their associated customs are recognized to this day.

'Āiga Sa Fenunu'ivao

The origin of the 'Āiga Sa Fenunu'ivao (family of Fenunu'ivao) is traced to Tupua Fuiāvailili who lived in approximately the early 18th century.[25] His adopted mother was Fenunu'ivao, who gave her name to the *'āiga*. Muagututi'a, son of Fonotī, married Fenunu'ivao, a daughter of Leutele of Falefā. Because they had no children of their own, they adopted Fuiāvailili as their son. Fuiāvailili's biological father was Fuimaono, a direct descendant of Salamāsina's son Tapumanaia, who was also known by the name Tapufautua (Tupua 1995:7). Tupua Fuiāvailili, through his ancestry and adoption, re-united the Salamāsina lineage through his ancestor, Tapumānaia (the Fuimaono line) and Muāgututi'a's ancestor, Salamāsina's daughter, Fofoaivao'ese (Muāgututi'a line).[26] Henceforth, the 'Āiga Sa Fenunu'ivao was responsible for appointing holders of the Tupua title, after having consulted 'Āiga Sa Tuala.[27] 'Āiga Sa Fenunu'ivao includes Talo and Tofoiofo'ia (the high-ranking *tulafale* of Faleālili), and Moe'ono and 'Iuli (high-ranking *tulafale* of Falefā village and genealogically related to Leutele and the other *ali'i*, Leala'isalanoa) who are the spokespeople of the Sa Fenunu'ivao family not only on all matters concerning the Tupua title, but also on matters concerning other *'āiga*, such as Sa Tuala and Sa Levālasi. Moreover, they are members of Ātua's great council which met at Lalogāfu'afu'a, the meeting place of Ātua district in Lufilufi village. Leutele is greeted *O le tinā o Tupua* (the mother of Tupua). Leala'isalanoa is greeted *O le tei o Tupua* (the brother of Tupua). Fuimaono is greeted *Ole gafa tasi* (literally, of the same genealogy – both Fuimaono and Muāgututi'a's wife, Fenunu'ivao, descended from the Leutele title of Falefā. Moreover, Fuimaono had close genealogical connections to both the Tui Ātua and Tui Ā'ana titles).

'Āiga Sa Tunumafono

The 'Āiga Sa Tunumafono (family of Tunumafono) is traced to the four sons of Tunumafono. Tunumafono had a sister named Fe'eonu'u. Fe'eonu'u married Va'afusu'aga, the brother of Fonotī and Samalaeulu', and gave birth to Tole'afoa. Tole'afoa took over the leadership of his father's supporters in the same war in which, as previously discussed, Fonotī emerged victorious (Tupua 1995:6). Tunumafono's sons and all their allies supported their father's sister's son, Tole'afoa, according to the traditional obligation of *feagaiga*.[28]

'Āiga Taulagi

The 'Āiga Taulagi originates with other descendants of the same Va'afusu'aga who fought his brother, Fonotī for the right to succeed to the titles formerly held by their father. 'Āiga Taulagi literally means 'the *āiga* whose many plans to attack their enemies during this war were never carried out' (Leala'i'auloto and Fuataga 1985:51). 'Āiga Sa Tunumafono and 'Āiga Taulagi were to be very important in the 19th century because of their support for Tuimaleali'ifano Sualauvi (a descendant of both these *āiga*), not only as their kingship candidate, but because he held the Tui Ā'ana and Vaetamasoāli'i *pāpā*.[29]

The *Tafa'ifā*

The *Tafa'ifā* is an institution which is usually referred to as 'four-in-one' in reference to the four *pāpā*, which, when held by one person, make that person the *Tafa'ifā* (see, for example, Stair 1897:81). However, the *Tafa'ifā* literally takes its name from the fact that each of the four *pāpā* had associated with it two *tafa'i*. This is the name given to the two *matai* who sit on either side of the *pāpā* holder during the ceremony at which the *pāpā* is conferred. *Tafa'ifā* literally means the four *tafa'i*, referring to four pairs of *tafa'i*. There are certain *matai* titles which carry with them the right to be the *tafa'i* for each *pāpā*. For the Vaetamasoāli'i *pāpā*, the *tafa'i* are Fuga and Mau'ava; for Gato'aitele, Fata and Maulolo; for the Tui Ātua, Tupa'i and Ta'inau; and for the Tui Ā'ana, Umaga and Pāsēsē. These traditions have been maintained to the present (Henry 1980:102–4). This tradition honours the legendary return of these *pāpā* to the political centres to which they originally belonged.

Having agreed to Levālasi's wish that the four *pāpā* be conferred upon Salamāsina, the Tonumaipe'a family returned the *pāpā* to the *fale'upolu* of their respective political centres. Each centre in turn conferred their *pāpā* on Salamāsina.[30] Thereafter, the order in which the *pāpā* were conferred was maintained. The Tui Ā'ana was conferred first, followed by the other two *pāpā*, and the conferral concluded with the Tui Ātua (Stair 1897: 79–81, Tupua 1995:4, 10). In the 19th century the preferred candidates for succession to *pāpā*, and rivals for the *Tafa'ifā*, came to be known as *O tama-a-'āiga* (sons of the families), originally referring to rival claimants in the Mālietoa and Tupua lineages to the *pāpā*, and in the right to become king of Sāmoa under a new central government.

There are several points to note about the institutions of *pāpā* and the *Tafa'ifā*. First, when the incumbent *pāpā* holder passes away, the *fale'upolu* who confers the *pāpā* has the right to decide who the next holder should be, a right that may at times bring them into conflict with the *'āiga*, although normally only the descendants of previous *pāpā* holders are considered ('Ai'ono 1992:120). In pre-Christian times, only a select few had the appropriately divine ancestry and associated qualities to be considered. The nature of the political relationship between the *fale'upolu* and the *pāpā* holder would be a factor in issues of succession. Only the descendants of past titleholders (and, in pre-Christian Sāmoa, only the children of their spouses of high rank) are eligible to have bestowed upon them the *pāpā*. The line of descent narrows over time so that only a particular branch inherits the title, leaving the other sub-branches (the *'āiga*, previously discussed) with only the right to be consulted should a new holder be elected.

The relationship between the *Tafa'ifā* and the people associated with the holder, differs from that between a king and his subjects as in pre-constitutional European monarchies, where all authority is derived from the power residing in the monarch. As with the holders of individual *pāpā*, the *Tafaʻifā* has no independent power: He *had* supernatural power attributed to these titles in pre-Christian times (Meleiseā 1995) but the political authority of the title was and still is collectively shared with the *faleʻupolu* who confer the *pāpā*.[31] A *Tafaʻifā* holder, and the institution of the *Tafaʻifā* in general, become the central point around which all the people associated with the *pāpā* titles unite. The congregation of interests and alliance of polities around this central point is the closest political framework Sāmoa had to that of a central government as it is understood in the modern sense.

Political organization and institutions

Tūmua and *Pule*

The various political centres of Sāmoa were associated with paramount titles, or became associated with them. The political centres in Upolu are identified with *Tūmua*, an institution that explains the political significance and the collective authority of the two classes of *matai* – *tulafale* and *aliʻi* (see Appendix 5). The two original *Tūmua* were Lufilufi in Ātua and Leulumoega in Āʻana.[32] The names Lufilufi and Leulumoega were names of places in their respective districts the origins of which can also be traced to certain traditions. *Tūmua* specifically refers to groups of *tulafale*, also referred to as *faleʻupolu*, who represented allied polities in the district, and who met in those places. *Tūmua* derived their importance from their association with the paramount titles of their respective districts, which gave them administrative power (discussed later).

As mentioned, the Tui Ātua and Tui Āʻana were the paramount titles of Ātua and Āʻana districts respectively, and their original holders were traced to the god Tagaloa-a-lagi (Ella 1895:599; Kramer 1994:24): Western Polynesians associated with the god Tagaloa-a-lagi seem to have settled Sāmoa from the east. *Tūmua*, on the other hand, implies founders, or people who were already occupying the Sāmoan islands. One oral tradition holds that the founders of the *Tūmua* centres arrived in Sāmoa from the *west*, from Pulotu or modern-day Fiji (Lāfai 1988:249, Anon. nd:4–5).

The word *fale* (house) has similar metaphorical usage in Sāmoan as in English, and can connote a lineage, clan or dynasty. The term is also used to refer symbolically to the relationship between *aliʻi* and *tulafale*. The *Tūmua* (because its leaders and members were *tulafale*) symbolizes the 'foundation' and the 'top beam' of the house. The parts of the house between the top beam and the foundation symbolize the *ali'i*. The Tui Ātua and Tui Ā'ana are the highest-ranking *ali'i* of their districts. Complete political authority therefore requires the presence of both paramount titles and the districts' respective *Tūmua*. In other words, neither *ali'i* nor *tulafale* alone have supreme authority (Gilson 1970:234). This political phenomenon permeates all aspects of Sāmoa's political system, and is also seen in the workings of village governments.

A similar institution – termed *Pule* – existed in Savai'i. Like the *Tūmua* in Upolu, *Pule* identifies the political centres of Savai'i, although not all of these centres acquired this traditional designation at the same time. The traditional designation of *Pule* gives certain political centres the legitimacy (or traditional right) to take the leading role in the conduct of Savai'i's socio-political affairs.

The legendary origin of *Pule* is traced to the brothers Letufuga and Le'aula, who lived in approximately the 12th century (Anon. nd:17). They were fifth generation descendants of Lealali, who lived at the same time as Fune who acquired the Le Tagaloa title. Like Fune, Letufuga during his time seems to have been a respected man with great influence and fighting prowess – if not throughout Sāmoa, at least on Savai'i. Part of his influence might have been related to the fact that he married a daughter of the Tui Ā'ana (Anon. nd:8).

The 'legitimacy' of Letufuga's and his brother's authority seems to have been associated with the first holder of the Mālietoa title, and perhaps with the establishment of a new political order at that time. It seems likely that they helped out in the events that culminated in the conferring of the Mālietoa title upon its first holder. Oral traditions tell of the two men going to the original holder of the Mālietoa title and asking for a share in the administration of his government. After much counselling from one of his main supporters, the holder of the Mālietoa title granted the two men the privilege, which their descendants still cherish to this day (Anon. nd:17). Letufuga and his brother, Le'aula, respectively, founded the villages of Sāfotulāfai, named after their father, and Sāle'aula, after Le'aula, and meaning 'the family of Le'aula' (Kramer 1994:110). These two villages have since been referred to as the original *Pule* on Savai'i. The political affairs of Savai'i were discussed and organized around the authorities vested, by tradition, in the *Pule* centres (Eteuati 1982:23). Sāfotulāfai and Sāle'aula are the political centres, or capital villages, of Fa'asālele'aga and Gāgā'emauga districts, respectively.[33] The rival political centres on Savai'i, which did not have the same status, contested that right for years (Eteuati 1982:23).

Each of the political centres in Savai'i was associated with paramount titles. The Le Tagaloa title was associated with four political centres; Vaisala (on the north-western end of the island), Sāfune-i-taoa (on the mid-northern coast of the island), Vai'afai (on the eastern coast of the island) and Sili (on the south-eastern side of the island). Collectively, the political centres of Le Tagaloa were, and still are, known as Sāfune. They were incorporated into the political districts established later.

Political centres associated with the Tonumaipe'a title were later established at Sātupa'itea (on the south-eastern side of the island) and Āsau (on the north-western side of the island). Sātupa'itea and Āsau became the capital villages of Sālega and Vaisigano political districts, respectively. Vaisigano district incorporated the Sāfune political centre of Vaisala. Two of the political centres that developed in association with the Lilomaiava titles were Vailoa (on the south-eastern side of the island) and Sāfotu (on the mid-northern coast of the island). The third political centre associated with the Lilomaiava title was on Upolu island and had been incorporated into Ā'ana district. Vailoa and Sāfotu became the political centres of Palauli and Gagaifomauga districts, respectively. Palauli and Gagaifomauga incorporated the Sāfune centres of Sili and Sāfune-i-taoa, respectively.[34] These four political centres (Sātupa'itea, Āsau, Vailoa and Sāfotu) acquired *Pule* status at different times in the 19th century. With the original *Pule* centres of Sāfotulāfai and Sāle'aula, they became the six *Pule* centres in Savai'i, the capital villages of their respective districts (Leala'i'auloto and Fuataga 1985).

Although the original *fale'upolu* on the island of Upolu were the *Tūmua* of Leulumoega and Lufilufi, new *Tūmua* centres, Malie and Afega, developed long ago on Upolu. As *Tūmua*, Malie and Afega are alternatively known by their *fale'upolu* names of 'Auimatagi and Tuisāmau, repectively. Hence, when Sāmoans refer to the four *Tūmua*, they mean Lufilufi in Ātua, Leulumoega in Ā'ana, 'Auimatagi in Malie, and Tuisāmau in Afega (Tupua 1994:73).

Malie gained the distinction as a *Tūmua* because it was the original seat of the Mālietoa title (Henry 1980:45), and its *tulafale* confers the Mālietoa title in Upolu.[35] The war in the 1440s that culminated in the establishment of the Gato'aitele name as a *pāpā* title established Afega village as one of the political centres of Upolu. Afega sided with the descendants of Mālietoa La'auli against neighboring Malie village, which supported a rival, Mālietoa La'auli's adopted son, Falefatu (Tupua 1994:73). Sometime later, Afega village also adopted the *Tūmua* designation, not only to distinguish itself from the political centres on Savai'i, but also to equate itself with the original *Tūmua*, Leulumoega and Lufilufi.

Other political districts of Upolu

Other political districts of importance in Upolu are Sāfata and Faleata; they are associated with the initial establishment of the Mālietoa title. Sāvea, the original holder of the Mālietoa title, had two brothers whose names were Tuna and Fata. They founded Faleata and Sāfata districts, respectively (Henry 1980:45-6). However, because of intermarriages and alliances, these districts became closely identified with the wider Tuamāsaga district, which, as discussed previously, was founded in distant, legendary times. Malie and Afega were its political centres when issues associated with the Mālietoa title were discussed.

Two other important districts, 'Āiga-i-le-Tai and Va'a-o-Fonotī, have different historical origins, and maintain their independent political status to this day. Va'a-o-Fonotī literally means the boat of Fonotī. This is the same Fonotī who emerged victorious in the war of succession against the combined forces of his brother, Va'afusu'aga, and sister, Samalā'ulu. The Va'a-o-Fonotī district comprises the village of Faleāpuna and the sub-district of Fagaloa, all situated in the northern region of Ātua district. People in these places not only sided with Fonotī but their fleets also contributed greatly to Fonotī's victory. In reward, Fonotī designated them an independent political district in its own right (Tupua 1995:6).

'Āiga-i-le-Tai district comprises the villages on the small islands of Manono and Apolima, which lie in the straits between Upolu and Savai'i, and their associated villages along the north-western tip of Ā'ana district; they also sided with Va'afusu'aga and Samalā'ulu against Fonotī in the same war (Tupua 1995:6). Probably in an effort to reconcile old differences, Fonotī designated these villages an independent political district in its own right – thus the political district 'Āiga-i-le-Tai, literally family on the seaward side (Lāfai 1988:187).

The five political districts in Upolu and six *Pule* centres of Savai'i to-

gether comprise the eleven traditional political districts of Sāmoa. The incremental subdivisions of these political districts in the period following
European contact resulted in the 41 electoral constituencies Sāmoa had by
the time of independence.[36]

Political districts, capital villages and pāpā titles

Sāmoan political districts are based on *faigāmālō* and *itūmālō*. *Faigāmālō*
refers to a political arrangement in which two or more villages agree to a
limited form of unity for the common purposes of protection and mutual
assistance. An *itūmālō* (which, in modern Sāmoan translation, also refers
to a district government) is a political arrangement in which two or more
faigāmālō have agreed to be united under one paramount title as the ceremonial head of their united government (Ma'ilo 1972:21). Under such
arrangement, the capital village, the seat of the title that is paramount in
the district, becomes a coordinating centre for all activities in which all
the villages comprising a political district are involved. In Ātua, the capital
village is Lufilufi. Lufilufi comprises six *tulafale*, and they confer the Tui
Ātua title and summon what can be called the 'parliament' of Ātua district
to ascertain its members' views on a prospective holder of their *pāpā* when
the title is vacant. The 'parliament' of Ātua comprises the six *tulafale* of
Lufilufi and 13 other *matai* of Ātua. Of those 13 *matai*, nine are *tulafale*
and four are *ali'i*. The members of Ātua's 'parliament' form an exclusive
group (Tupua 1992:11). Not every *matai* in Ātua can sit in it. As such, the
rest of the *matai*, let alone non-*matai*, cannot participate equally in the
selection of a *pāpā* titleholder, nor can they compete to be members of that
parliament. The reasons why only certain *matai* have the rights to be in
Ātua's parliament have been determined by various traditions, and are not
of immediate interest to this study. Once the right to be in this parliament
is established, it becomes hereditary, and it is jealously guarded.

The functions of a capital village vis-à-vis the other villages and subdistricts comprising a district are illustrated by the roles of Malie and Afega
villages in relation to the affairs of Tuamāsaga district.[37] This shows how
traditional politics work at this level. Tuamāsaga has some unique varia-
tions reflecting the various *faigāmālō* that comprise it. The initiative to hold
a Tuamāsaga district meeting can originate from either the villages comprising the district (the periphery) or from Malie and Afega (the centre).
In the former case, either Malie or Afega has to be notified first, although

certain villages go to Malie and others to Afega for reasons to be explained later. Regardless of whether Malie or Afega is notified, these two villages will then consult each other before sending out messengers to the villages on the periphery. Malie and Afega do the same if a meeting is initiated by them.

Thus, Afega sends out a messenger to X in Faleata subdistrict. Having received the message from Afega, X then performs two duties; first, he relays the message to Y in Sāfata sub district; second, he relays the message to certain people in the villages comprising Faleata subdistrict. In turn, Y relays the message to certain people in certain villages in Sāfata subdistrict. In this way the message from the centre is sure to get to the end of the communication line. The members of Tuamāsaga's 'parliament' then meet at Afega – if the agenda item is to prepare for war – or at Malie – if it is a meeting in time of peace. (Kramer 1994:287, Gilson 1970:54). Malie, on the other hand, would notify a number of villages known collectively as Faleono-o-Leatigana.

Two traditions established the basis of Malie's responsibilities. The first relates to the establishment by the children of Sāvea, the first Mālietoa titleholder (who lived in approximately the 12th century), of the villages and subdistricts known collectively as Faleono-o-Leatigana. The second relates to the founding of Malie village and its relationship to the Mālietoa title. The founder, Mālietoa Sāvea, married twice. His first wife bore three sons. Two of them, Upolusāvea and Umusāvea, established settlements which, since then, have been called Sāleupolu (the family or descendants of Polu – a shortened name for Upolusāvea) and Si'umu (after Umu – short for Umusāvea). The third son, Ganasāvea, succeeded his father to the Mālietoa title. Mālietoa Ganasāvea married Pate, a daughter of the Tui Tonga, and from that union fathered six sons. These sons were appointed by their father either to settle in certain villages or found new settlements. Seupule, Taogaga and Niuāli'i were told to go and live at the village of Fale'ula. Thereafter, their descendants have lived there and these titles are among the high-ranking titles, if not the highest, in Fale'ula village today. Fuataogana and his uncle, Upolusāvea, founded settlements in what is today the subdistrict of Vaimauga. Sāveatama and his uncle, Umusāvea, founded what is today the subdistrict of Si'umu. The sixth son, Poluleuligana, founded the settlement which is known today as Sāle'imoa, and which comprises the three subvillages of Levi, Loťoso'a and Salepou'a'e. The villages and subdistricts founded by these six sons of Ganasāvea are today known collectively as Faleono-o-Leatigana (the six houses of Gana, or the six houses which come to the support of Gana – Gana being short for Ganasāvea) (Anon. nd:12–13, Henry 1980:49–50, Kramer 1994:314–5).

Although Malie is the original seat of the Mālietoa title it was not until the time of his children that Malie's *fale'upolu* was founded. Pate, the wife of Mālietoa Ganasāvea, had a female cousin, a daughter of her mother's sister, whose name was Fa'ane'ene'eiai. Fa'ane'ene'eiai married the Tui Fiti, the paramount titleholder of Fiji, and gave birth to Tuife'ai (Tui the savage). Tuife'ai came to Sāmoa to be with his female cousins. He was responsible for the establishment of Malie's *fale'upolu*, which henceforth became known as 'Auimatagi ('to side with the wind', this name probably given in remembrance of Tuife'ai and his retinue's trip from Fiji to Sāmoa) (Kramer 1994:321, 340). 'Auimatagi comprises seven *tulafale* known collectively as *O pou e fitu o le fale o Mālietoa* (the seven posts of the house of Mālietoa). As well as conferring the Mālietoa title, 'Auimatagi was responsible for notifying the seven children of Ganasāvea about all affairs associated with the Mālietoa title.[38] This framework of communication, said to have been established approximately seven hundred years ago, is still the practice today.

Afega village was founded in approximately the 12th century by Fata and Maulolo, the two brothers of one of Mālietoa Sāvea's wives (Henry 1980:45). Afega's political status was enhanced following events which culminated in the bestowing of the Gato'aitele *pāpā* in approximately the early 14th century. A little later, Taulapapa established other traditions. Taulapapa had four marriages, from one of which issued Seiuli. Seiuli not only succeeded Taulapapa to the Mālietoa title, but was appointed by his father to reside at Faleata where he would be one of the high-ranking *ali'i* in that subdistrict.[39] Thereafter, the Seiuli title has resided in Faleata subdistrict. Among the reasons for requiring Seiuli to reside at Faleata was that the mother of Taulapapa's paternal grandfather was a daughter of one of the high-ranking *tulafale* of Faleata (Kramer 1994:345). This *tulafale* is 'X' mentioned above. When Seiuli was appointed by his father to reside at Faleata, he was entrusted to the care of X, who was (and still is) among the leading *tulafale* of Faleata. Thereafter, in any issue associated with the Mālietoa title, Afega would first consult X, as Seiuli – as a title – is a son of the Mālietoa title.

The custom of X notifying Sāfata subdistrict was established by a different tradition. Tunumafono (after whom the 'Āiga Sa Tunumafono is named) and his sister Fe'eonu'u (who married Va'afusu'aga – Fonotī and Sāmalā'ulu's brother) are direct descendants of a high-ranking *matai* of Faleata (Kramer 1994:388, Anon. nd: 13). Sāfata subdistrict is tradition-ally referred to as *O le gafa o Faleata* (Faleata's descendants). For this rea-son, 'X' of Faleata also notifies Sāfata in all issues associated with not only the Mālietoa title but also Tuamāsaga affairs in general. In other words X extends to Sāfata his traditional responsibility vis-à-vis Faleata, be-cause, among other reasons, Sāfata is genealogically a part of Faleata. As in Tuamāsaga, the customs currently practised in Leulumoega and Ā'ana District can be traced to several ancient traditions.[40]

When two districts meet, each is represented by *matai* of the capital vil-lage whose titles carry the hereditary right to be spokesmen for the district. He speaks on behalf of his district. The right to speak on defined occasions or for specific *ali'i* is associated with many local and nationally important *tulafale*, explaining why the term *tulafale* is often interpreted in English as 'orator'. A number of complicated relationships, established by various traditions, define the nature of the relationship between certain capital villages, the order in which capital villages speak in an all-Sāmoa meeting, and so forth. It was through these traditional administrative and commu-nication channels that the affairs of indigenous Sāmoa were conducted at the supra-district level (see also Gilson 1970:51–9, Davidson 1967:25–9). Because of the prominent role of village governments in both traditional and modern-day politics, they require more detailed discussion.

The *nu'u* and its *matai*

The English word 'village', which will be used in this discussion, is an approximation of the Sāmoan term *nu'u*, for which there is no literal English translation. A *nu'u* is more than a settlement implied by the term 'village'; it comprises a territory usually defined by boundaries from the central mountain ridges of the main islands, to the outer reef. It is an in-dependent political entity comprising a number of '*āiga* and their houses and lands; most of these '*āiga* will have genealogical connections to '*āiga* in other villages and to the large overarching '*āiga* or maximal lineages as-sociated with paramount titles. However the identity of the '*āiga* will be closely linked to the village. Each '*āiga* is associated directly or indirectly with a *matai* title linked to the foundation of the village, and the holder of this title represents them and takes part in its governing council.

The major titles of the *'āiga* of *pāpā* all belong to particular villages, and in some cases they hold titles associated with the founding of the village. Those who do not hold founding titles settled in their villages through family connections, or because they were given land as a reward for service; some are there as an outcome of wars. Two villages have historical legends narrating how an aristocratic infant was taken to be raised in the village so that the village could have a high-ranking *ali'i* to enhance its dignity and status vis-à-vis others. Because of this, certain villages maintain special relationships with others through a connection to a particular high-ranking title, while at the same time maintaining their autonomous status.

As far back as the 12th century, the period from which institutions discussed in this study originated, villages began to be established (see, for example, Appendix 2).

A *nu'u māvae* (foundation village) always has a *fa'alupega* (a set of ceremonial greetings) which is like a constitution for the village, defining the rank and alluding to the historical origin of each title. A village that is not a *nu'u māvae* (and this includes most modern settlements) is not acknowledged as part of the 'legitimate' indigenous system, because it has no *fa'alupega* and it has no *matai* – and only *matai* may legitimately communicate with other *matai*.

Every village has a unique history which shapes its particular socio-political structure, traditions, customs and protocol. In some villages, the foundation titles are mainly *ali'i*, while in some they are all *tulafale* – but most villages have both. The collective authority of *matai* requires the functions associated respectively with *tulafale* and *ali'i*. The *fa'alupega* listing the foundation titleholders, usually in order of rank, is recited on all formal occasions, affirming the status of its members. This avoids competition of the type inherent in democratic political systems, which gives every individual the right to compete for all positions of power. Every *matai* in a village knows where he, or in some cases she, fits in the socio-political hierarchy. Severe punishment may be dealt out to anyone who tries ambitiously to alter the status of their title from that confirmed by the *fa'alupega* and the hierarchy it states.

Titles, both foundation and subordinate titles, may be held by a number of incumbents, a practice that may or may not be of recent origin. This is a complicated subject, but in the context of this discussion it is enough to say that the rank, rights and duties of the title belong to the title itself, not to individuals. Accordingly, when the same title is held by two or many incumbents, they work out amongst themselves who of them will exercise the rights and duties of the title and in what contexts.

Subordinate titles, in contrast to foundation titles, may be titles that came into the village in the past from elsewhere – they are, therefore, not considered foundation titles – or those which have been created over long periods of time by foundation *matai*; these titles may be either *tulafale* or *ali'i*. New titles are created for various reasons – for example, there may be older members of the *'āiga* who did not receive its main title but who deserve a higher status. Sometimes, the family, or the foundation title-holder, decides to confer more titles to help the foundation titleholder in the administration of family affairs. There is always, however, a distinction between a foundation titleholder and the holder of a subordinate title, one which is expressed in political decision-making processes.

Matai election[41]

The election of a person to a subordinate title by family members is not as weighty a matter as is electing a person to a foundation title. Every family member, in theory at least, is entitled to be elected to hold its *matai* title or titles, but in practice the choice is based on ancestry and ability to contribute to family affairs – which nowadays includes wealth and education, leadership ability, and trustworthiness. Younger members of the family do not contribute equally to the selection of their *matai*; the family decision-making council (*'āigapotopoto*) usually only comprises its titleholders, other distinguished members such as church ministers, and women and men from the oldest generation. Once elected to hold a *matai* title, the title is usually held for life, even if the *matai* does not live up to what their families expected of them. Although families have the power, they rarely decide to strip someone of their *matai* title (Le Tagaloa 1991:102-7).

The affairs of every village are controlled by its council of *matai*. It makes village rules, and enforces and adjudicates them. It provides an umbrella authority above the family level over all village lands, and legitimizes the conferral of *matai* titles on village members. Performance of the second responsibility requires the presence of the council of *matai* in a title-conferring ceremony, thereby indicating the acceptance of the new titleholder into the village council. Villages have sub-organizations such as *faletua ma tausi* (wives of *ali'i* and *tulafale* respectively), *aualuma* (unmarried village girls and village women who have either divorced their husbands or whose husbands have passed away), *taulele'a* (untitled males) and *avā taulele'a* (wives of untitled men). Members of these sub-organizations perform certain functions for the general welfare of village members. Ultimate authority over them rests with the *matai* council. The following case study of 'Tasi' village will illustrate how one village operates.[42]

Tasi Village

There are five foundation *matai* (*matai fa'avae*) of Tasi. Of them, three are *ali'i* – Lua, Tolu, and Fa. The other two are *tulafale* – Lima and Ono. *Ali'i* Lua and Tolu and *tulafale* Lima trace their origin, if not genealogically at least in association with the establishment of Tasi, to a noted historical figure. Part of the agreement, or tradition, when Lua, Tolu and Lima first settled Tasi was that Lima was to be the *tulafale* of Lua and Tolu. That tradition has remained to the present. Lima's responsibilities include speaking on behalf of Lua and Tolu in all affairs in which they are involved, whether in Tasi or outside it. In the performance of such duties, Lua and Tolu present to Lima gifts, such as fine mats, money and other items. Likewise, when Lua, or Tolu, or both, attend events, such as weddings and funerals in which Lima is involved, Lima has to present them with gifts of the same type.

Genealogically, *Ali'i* Fa traces his ancestry to different historical figures than those to whom *ali'i* Lua and Tolu trace their descent. However, certain events in the past brought Fa together with Lua and Tolu and these events resulted in the founding of Tasi. *Tulafale* Ono has a different origin. His association with Tasi was more to do with uniting Tasi with the other five villages that comprise the subdistrict of Itu, of which Tasi is part. When Tasi was founded, each of the five foundation *matai* was allocated a piece of land on which each has resided, to this day. As the only *tulafale* in Tasi, Lima and Ono alternate between them the leadership role in village affairs, including speaking on behalf of the whole village to other villages, whether in Itu district, or outside it. As on all occasions where *tulafale* speak on behalf of others, Lima and Ono, in performing those duties on behalf of Tasi, are presented gifts.

Another custom in Tasi is that which implies the differences in rank between Lua and Tolu. Traditionally, Sāmoan village meetings are held in Sāmoan *fale*, which were traditionally round or oval, but nowadays are more likely to be rectangular in shape. These houses comprise raised foundations of stone or cement, in which posts are set supporting a roof. In traditional architecture these roofs were high and of a dome shape. The ranking *ali'i* sit at the sides, while the ranking *tulafale* occupy the front (the side closest to the road); those of lesser rank sit at the back of the fale. In Tasi village, Lua and Tolu occupy one side and Fa the other. Lua always sits in front of the centre side post, the position of highest rank, while Tolu sits in front of any post between the centre side post and the front side of the house. These ranked seating positions are jealously guarded, as are other indicators of rank. They discourage the possibility of competition – a foundation *matai* entertaining the thought of one day usurping the other foundation *matai*'s roles, privileges and authority associated with them.

The procedures involved and practices used in village decision-making lend themselves to maintaining the influence of foundation titleholders on village affairs. For example, in Tasi, either *tulafale* Lima or Ono opens the meeting and *Ali'i* Lua, *Ali'i* Tolu or *Ali'i* Fa respond. The floor is then open to any speaker regardless of rank. Normally, the subordinate titleholders say little or nothing because the foundation titleholder speaks on behalf of their respective families. If subordinate titleholders do speak, less weight is attached to their opinions than to those of a foundation *matai*.

In Tasi, at the end of any discussion, either Lua, Tolu or Fa speaks on behalf of all three. Normally the oldest *ali'i* presents their collective opinion, seniority being associated with age. The response to confirm the opinion of the *ali'i* is made by either *tulafale* Lima or Ono. This then is the council's decision, representing a qualified consensus. The decision is regarded as a consensus because, although *ali'i* have the final say, ideally at least they are considered to have listened to all arguments, assessed the respective merits of these arguments, and then come up with what is considered the best resolution. Ultimately, then, the final decision rests with one person; it is not an expressed majority view as indicated through a ballot, as in a democracy. Consensus politics are seen as the legitimate way to reach such decisions, and in most villages, the foundation *matai* usually have the predominant influence.

This chapter has shown that, although Sāmoa is a highly competitive society, and its many wars are evidence of this, competition was, and is, restrained by the traditional political order. Sāmoans envisage their political system as one based on a fixed order, legitimized by historical events, in which all *matai*, whether *tulafale* or an *ali'i*, know their place in society. This is reflected in the well-known Sāmoan saying: *O Sāmoa ua 'uma ona tofi* (In Sāmoa all positions have been allocated).[43] Competition, in the democratic sense, is discouraged because of the understanding that there are no more positions to be filled, and the established positions are already jealously guarded by those who have inherited them. Once established through the historical processes which have been described, the rank of *matai* titles is fixed. Accordingly, the traditional rights and privileges of major titles and of the districts, villages and families and other titles associated with them, belong exclusively to, and are inherited by, the descendants of those titles. Participation in political activities is limited to those holding recognized positions. Furthermore, there are no accepted processes for conducting political affairs other than those established by tradition and maintained through custom. Because the authority, influence, recognition, pride and prestige of each district and village, and each *matai* are given legitimacy by these customs and traditions, they are jealously guarded.

Traditional competition was expressed in district councils and, if these failed, on the battlefield. While democratic competition occurs via the ballot box in the contemporary era, it does not constrain traditional competition in Sāmoa. Competition is not allowed to erode the traditional order, and is restricted to actions that uphold and enhance traditionally acquired influence, status and rank. Participation in decision-making at all levels is the prerogative of *matai* with 'allocated' positions. Participation in electing titleholders is a once-in-a-life-time affair, although the increasing number of titles being bestowed by some families has also increased the number who may participate in title elections. In terms of civil and political liberties, traditionally established procedures by which affairs of village and district governments are conducted prevent non-traditional political mechanisms, such as social movements and pressure group, seeking to influence those who make decisions. Untitled people have no formal rights in traditional politics.

Among important innovations in Sāmoa's path towards democracy was the establishment of a central government with deliberative powers, under which all islands and districts of the western group were unified. Against this background, the next chapter examines political developments in the 19th century which culminated in Sāmoa gaining its independence in 1962.

Notes

1   For examples, see Meleiseā 1995 and Schoeffel 1999, both of whom argue that the political system was transformed by the adoption of Christianity, and Tcherkezoff 2000, who argues that the term *matai* has only come in to common use in the past two centuries.

2   The indigenous system is very complex. This account, which, for the purpose of this study, somewhat simplifies things, shows the way it is ideally perceived today. The dilemma is that by trying to simplify it in a few words, the complexity of the system and the past is diminished.

3   For the locations of places mentioned in this study, see Figures 1–3.

4   See also, Anon. nd, an anonymous Sāmoan document which appears to be a solidly researched source. It is entitled *O "Gafa" 'Ese'ese o Sāmoa ina ia Faitau i ai Tupulaga Tu'ufa'asolo i le aga'i i luma* but has no date of printing or publication. The document comprises sets of genealogies and other traditions associated with the creation and settlement of the Sāmoa island group, and was given to me by a retired government school teacher.

5   Tagaloa-a-lagi was personified by the Tui Manu'a (Tupua 1995:3), the paramount titleholder of the Manu'a island group on the eastern-most side of the islands of the Sāmoan group.

6   The word *Tui* is a contraction of the Sāmoan phrase *tu-i* (stands, lands, or resides, at a place) (see also 'Ai'ono 1992:120). Thus *tu-i-Ātua* means he/she who had stood, landed, or resided at Ātua district. *Tui* therefore gives the connotation of someone who came in from outside.

7   It is not the purpose of this book to discuss in detail the manner in which the paramount titles of Upolu and Savai'i originated; such would involve extensive historical analysis of oral traditions. My purpose here is to identify these titles because of their significance in Sāmoa's political history, and because of the political centres that became associated with them. They form the basis of indigenous institutions at the supra-village level, and became very important in the 19th century when the Sāmoans attempted to establish a central government.

8   The Tui Ātua title is currently held by Tupua Tamasese 'Efi, who, for a long time, was the leader of the opposition Sāmoa National Development Party (SNDP) but was, on 21 December 2004, appointed to the council of deputies. He was appointed head of state of Sāmoa on 19 June 2007, following the passing away of the late head of state, Mālietoa Tanumafili II, on 11 May 2007.

9   Gurr was one of the judges in the 1898 court case to decide who would be the next king of Sāmoa following the death that year of King Mālietoa Laupepa. His records were based on evidence given before him by a number of prominent Sāmoans, and on handwritten copies of some of the statements written, although unsigned and undated, in Sāmoan by Sāmoans. Other notes were taken by him during conversation, or at meetings of prominent Sāmoans, outside the court.

10   See Appendix 1 for an explanation of the manner in which the chronology used in this study has been calculated. It is necessary to use such a chronology to give an idea of the time at which events took place that gave rise to various aspects of indigenous institutions. The period in which Leutelele'i'ite lived gives a good starting point from whence to trace the indigenous institutions currently recognized in Sāmoa. The earliest date to which historical events identified in this and other chapters can be traced is the time Leutelele'i'ite is estimated to have lived.

11   The last holder of the title was the late Mālietoa Tanumafili II.

12   The current holder of this title was the leader of the *Temokalasi Sā moa Fa'amatai* political party in 1996. He lost his parliamentary seat in the 2001 general election. For more information on people and villages associated with this title, see Appendix 2. Because of intermarriage, the descendants of the title were later associated with the traditional 'Āiga Sa 'Amituana'i (the family of Amituana'i). See also Appendix 4.

13   The article Sa denotes an *'āiga* (or family) and the name that follows it is the person whose family that is.

14   People who descended from this title and others associated with it are known collectively as Sa Moelēoi (the family of Moelēoi). For more information on people associated with this title, see Appendices 2 and 4.

15   People who descend from this title are known collectively as 'Āiga Sa Lilomaiava (the family of Lilomaiava). See also Appendix 2, Kramer 1994:242–43, 398, and Anon. nd: 20,24.

16   A number of examples illustrate this point. Selaginatō (who lived in the 1470s), Le Tagaloa Fa'aofonu'u's son, married Vaetamasoa who gave birth to Tama-a-le-lagi (*Anon*, p. 8). Tama-a-le-lagi married Vaetōifaga, a daughter of the Tui Tonga, and had Salamāsina, who was Sāmoa's 'first *Tafa'ifa*. Salamāsina's daughter, Fofoaivao'ese, who lived in the 1540s, married Tauatamaniula'ita, who was a direct descendant of the Tonumaipe'a title (Kramer 1994:124-5). Later marriages of other descendants of Salamāsina established genealogical connections with the Lilomaiava title (LC 8384 – Submission by the descendants of Seutātia). Records of the Land and Titles Court of Sāmoa are kept in files, which are identified by either the letters LC or ALC. The number that follows these letters specifies a particular file. The same system is used in this study when referring to the records of the Land and Titles Court. Each file comprises records of various hearings related to either the same issue or issues associated with the same title, decisions on those hearings, and submissions by various parties involved in those hearings. In this study, as well as stating the file number, references identify the party, or parties, from whose submissions the information referred to has been taken.

17   ALC 11. Submission by 'Aiolupo M Ta'atiti and *ali'i* and *tulafale* of Ālātaua. See also Tupua 1994 and Henry 1980:70-75.

18   ALC 11 – Submission by Aiolupo M. Ta'atiti and *ali'i* and *tulafale* of Alataua.

19   The Sa Levālasi family is slightly different from the other *'āiga* of *pāpā* in that people who originally comprised it were not direct descendants of Levālasi.

Rather, they were people upon whom Levālasi bestowed the honour as a family of the *pāpā*. However, through genealogical connections, members of this family later became directly associated with both the Tui Āʻana and Tui Ātua titles. For example, Talaleomalie, Fonotī's mother, was a direct descendant of Sa Levālasi. Fonotī held both the Tui Āʻana and Tui Ātua titles in the 1640s. Associated with Sa Levālasi (see Appendix 3) are ʻĀiga Sa Tago and ʻĀiga Sa Amituanaʻi (LC 852 – Submission by Sa Levālasi). See Appendix 4.

20   See also Tupua (1995:4) who maintains that the Sa Levālasi family was named by Salamāsina, not Levālasi.

21   For more information on ʻĀiga Sa Tuala, see Appendix 3.

22   Submission by Sa Tuala.

23   Submission by Sa ʻAiʻonō LC 8384.

24   Information from Leātuāvao Faʻalata (a member of Sa Tuala, like Taimalieutu mentioned in the text). Interview, 12 October 1993. See also Kramer (1994:270) who notes the same tradition.

25   LC 2440. For more information on ʻĀiga Sa Fenunuʻivao, see Appendix 3.

26   The Fuimaono line from Salamāsina is – Salamāsina, Tapufautua, Sifuiva, Fuimaono, Tupua (Tupua 1995:7). The Muāgututiʻa line from Salamāsina is – Salamāsina, Fofoaivaoʻese, Sina, Faumuinā, Fonotī, Muāgututiʻa (LC 8384 – Submission by Sa Tuala). Tapumanaia and Fofoaivaoʻese had different fathers.

27   Land and Titles Court decision (6 August 1987). LC 8384.

28   The *feagaiga* (covenant) defines the brother-sister relationship. Among cultural obligations associated with it is that the brother comes to the protection of his sister. Feʻeonuʻu was Tunumafono's *feagaiga*. Likewise Feʻeonuʻu's children were the *feagaiga* of Tunumafono's children. This *feagaiga* relationship was one of the important reasons, if not the most important one, why Tunumafono's four sons stood firmly behind Toleʻafoa, Feʻeonuʻu's son, in the war in the 1640s. Tunumafono's four sons (Mauga, Pule, Taoa and Afemata) and others who descended from them founded some of the prominent villages in Sāfata subdistrict. All these villages are known collectively as Sa Tunumafono (the family of Tunumafono).

29   For more information on ʻĀiga Taulagi, see Appendix 3.

30   Submission by Lufilufi village LC 8384.

31   LC 8384. This is the author's personal assessment of the evidence that was presented before the Court in this hearing. Eventually, the court decided that Lufilufi has the authority over the Tui Ātua *pāpā*. More important is the reason for giving Lufilufi that authority: That Lufilufi has the right to refuse to confer the *pāpā*. The historical proof of Lufilufi's right of refusal is the tradition of *saesaelaufaʻi* (explained under the section 'Pāpā holder and *pāpā* bestower'). Although *matai* originally gained their authority from the gods to which they could trace descent, the political reality is that people (regardless of which god they descend from) cooperate if their authority is to be maintained.

32   This is based on a personal assessment of a number of oral traditions relating to the establishment of *Tūmua* centres.

33   Hereafter 'political centre' and 'capital village' is used interchangeably. However, there are slight differences in meaning. Political centre describes political organizations that developed in association with the Upolu and Savai'i paramount titles. 'Capital village' on the other hand refers to the villages that eventually became the political centres of political divisions (or what I refer to in this study as political districts) when those political divisions acquired their current status as 'autonomous political organisations'. For example, Vailoa village (in Palauli district), originally developed as one of the three political centres associated with the Lilomaiava title, became the **capital village** of 'Palauli district', or the **political centre** of Palauli district.

34   The forth Sāfune political centre of Vai'afai was incorporated into Fa'asālele'aga district. See Appendix 2.

35   Submission by the heirs of Mālietoa Mōlī (14 December 1939, LC 853). The previous head of state, the late Mālietoa Tanumafili II, was a direct descendant of Mālietoa Mōlī. The seven *tulafale* of Malie, one from Fale'ula village and one from Si'umu are the ones who elect a Mālietoa titleholder.

36   Constitutional Convention Debates. CCD1954, Vol. I, p. 157.

37   This information is based on interviews I had with Fata Meafou (1 September 1993). It is similar to that given in Kramer (1994:288), Gilson (1970:54-5) and Ma'ilo (1994:12-3).

38   LC 853. Submission by the descendants of Mālietoa Mōlī (14 December 1939).

39   Submission by Gale Suaesi, Utututu Nātia, Lesoa Koko, Mala Puna and Tagaloa E Gale ALC 3597. Anon. nd:13.

40   Appendix 6 discusses the relationship between Ā'ana District and its capital Leulumoega.

41   In this discussion I am taking a leap into the situations that exist in the post-European and post-independence periods in order to avoid having to repeat the same sort of discussion in later chapters.

42   The name is fictitious, as are all names used in this case study. In examining the political affairs of this village, I am linking the traditions, which established not only this village but the political relationships among its founding members, and the way those traditions influence the manner in which the affairs of this village have been conducted down to the present. Hence, I am linking the past to what is actually happening today. 'Tasi' is one of the six villages on the south-western coast of Ā'ana district where the author conducted interviews during his field-work in 1993. The author also spent most of his life there, observed its affairs on a daily basis, and was able to discuss its political aspects informally with most of its foundation titleholders.

43   *Tofi* means to appoint, or to designate. In this Sāmoan saying I am translating it as 'positions being allocated' to capture the meaning of the Sāmoan saying. Literal translation of that word, as used in the saying, can make the saying either misleading or meaningless.

2 | Foreign influence 1830–1962

THE FIRST HALF OF THE 19th century saw an influx of European settlers into Sāmoa, a series of civil wars in which foreigners became increasingly involved, and, in 1899, an international agreement to annex and partition Sāmoa between Germany and the United States. This period has been covered by many historians, most notably R.P. Gilson (1970), and the focus here will be on the impacts of the period on traditional Sāmoan political institutions.

The first written codes of law

The first Europeans to discover Sāmoa were navigators and explorers. They were followed by British, American and Australian whaling ships, which started to frequent Sāmoan waters in the early 1820s. Next came British missionaries. John Williams of the London Missionary Society (LMS) landed at Sāpapāli'i on Savai'i on 18 July 1830 bringing with him six missionaries from Rarotonga and Raiatea. Missionaries of the Wesleyan mission arrived five years later, followed by the French Catholics in 1845, and the Latter Day Saints in early 1863. The establishment of missions helped to dispel the rumours that Sāmoans were a particularly aggressive people, which had arisen from a violent encounter between the French explorer La Perouse and Sāmoans in Tutuila in 1787.

By the late 1830s, increasing numbers of Europeans began to settle in Sāmoa as traders. The missionaries detested the behaviour of men, mainly seafarers, whose drinking and womanizing were undermining their efforts to establish a Christian moral order. One issue for them was the regulation of relations arising from the growing trade between the Sāmoans and visiting ships and foreign settler-traders. Military conflicts between districts also threatened the security of the settler community and their commercial interests. Law and order problems became increasingly important issues for resolution. Consular representatives for the British, American and German settlers in Sāmoa were soon appointed to defend the interests of their nationals, but the only formal mechanism to mediate relations between Sāmoans and foreign settlers was Sāmoan customary law, which of course was unacceptable to the settlers. It was in this context that Western codes of law were introduced.

The first written code of law in Sāmoa was that drawn up by Captain Drinkwater Bethune of the HMS *Conway,* who arrived in Apia in January 1838.[1] Bethune first anchored at Tutuila where he also drew up a port code for that island. Among its provisions were those for Sāmoans to apprehend sailors who had deserted their ships and for ship captains to pay their port fees. The missionaries' attitude to the code (generally referred to as the port ˙regulations) was stated by Rev. Murray of the LMS, who said, 'We find them highly advantageous although it is a matter of no small difficulty to get them enforced, owing to the weakness and ignorance of the natives and the wickedness of visitors and foreigners living on shore'.[2]

Captain Charles Wilkes of the United States Exploring Expedition arrived in Apia on 26 November 1839. Part of his mission was to investigate America's interests in the whaling industry. Shortly after his arrival, Wilkes called a meeting with 'representatives' of the Sāmoan 'government' to endorse the revisions and additional provisions he proposed for the Bethune code. His main objective was that the laws 'might secure to our whaleships a certainty of protection and security, and at the same time to prevent impositions being practised by them upon the native government, of which complaint had been made' (Wilkes 1845: 103). Among those present at the meeting were Pe'a of Apia (who later became Seumanutafa Pogai); Mālietoa Vaiinupo (who presided at the meeting); Taimalelagi, Mālietoa's half-brother and successor to the Mālietoa title; Mōlī, Mālietoa's son; To'oā Sualauvi, Mālietoa's father's sister's son; and Matetau, the renowned warrior chief of Manono. The signatories to the Wilkes code were Mālietoa, Taimalelagi, Matetau, Pe'a, To'oā, Mōlī and Saga (who was probably Afamasaga of Fasito'otai village in Ā'ana district). They represented an alliance between Manono and its Sa Mālietoa allies which had emerged victorious from a war fought in the mid-1830s to avenge the death of Tamafaigā. All were leading figures in the *mālō,* which in this sense refers to the victorious and thus dominant party. They represented the closest approximation of a national government of those days, but one which in no way corresponded to Western notions of a government with authority over the people. They would never have been able to enforce the provisions they had signed to uphold.

The only signatory with some influence to enforce the code was Pe'a, and this was because he had moved from Manono to reside permanently in Apia, where he later held the important title, Seumanutafa. But that in itself was also a problem. Apia was a subvillage closely attached to two other subvillages Matāutu and Tanugāmanono. The collective authority which controlled the affairs of the people in these subvillages was the prerogative of the village council, comprising all *matai*. One of the ranking *ali'i* of the village council was Seumanutafa who was of the same rank not only as his 'brother' chief To'omalātai, but also as the other *ali'i* – Tupuola, Tamaseu and Faualo of the *fuaifale* (branch) of Sa Levālasi.[3] Moreover, among the high-ranking *matai* were the *tulafale* Lēta'a, Tuiletufuga, Lima and others (Leala'i'auloto and Fuataga 1985:225). Unless deliberated upon and agreed by the village council, no 'policy', or any other decision for that matter, was deemed binding upon the villagers of the three subvillages. However, Seumanutafa's land happened to be immediately adjacent to the main part of Apia bay within which were the harbour ports. He was, therefore, able to represent himself as the principal chief of the area and to collect port fees and to act as a broker for trade between whaling ships and Sāmoans.

The Wilkes code remained the basic code of law on the islands until the late 1860s. By the 1860s, efforts were being made to establish law codes at the district level in some of the districts of Upolu. The European settler community, in particular the missionaries and the business community, hoped that, if the district leaders assented to a code of law, they would eventually agree to establish a central government to administer Sāmoa's national affairs. A missionary, Murray, wrote to a colleague, remarking that:

> A decided step has been taken towards the formation of a regular government … The laws came into force at the commencement of the year and their operation has been highly beneficial. The movement originated in the district of Apia and for a time was confined to that district. It had been extended to Faleata, the neighbouring district, and eventually

it will, I doubt not, extend all over the group (LMS/SSL, Murray to Tidman, 20 August 1861).

For many years the representatives of the settler community had hoped to see laws and a 'modern' government of Sāmoa established. The growing port-town of Apia was situated within Tuamāsaga, as were most of the commercial plantations. The settlers hoped that the establishment of a government there would regulate relations and transactions between settlers and Sāmoans. In 1865, the British consul, J. C. Williams, attempted to introduce political reform. Williams owed his influence to the fact that he was the son of revered pioneer missionary John Williams. Williams served as American consul as well as that of Britain and was a businessman with a personal interest in establishing a strong government, at least within the Vaimauga area, so that he and others in the business community could pressure the chiefs to require the degree of law and order necessary for successful trade. Williams called a meeting at Apia of the 'principal *matai*' of the districts. The outcome of the meeting was the declaration of a code of law binding upon the whole Tuamāsaga district. Sāmoan leaders may have been reluctant to heed the advice of Williams, who did not have the traditional authority to call such a meeting and who was bypassing traditional channels of communication in Tuamāsaga. Williams wrote, 'I have had a long struggle and a hard one to get then to adopt laws'.[4] However, Williams was able to back his struggle with some British naval support, in a manner that was to become all too familiar to Sāmoans for the next 35 years. In July 1866, Captain Charles Hope of HMS *Brisk* told the local leaders that Britain supported the consul's plan.

The headquarters of the Tuamāsaga government was at Matāutu on the outskirts of Apia; this was not a traditionally recognized political centre in Tuamāsaga and the selection of the location signified the interest of foreign communities in establishing a government that would serve their commercial interests. Over the next 35 years a great deal of blood was spilt in trying to get Sāmoans to adjust to this vision.

The war of the Faitasiga

The question of who would be head of the new government of Tuamāsaga district was the cause of civil war in 1869–73. Initially, conflict was over who would be the king of the Tuamāsaga district government, then the question became entangled in the Sāmoan politics of succession. Tuamāsaga was particularly associated with the Mālietoa title, and a holder of that title seemed the appropriate person to appoint as head of the government. However, there was a contest over sucession to the Mālietoa title between factions backing the heirs, Laupepa and Talavou. Laupepa was of the younger generation, a faithful Christian who had attended the Mālua Seminary, and was favoured by the highly influential London Missionary Society. His father, Mōlī, was Mālietoa Vaiinupo's son, who received the LMS missionaries in 1830, and who had been a mission teacher, and had promoted Christian teaching on peace. He not only remained neutral in the earlier war of 1847–56, but also campaigned for peace. Talavou was half-brother to Mōlī and Laupepa's generational senior. However, Talavou was seen by the settlers and the missionaries as a warlike traditionalist, one who rebelled against missionaries teachings on Christian peace.[5] In 1844, as a leader of Sāfotulāfai, he had fought with his senior kinsman Mālietoa Taimalelagi against the combined forces of Palauli and Sātupa'itea on Savai'i. Talavou also fought with Manono alliance against the allied forces of Ā'ana and Ātua during the1840s and 50s.[6]

The title was conferred on Laupepa, probably with lobbying from leading members of the settler community and the LMS missionaries. On 25 February 1869, Mālietoa Laupepa was brought to the headquarters of the Tuamāsaga government at Matāutu in the Apia area, and proclaimed the only Mālietoa, and king of Tuamāsaga. This was despite the fact that the conferral of the Mālietoa title requires the support of the parties with traditional rights to be consulted. These include the groups of *matai* known as Faleono-o-Leatigana (the six houses of Leatigana), 'Āiga e iva (the nine families of Mālietoa) and the nine members of the Fale-Mālietoa (house of Mālietoa). The Fale-Mālietoa include seven *tulafale* known as 'Auimatagi, *fale'upolu* of Malie village, and representatives from Fale'ula and Siu'mu.[7] Faleono-o-Leatigana and Fale-Mālietoa belong only to Tuamāsaga. However, the nine families of Mālietoa all live in villages outside Tuamāsaga. They are individual titles, who, because of kinship and past alliances with Mālietoa titleholders, had been recognized as families of Mālietoa. These people had no interest in a Tuamāsaga government; their main interests were their association with the Mālietoa title.

After Mālietoa Mōlī died in 1860, there was no full consultation with the nine families and so there was no consensus on the bestowal of the title; therefore, the bestowal of the title on Laupepa was violently contested. One of the reasons for the conflict lay in the past: Tuamāsaga had undermined some of Mālietoa's allies in the wars of the early 1800s. Among these were Sāfotulāfai – one of the two original *Pule* centres in Savai'i – and Manono, who were, and still are, two of the nine families ('Āiga e iva) of Mālietoa. By the late 1820s, the centre of political power in Sāmoa was in Manono, whose leader, Lei'ataualesā Tonumaipe'a Tamafaigā, had subdued all the districts of Upolu and the political centres in Savai'i (Tupua 1995:12–15). Following the death of Lei'ataualesā, not long before the first visit of the Rev. John Williams to Sāmoa in 1830, Manono and Sāfotulāfai stood by Mālietoa Vaiinupo in the war to avenge Tamafaigā's death. This war culminated in the conferral of the four *pāpā* on Mālietoa Vaiinupo, thereby making him one of Sāmoa's *Tafa'ifā*. In the intermittent wars from the late 1840s to the late 1850s, between the allies of Mālietoa and the combined forces of Ātua and Ā'ana, Manono and Sāfotulāfai, the latter usually supported the Mālietoa forces.[8] Yet Tuamāsaga had conferred the Mālietoa title without consulting Manono and Sāfotulāfai, among others (*SR* 1 Feb 1870).

Manono and its allies supported Talavou's right to hold the Mālietoa title. Talavou's wife was from Manono (see, Kramer 1994: 320). He held the prestigious Tonumaipe'a title, and Manono had played a major role in having that title conferred on him. Thus, the pre-European alliance between Sātupa'itea – one of the political centres of the Tonumaipe'a title – and Manono was retained through Talavou (Tupua 1995:12, 71). As a rival candidate for the Mālietoa title, Talavou had strong political and military support from Manono, Sāfotulāfai and Sātupa'itea.

Other political issues concerning Laupepa's accession to the title, and his appointment as the king of Tuamāsaga, were associated with the question of which district was the 'legitimate' traditional seat of the Mālietoa title. The Mālietoa connections were predominantly from Tuamāsaga district, with some from other villages scattered throughout Ātua and Ā'ana district on Upolu island, and villages on Savai'i. The residence of the Mālietoa title in Sāpāpāli'i was famous in the Christian era as the place where Mālietoa Vaiinupo lived in 1830, when he sponsored the introduction of the Gospel to Sāmoa by giving his patronage to the LMS missionary, John Williams. The Mālietoa residence there was established relatively recently, in the 1770s, following the marriage of Mālietoa Ti'a to a woman of that village, from which issued Mālietoa Fitisemanu, the father of Mālietoa Vaiinupo and Taimalelagi. Originally, the only seat of the Mālietoa title was in Malie village on Upolu. Mālietoa Mōlī was buried in Malie and his son, Laupepa, had grown up there. 'Auimatagi of Malie bestowed the Mālietoa title on Laupepa, with the need for a king of the Tuamāsaga district government in mind. In this way, Malie asserted that *it* was the legitimate seat of the Mālietoa title, and not Sāpapāli'i, and that it alone had the traditional prerogative to confer the Mālietoa title, regardless of which candidate was preferred for the title by connected parties in other villages.

In defiance of the proclamation by the Tuamāsaga government that Laupepa was king and sole holder of the Mālietoa title, Talavou and his supporters successfully sought allies from Savai'i and Manono from among those closely associated with the Mālietoa title there. Among those were Leulumoega and Lufilufi, both former enemies of Talavou; but the majority of Ātua and Ā'ana remained neutral until later in the war, when they joined the Laupepa side (*SR* 1 Feb 1870). Their leading villages, Leulumoega and Lufilufi, joined the Manono allies on Talavou's side against the wishes of the majority of Ā'ana and Ātua people. Thus, when fighting began, only one village of Ā'ana went with Leulumoega and about a dozen Ātua people joined Lufilufi. This war divided the people of Ā'ana and Ātua. Some prominent *matai* of Tuamāsaga who also sided with the Talavou faction, were probably alienated by 'Auimatagi's seeming high-handedness. Leulumoega and Lufilufi originally had been involved as mediators, but their main intention seemed to have been to establish a single government for Sāmoa. Talavou's supporters, claiming to truly represent all Sāmoa, established themselves at Mulinu'u Peninsula on the western side of the Apia area facing the headquarters of the Tuamāsaga government. Eventually, the confrontation erupted into an all-out war, which was fought intermittently from late March 1869 till May 1873.[9]

This war was called *O le faitasiga o le Tuamāsaga* (the alliance against Tuamāsaga) – or in short, *Faitaisiga*. The name of the war did not necessarily mean that all the people in other villages of Sāmoa were fighting against Tuamāsaga. It nevertheless, portrayed how the concept of kingship was perceived by the non-Tuamāsaga people.

Lufilufi and Leulumoega's involvement in what was primarily a dispute associated with the Mālietoa title was related to their positions as the *Tūmua*. They were not prepared to sit back and await the outcome, because that might result in the Mālietoa title increasing in importance over the Tui Ātua and Tui Ā'ana titles. Elevation of the Mālietoa title above the other paramount titles also implied elevation of people associated with it, such as the *fale'upolu* of Malie and Afega. The status of Lufilufi and Leulumoega and their recognition in traditional politics vis-à-vis supra-district affairs was threatened by the establishment of the Tuamāsaga government. It was the explicit intention of Tuamāsaga district in establishing their government to promote Apia as the future capital of the country (*SR* 1 Feb 1870), although the traditional meeting place of all the districts of Sāmoa was probably at Ma'auga, in Leulumoega, Ā'ana district (Tupua 1994:196, Tupua 1995:17).

The nomination of a new and foreign-dominated centre must have threatened *Tūmua*. In lending their support to Talavou, the allies, Lufilufi and Leulumoega, were acting against the wishes of the majority of Ā'ana and Ātua people (*SR* 1 Feb 1870). This suggests that, rather than seeking a district consensus through the traditional meetings of their respective 'parliaments', Lufilufi and Leulumoega went ahead in defense of their vested interests. Moreover, in the 1847–57 war, Tuamāsaga had been the side defeated by combined forces from Ā'ana and Ātua and their allies in Savai'i. Accordingly, Lufilufi and Leulumoega were suspicious that Tuamāsaga, under the guise of establishing a district government, were trying to reassert dominance over Sāmoan affairs. (Tupua 1992:4).[10]

Lufilufi and Leulumoega preferred a single government for Sāmoa because this would allow them to maintain their traditional influence, and prevent the Mālietoa title and those associated with it from becoming dominant in Sāmoan affairs and undermining the historical precedence of Ā'ana and Ātua. Sāmoans, and some foreigners as well, equated the position of a king to that of the *Tafa'ifā*. But in a monarchy, succession is based on hereditary principles familiar to Europeans, whereas under the Sāmoan equivalent, *Tafa'ifā*, hereditary rights of succession are modified by the processes of appointment (see previous chapter). Following Mālietoa Vaiinupo's death in 1841, the four titles of the *Tafa'ifā* had been held by different men, and their reunification in this period required either the achievement of a national consensus, or a war of conquest. The prospect of a Tuamāsaga government with its own monarch was unacceptable to most of the districts, as well as to some villages and subdistricts within in Tuamāsaga. There was no collectively recognized paramount chief of Tuamāsaga. While most of its leading *matai* could trace their ancestry to the Sā Mālietoā, others belonged to various lineages and alliances associated with the Tui Ātua and Tui Ā'ana titles (hereafter called Sa Tupuā), including some of the *matai* in the subvillages of Apia, whose paramount chief belonged to a branch of the Sa Tupuā.

A break in the fighting in July 1870 provided an opportunity for attempts at mediation between the two parties by the British consul, missionaries and Sāmoan teachers.[11] By this time the majority of Ā'ana and Ātua had thrown their support behind the Laupepa party, leaving *Tūmua* in opposition with their allies in Savai'i.[12] The new Laupepa alliance was led by To'oā Sualauvi, whose ancestral and marital connections united the majority of Ātua, Ā'ana and Tuamāsaga. By the early 1860s, To'oā Sualauvi held two of the four principal titles of Upolu – Tui Ā'ana and Vaetamasoali'i – and the Gatoaitele *pāpā* was also conferred on him at some time during the 1860s.[13] Further, his Ātua supporters were looking upon him as a candidate for the vacant Tui Ātua title, which would have made him *Tafa'ifā*.[14] However, To'oā Sualauvai died during the mediation process in August 1870[15] and, without his unifying presence, fighting erupted again in February 1872.[16] It was not until after further mediation by the three consuls, three LMS missionaries, one Wesleyan missionary, the Roman Catholic bishop and several priests on 1 May 1873 that both parties agreed to end the war, and Talavou agreed to return to reside in Savai'i.[17]

The first central government

The constitution of the first united Sāmoan government was drafted by its representatives at Mulinu'u and adopted on 21 August 1873. The government's flag was raised at Mulinu'u on 7 October[18], and was recognized by Commodore Goodenough of the HMS *Pearl* on 11 November.[19] With few modifications, the basic structures of the central government established under the 1873 constitution, and its 1875 revised version, remained intact until 1900, the year when Germany took control of the western islands as its colony. The constitution provided for one *ta'imua* (leader) for each of the country's seven major political divisions. These included three divisions of Savai'i (Itūotane, Itūoteine, and Fa'asalele'aga), three districts of Upolu (Ā'ana, Tuamāsaga and Ātua) and one comprising Apolima and Manono. The *ta'imua* for Ātua also represented the island of Tutuila. Because of the competitive issues inherent in the appointment of a king, clause 24 of the law code specifically stated that no *Tūmua* or any other person might bestow on an *ali'i* or anyone else a *pāpā* in order to make that person king. Recognizing that competition for *pāpā* titles often led to war because of the existence of divisive cross-cutting loyalties in Sāmoan politics, the 1873 law code specifically stated that any *matai*, or group of *matai*, who conferred a *pāpā* title were committing a crime comparable to murder. It allowed a king to be appointed only when the government unanimously agreed upon a candidate. The constitution aimed to reflect some elements of the Sāmoan order; each of the seven *ta'imua* constituencies comprised 40 *faipule* (authorities), who in turn elected the seven *ta'imua*. Only *matai* were eligible to be candidates and to elect the *ta'imua* and *faipule*. The elections were held, not by a secret ballot, but by the consensus of *matai* in village councils, thereby continuing traditional modes of decision-making. The constitutional provisions enabled the opinion of all districts and most villages to be brought to bear upon government policy, but created a cumbersome deliberative body that kept a very large number of *matai* from their ordinary duties. The division of the country into seven electorates implied political equality among the divisions, and between Upolu and Savai'i. However, the traditional districts retained their traditional political organization while participating on an equal basis at the supra-village level, much as they did under the existing indigenous system. The large size of *faipule* per *ta'imua* constituency ensured the participation of as many villages as possible in the affairs of the central government. Because the *faipule* elected one of their number as their *ta'imua* representative, the precontact method of discussing district affairs at the district 'parliaments', and of consulting district villages through traditionally established channels of communication were unaffected. From the Sāmoan viewpoint, the arrangement was acceptable inasmuch as it emphasized the continued importance of the tradition of village autonomy. Clause 21 of the 1873 constitution was drafted specifically to guarantee the retention of traditional powers by district and village authorities. Accordingly, the government was to have no power in respect of village government and *matai* authority; a provision that has been upheld to the present day. The provision was clearly intended for the resolution of disputes between Sāmoan polities, rather than to give the government direct authority over them. As Gilson (1970:293) explains:

> It is significant … that the central government was meant to have, in its own right, no direct authority over Sāmoans, except at Mulinu'u and on

the Beach at Apia Bay. Rather, it was to try to settle Sāmoan disputes referred to it and to negotiate uniform laws and rules of administrative procedure for local enforcement and observance.

In addition to the law-making responsibilities that they shared with the *faipule*, the *ta'imua* were responsible for the executive government, which conducted relations with foreign powers, maintained law and order in the Apia area (in association with the village *fono* and the consuls), and appointed certain district officials. The constitution also provided for the first nationwide administration comprising judges, clerks and police to be appointed for districts and subdistricts, and rules were made for their guidance. These appointments were made locally but commissioned by the *ta'imua* in the name of the Mulinu'u government. The *ta'imua* were further empowered by the constitution to appoint four governors with administrative functions, but it is not known whether or not they were allocated to traditional districts at that stage.

By early 1875, there was pressure from the consuls to have the 1873 constitution modified. Among the important changes they sought was the appointment of a king, an office held by a single person and his heirs. Proposals by the consuls to increase centralization of power by reducing the number of *faipule* and downgrading their role were resisted by the *matai* at Mulinu'u.[20] The compromise was to retain the number of *faipule* and double the number of *ta'imua*, whose election was to be the responsibility of the *faipule*. The *faipule* were also to be responsible for selecting one representative from both Sa Tupuā and Sa Mālietoā to be joint-kings, whose responsibilities were to jointly convene government councils, supervise and participate in those bodies, and determine whether or not measures passed by them should go into force. There was also provision that the two kings might be impeached by a majority of four-fifths of the *faipule*. The consuls were granted rights to share in all jurisdiction over foreigners, whatever their instruction from their home governments.

The identification of two eligible lineages, Sa Mālietoā and Sa Tupuā was a major adaptation of the Sāmoan system, a response to accommodate foreign pressure to establish a centralized monarchical government. Henceforth, the Sāmoans referred to these families as the two 'Āiga Tupu of Sāmoa. The term *tupu* is often translated as 'king' in the historical literature; however, it literally means 'grow' and refers to 'one from whom people descend or grow'. It implies that the connection between a title and the district in which it is paramount is based on shared ancestral connections. It does not imply sovereignty. The formal recognition of two lineages as 'Āiga Tupu denied other traditional cross-cutting aristocratic connections among the leading centres, and the problems inherent in this compromise were reflected in the subsequent shifting alliances and wars over who should be king. Although the institutions of king, *ta'imua*, and *faipule* were to remain the basic structure of Sāmoa's central government for the next 25 years, the reconciliation of the institutions of *Tafa'ifā* and monarchy proved impossible. The situation was further complicated by foreign powers' interference in local politics on behalf of various settler interests.

The 1875 constitution increased the number of *ta'imua* to 14, and appointed the king. The *ta'imua* were to have included two from the eastern islands (Tutuila, Manu'a, Olosega, Ofu, and Aunu'u), two from Ātua district, two from Tuamāsaga district, two from Ā'ana district, one from Manono and Apolima islands, and four from Savai'i. However, those actually appointed were one from the eastern islands, one from Manono and Apolima, two from each of the three districts on Upolu island, and five from Savai'i. The five from Savai'i represented the six political centres, which in 1880 were 'officially recognised' as *Pule*.

The people of Sa Mālietoā were unanimous in their choice of Mālietoa Laupepa to be their representative, however Sa Tupuā was divided between Matā'afa Iosefo and Pulepule Tupesiliva (Gilson 1970:312). The latter was chosen from among a number of ranking *matai* in the line of Galumalemana. Pulepule was a descendant of the original Tūpolēsava, one of Galumalemana's five sets of male descendants, whom he had designated *Aloali'i*. During the Faitasiga War, the aspirants to the Tupua title were the *Aloali'i* Tuālau from Palauli, Titimaea from Āsau, and Pulepule of Solosolo. Sa Tupuā had to settle the issue of who, among Galumalemana's descendants, was to hold the Tupua title, and which of the descendants of the Galumalemana and the Matā'afa titles was to hold the Tui Ātua title. The various factions could not come to an agreement, although *Tūmua* indicated that they preferred Titimaea. Among other qualities, Titimaea was said to be hospitable and generous (*tama gāsese mea lelei*), and the name Tamasese was derived from this appellation, by which Titimaea and his descendants have been known ever since. With the representative of the Sa Tupuā unresolved, it was agreed that Mālietoa would be king first, and would be succeeded by a representative of Sa Tupuā when it had made its selection.

The proposal that the two lineages provide alternate kings came from an American who had become influential in Sāmoan affairs. Albert Steinberger claimed to be the 'special agent' of President Grant of the United States of America. The Sāmoans, convinced that the United States wanted to help them establish their government, made Steinberger their premier under the newly promulgated constitution of 18 May 1875.[22] However, the rivalrous settler community soon discovered that Steinberger had no authority from the United States and had secret dealings with German commercial interests.[23] In 1876, Steinberger was removed from Sāmoa by a British naval ship.[24] It is not clear whether Steinberger had made his deal to advance the interests of German plantation company Godeffroy und Sohn before he arrived in Sāmoa, or after he had become premier, or whether the Sāmoan leaders knew anything about it. Steinberger saw himself as Sāmoa's sole powerbroker, whereas the Sāmoans thought that his authority, being derived from them, was limited. Mālietoa Laupepa resisted the American and British consuls' determination to arrest Steinberger, telling them:

> If Steinberger had done anything wrong or had violated his oath, it was the business of the Sāmoan government … We are responsible for his acts, and we do not consider that he had violated his duty … We were aware of everything that transpired in reference to Colonel Steinberger before we appointed him premier of our government. We did not wish him to have a commission from the United States of America to establish our government; he had taken the oath of allegiance to our government, and we will protect him. We would now this day demand of your Excellency what is the meaning of this examination of our premier? Who is it that doubts he is our premier; which of the consuls is it that does not know he had been appointed by us? (Stathis 1982:98)

Eventually, Mālietoa gave in to pressure and signed the document on behalf of the Sāmoan government to have Steinberger removed from Sāmoa. However, *ta'imua* and *faipule,* still convinced that Steinberger was of value to Sāmoan interests, were angry that Mālietoa had acted without their sanction. In early 1876 they deposed him.[25]

The wars to control the central government

Mālietoa Laupepa and his supporters retired to Leulumoega, where they established a rival government called the *Puletua* (the authority at the rear). They intended to re-establish themselves at Mulinu'u, but *ta'imua* and *faipule*, on the other hand, were determined that there was no government other than the one at Mulinu'u. Under the leadership of Tupua Tamasese Titimaea (hereafter, Tamasese), *ta'imua* and *faipule* fought *Puletua* at Fale'ula (a village about five miles from Mulinu'u) in July 1877. *Puletua* was defeated, thereby enhancing the status of the Mulinu'u government. Meanwhile, the Mulinu'u government had become aligned in the rivalry between German, American and British interests. In 1878 they signed a treaty granting the USA exclusive jurisdiction over the Pagopago harbour and, in January 1879, granted trade privileges to the Germans. The Mālietoa side became stronger when the previously divided supporters of Mālietoa Talavou and Mālietoa Laupepa joined forces in a bid to establish themselves at Mulinu'u. In May 1879, while *ta'imua* and *faipule* were away from Mulinu'u in what was expected to be a short recess, the two Mālietoas and their supporters re-established themselves at Mulinu'u as the *Pulefou* (new government). Talavou and Laupepa became king and vice-king respectively (*ST*, 84, 10 May 1879). However, *ta'imua* and *faipule* did not accept this bloodless defeat; they established themselves at northern Ā'ana awaiting their opportunity to regain Mulinu'u. When war broke out, the German warship *Bismarck* intervened to impose peace terms. The *Bismarck* agreement endorsed the positions of Talavou and Laupepa for life, and provided for the appointments of new *ta'imua* and *faipule* from members of both parties. The new government was recognized by the three powers (Great Britain, Germany and the United States) in March 1880 (Kennedy 1974:24; *ST*, 128, 13 March 1880). In July 1880, an agreement was signed between the representatives of the Mālietoa government and Matā'afa Iosefo's supporters in Ātua on board the German warship HMS *Nautilus* at Sāluafata. Ātua agreed to send their *ta'imua* and *faipule* to Mulinu'u and to persuade their allies in Ā'ana and Savai'i to do the same (*ST*, 146, 17 July 1880). Leulumoega and Lufilufi (as representatives of Ā'ana and Ātua) proceeded to Savai'i on this mission, but their true intention was to bestow *Tūmua* status on these Savai'i political centres, thereby diverting its support away from Sa Mālietoā to Sa Tupuā. Sa Mālietoā and its supporters responded to this move by bestowing the powerful status of *Pule* on four political centres in Savai'i that had not tradtionally enjoyed this honour, thereby increasing the total of *Pule* centres on Savai'i to six (Eteuati 1982:23; *ST*, 149, 7 August 1880). (Previously, only

Sāfotulāfai and Sāle'aula had been recognized as *Pule* centres.) Apart from their association with the Mālietoa title (despite which Sāle'aula was a strong supporter of the Tui Ātua/Tui Ā'ana alliance), they saw Lufilufi and Leulumoega's actions as an intrusion into traditional jurisdiction and sent war parties to meet the mission from Lufilufi and Leulumoega.

It had been agreed by all present at the *Nautilus* meeting on July 1880 that the next king would be from Sa Tupuā. Matā'afa Iosefo joined the government and became premier (*ta'imua sili*) (*ST,* 162, 6 November 1880); however, fighting continued, despite the consuls' recognition of Mālietoa Laupepa as king in March 1881[26], following Mālietoa Talavou's death on 7 November 1880.[27] Sa Tupuā and their supporters established a rival government at Leulumoega, where Tamasese was crowned king on 20 April 1881, after his installation as Tui Ā'ana *pāpā*.[28] On 12 July 1881, after further foreign intervention, the Lackawanna peace settlement recognized Mālietoa Laupepa as king, with Tamasese as 'vice-king' (*ST,* 198, 16 July 1881). When passed over as king, Matā'afa Iosefo left the Mulinu'u government and took up residence at Ātua.[29] The following year, Mālietoa Laupepa announced his intention to postpone the question of succession for seven years[30], but supporters of Tamasese Titimaea were discontented. In 1885, they withdrew from the Mulinu'u government and established a rival government at Leulumoega with Tamasese as their king.[31] After a short war, and with German backing, the Tamasese government was re-established at Mulinu'u on 25 August 1887 where Tamasese was proclaimed king, and recognized by Germany.[32] The Tamasese government appointed a German, Brandeis, as premier and demanded heavy taxes from the Sāmoans. Mālietoa Laupepa was exiled to the Marshall Islands with German backing. But this German coup did not crush the opposition; in Mālietoa's absence his supporters, and those of Matā'afa supporters on the Sa Tupuā side, made common cause behind Matā'afa Iosefo.[33] On 9 September 1888, at Fale'ula, Sa Mālietoā confirmed this alliance by conferring the Mālietoa title on Matā'afa. In June 1887 Leota of Solosolo and his Ātua supporters installed Mataáfa as Tui Ātua.[34] In response, Tamasese's Ātua supporters conferred the Tui Ātua title on Tamasese[35], and Su'atele of Mulivai in Sāfata bestowed the Vaetamasoāli'i title (another of the *pāpā* titles) upon him (*ST,* 7 10 November 1881). The Sāfata people, who were not consulted on the issue, were so enraged with Su'atele for giving this title to Tamasese that they threatened to have him killed. Another war broke out in 1888 culminating in the proclamation of Mālietoa Tui Ātua Matā'afa as king of Sāmoa on 3 October 1888 (*ST*, 6 October 1888). Pressured by their consuls, the three powers met at a conference in Berlin, and passed the *Berlin Act 1889*, which established a Supreme Court in the exclusive multinational settler zone, the Apia municipality. Although the Act provided that the Sāmoans would elect their own king, competing interests determined otherwise. Although Matā'afa Iosefo had the majority support of the Sāmoans (*ST*, 6, 3 November 1888), the Germans would not support him because he had defeated the German soldiers fighting with Tamasese. Tamasese was not acceptable to Britain and the U.S.A. because he had supported the German interests. Thus, before the Act had come into effect, there was a prior understanding among the powers that Mālietoa Laupepa would be brought back from exile to be king of a newly established government (Kennedy 1974:98-9). He was subsequently recognised king by the three powers on 8 November 1889 (*ST*, 16 November 1889).

This upset the Mālietoa alliance and divided its members. In defiance, Matā'afa supporters refused to pay taxes. Tamasese's supporters rallied to their Sa Tupuā kinsman, Matā'afa, following the death of Tamasese in April 1891. Matā'afa was taken to Malie where he was proclaimed king: In the context of Sāmoan politics, one cannot be the legitimate holder of a title if he/she does not reside at the official residence of that title. The move to Malie, the oldest of the two seats of the Mālietoa title, by Matā'afa and his supporters signalled to the supporters of the exiled Mālietoa Laupepa that Matā'afa was now the legitimate holder of the Mālietoa title. The seven *tulafale* of Malie (*fale-fitu*) whose prerogative it was (and still is) to confer the Mālietoa title, asserted this right, and soon after Matā'afa was declared king by his supporters at Malie (Tupua 1994:71, Stevenson 1892:282).

Meanwhile Mālietoa Laupepa's supporters in Ā'ana had conferred on Mālietoa the Tui Ā'ana title (Gilson 1970:419). Fighting between the two parties erupted in mid-1893 and continued intermittently until Matā'afa and some of his prominent supporters surrendered to the German warships on 18 July. They were taken away to be exiled in the Marshall Islands under German jurisdiction (Morrell 1960:300).

On 17 April 1891, Tupua Tamasese Titimaea died aged only 61 years (*ST*, 132, 18 April 1891). At the time of his death he held both the Tui

Ā'ana and the Tui Ātua titles. He made an oral will (*māvaega*) decreeing the establishment of a new lineage grouping, 'Āiga o Māvaega (literally, the family of his will). *Tūmua* of Leulumoega was accorded the prerogative of looking after it, thus increasing to four the number of 'a*iga* or major lineages for which Leulumoega was responsible – the other three '*āiga* being Sa Tuala, Taulagi and Tauā'ana. The 'Āiga o Māvaega comprised some of those from whom Tupua Tamasese Titimaea descended, including those who were among the military supporters of Tamasese. Members of the 'Āiga o Mavaega are scattered throughout villages on both Upolu and Savai'i islands. The villages on Upolu island are Luatuānu'u, Vaimoso and Faleasi'u; those on Savai'i island are Āsau, Ā'opo, Sāsina, Sāfune, Sāto'alepai and Sātaua (*LC*, 8384). Tupua Tamasese Titimaea was succeeded by his son, TupuaTamasese Lealofi I.

Fighting between the Mālietoa and Tupua parties broke out again in early 1894 (Kennedy 1924:103). By this time, Mālietoa Laupepa was old and sick and pressure was mounting to have Matā'afa returned to Sāmoa to succeed him. The majority of Matā'afa supporters at Ātua had joined the government and, the year before he died, 1898, Mālietoa Laupepa agreed that Matā'afa should be brought home. Upon Matā'afa's return, *Tūmua* and *Pule*, who claimed the sole right to appoint Sāmoan kings, declared in favour of Matā'afa and appointed him king on 12 November 1898. However, supporters of Mālietoa Tanumafili I (Mālietoa Laupepa's son) and Tamasese Lealofi I disputed Matā'afa's election. The issue was taken to the Supreme Court in Apia, which had been established by the Berlin Act. Chief Justice Chambers decided in favour of Tanumafili I on the grounds that the Berlin Conference of 1889 disbarred Matā'afa from the kingship (Holstine 1971:240). Matā'afa supporters refused to accept Chambers's decision. Fighting again broke out and Matā'afa supporters overwhelmed the combined forces of Tamasese Lealofi and Mālietoa Tanumafili. On 4 January 1899, the consular body recognised Matā'afa and his 13 *ta'imua* as the provisional government of Sāmoa. An international commission, comprising representatives of the three powers arrived in Sāmoa on 13 May 1899. Tanumāfili was induced to abdicate his kingship position, thereby permanently abolishing the 'Sāmoan monarchy'. He officially resigned the kingship on 10 June. Before leaving Sāmoa, the commissioners established a provisional government comprising the three consuls, with Dr Wilhelm Solf appointed as the president of the Apia municipality, and the American consul as the acting chief judge. This arrangement was made whilst await-ing an outcome of the commissioners' recommendations to the powers. A convention was signed by the powers on 2 December 1899 allowing for the partition of Sāmoa into Western and Eastern Sāmoa under the respec-tive control of Germany and the United States.

German rule

Germany's major interest in Sāmoa was its coconut plantations; Sāmoa was the hub of Germany's Pacific coconut 'empire', which included plan-tations in Fiji, Tonga, New Guinea and the Marshall Islands. The Ger-man objective was to create a political environment that was conducive to the commercial interests of the major plantation and trading company Deutsche Handels und Plantagen Gesellschaft. When the Sāmoan indig-enous power structures threatened, or became an obstacle to, the realization of German interests, the German governors in Western Sāmoa made it one of their objectives to undermine them (Meleiseā 1987a:46–63). Knowing Sāmoan institutions quite well, first German governor of Sāmoa, Dr Wil-helm Solf, recognized that most of the districts had backed Matā'afa Iosefo as king in the latter days of the 19th century. So he appointed Matā'afa to a specially created office of *ali'i Sili*. Solf's aim was to gradually erode the traditional polity and shift power from the villages and districts to the central administration. (Moses 1972:46). Upon Matā'afa's advice, Tupua Tamasese, Tuimaleali'ifano, Saipa'ia (of Sa Tupuā), and Fa'alata were ac-corded the title *ta'imua*. Unlike the pre-colonial *ta'imua* (the upper house of parliament), the new designation referred to an unspecified advisory role. Solf's *ta'imua* represented the paramount descent groups associated with four titles (Mālietoa, Matā'afa, Tupua Tamasese, and Tuimalali'ifano of the Sa Tupuā) that were at the forefront of the 19th century wars for su-premacy discussed in the previous chapter. Their appointment represented an attempt by Matā'afa and the governor to appease their families and districts. The titles had come to be known collectively as the *tama'āiga*, a contraction of *tama-a-'aiga*, and connoting 'the offspring' or principal titular representatives of two leading dynastic groups of Sāmoa.

When Matā'afa died on 12 February 1912, the position of *Ali'i Sili* was abolished and replaced by that of *fautua* (adviser), another important step in Solf's design to gradually undermine Sāmoa's indigenous political institu-tions. Mālietoa Tanumafili I and Tupua Tamasese Lealofi I became jointly the first holders of this office. These appointments formally recognized the status of *tama-a-'āiga* as the new focus of paramount rank, eclipsing the *pāpā* titles and the office of *Tafa'ifā*. This colonially engineered revision of tradition aimed to end efforts to establish a monarchy and avoid renewal of the 19th century struggles. The Germans wanted peace in order to promote their commercial interests.

New Zealand rule

German rule ended in 1914 at the onset of World War I when New Zealand sent a military expedition to seize the islands. New Zealand's rule in Sāmoa can be divided into three main periods: Military rule (1914–19), mandate (1920–45) and trusteeship (1945–61). Forty-eight hours after the outbreak of war with Germany in 1914, Great Britain suggested to New Zealand, 'as a great and urgent imperial service', that it occupy German Sāmoa on the understanding that the future of the islands rested with the imperial authorities (Boyd 1969:115, 1968:148). The New Zealand expedition occupied Sāmoa on 29 August 1914 without a shot being fired (Davidson 1967:90). The Germans had decided not to put up resistance because Sāmoa was not fortified. Moreover, the whereabouts of the German fleet was uncertain, while Britain was known to have nine men-of-war attached to the Australian station. Furthermore, Dr Erich Schultz, the governor, believed that Sāmoan loyalty could not be expected (Boyd 1968:148).

Having been dispatched to Sāmoa in haste, colonel Robert Logan, leader of the New Zealand military force, received from New Zealand no clear instructions concerning the manner in which the islands should be administered. His only instruction was 'to take such measures as he might consider necessary to hold the Islands and control the inhabitants' (Boyd 1968:151). The British flag was raised at Mulinu'u on 30 August and, on the following day, Logan told an assembly of Sāmoans at Mulinu'u that 'the government would be carried on by him on the lines established by the Germans' (Davidson 1967:91).

At Versailles, New Zealand's prime minister, W. F. Massey, successfully argued that German Sāmoa be administered by New Zealand 'as an integral part of her own territory' (Boyd 1969:124). Accordingly, the Treaty of Peace signed with Germany on 29 June 1919 enabled the League of Nations to confer on Great Britain the mandate, to be exercised by the

'Government of the Dominion of New Zealand' on her behalf, to administer the 'former colony of German Sāmoa'. Following confirmation of the mandate, the New Zealand parliament passed the *Sāmoa Act 1921,* establishing the administration in Sāmoa. This Act and its amendments were the basis of the New Zealand administration in Sāmoa, which lasted until 1962. Among major developments during the period of the British mandate was the Sāmoan resistance movement, *O le Mau* (The [Sāmoan'] Opinion), against the New Zealand administration.

The cause of the *Mau* has been a subject of many scholarly studies. Davidson maintains that the movement had been a result of both the intrusively paternalistic policies of Richardson (the incumbent administrator) and the determined attempts of the Sāmoans to resist Richardson's challenges to their traditional institutions, which he considered far stronger than the Germans' attempts to undermine Sāmoa's traditional institutions (Davidson 1967:112-3). Eteuati argues that, although other explanations may be valid (such as New Zealand racism – which forms the core of Wendt's [1965] and Field's [1984] arguments), the most significant underlying cause of the *Mau* was the pride and nationalism of the Sāmoans and their determination to control their own affairs:

> For most Sāmoans this meant freedom within the *'āiga* and autonomy within their villages. These things had been seriously threatened by Richardson's plans to individualize Sāmoan land and to change the system of administering the affairs of villages and districts (Eteuati 1982:336).

Meleiseā agrees that the *Mau* movement 'was a demonstration of Sāmoan solidarity to protect their institutions'. However, 'in terms of years, the *Mau* was a short episode in the continuing struggle by the Sāmoans to defend their system' (Meleiseā 1987a:128). I agree with Meleiseā, and consider that Sāmoans have always had a high regard for, and pride in, their indigenous institutions.

The *Mau* movement occupied the period from the 1920s to the 1930s. About 80 per cent of the population joined it (Eteuati 1982:336–37). A *Mau* procession on 28 December 1929, to await the arrival back in Sāmoa of one of their number who had been exiled by the administration, was fired upon by members of the police force during a scuffle between the policemen (who had tried to arrest the *Mau* secretary) and members of the *Mau*. One policeman and 11 Sāmoans were killed. Among the Sāmoans who died was the leader of the *Mau*, Tupua Tamasese Lealofi III. Although families, villages and districts were divided between *Mau* and government supporters, eventually, on 23 March 1934, a reconciliation between the two opposition groups restored amicable relations (Eteuati 1982:325-26). The *Mau* movement 'played a large part in sustaining political pressure which saw Sāmoa in 1962 ... attain full independence' (Eteuati 1982:337).

The victory of the Labour Party (NZLP) in the New Zealand general election in 1935 marked the beginning of a new relationship between New Zealand and Sāmoa (Davidson 1967:146). Soon after taking office, the new prime minister, Michael Savage, made a brief statement on Sāmoa, emphasizing his government's desire to work in cooperation with the Sāmoan people. Thus, in June 1936, a 'goodwill mission' consisting of Frank Langstone, the minister of lands, and James O'Brien, a Labour back-bencher, visited Sāmoa to discuss necessary changes (Eteuati 1982:148). However, New Zealand's involvement in the Second World War delayed not only efforts towards improving her political relationship with Sāmoa, but also the realization of the Sāmoan aspiration for self-government (Eteuati 1982:163).

The NZLP had maintained a nominal allegiance since the end of the First World War to the policy of internal self-government, under international supervision, for territories that were unable to exercise the full powers of an independent state. During the drafting of the United Nations Charter in 1945, the New Zealand prime minister, Peter Fraser – who was the chairman of the trusteeship committee – was one of the most convinced advocates of the trusteeship provisions. As Sāmoa was a mandated territory (the first class of dependencies listed in the charter as eligible for this form of supervision), the New Zealand government took it for granted that it would become a UN Trust Territory (Davidson 1967:163). The trusteeship agreement for Sāmoa was granted by the UN General Assembly on 13 December 1946. Under it, as the administering authority for Sāmoa, New Zealand was obliged to 'promote the development of free political institutions suited to Western Sāmoa'. New Zealand's trusteeship responsibilities were terminated at the attainment of Sāmoa's independence.

Notes

1   LMS/SSL, Heath, Apia, 6 January 1838.

2   LMS/SSL, Murray, Pagopago, 29 August 1838.

3   Seumanutafa and To'omalātai, according to genealogy, were brothers whose collective *fa'alupeaga* was, and still is, *Alo o Sina* (sons of Sina). In the 1590s, a descendant of the Tuiā'ana title named Fa'aolesā married Sina'ai'aiouga who gave birth to Seumanutafa and To'omalātai. Seumanutafa and To'omalātai were among those who founded the village of Apia.

4   LMS/SSL, J. C. Williams to Rev. E. Prout, Mission House, London, Apia, 10 September 1861.

5   LMS/SSL, Hardie to Tidman, Sāpapāli'i, 11 March 1844.

6   LMS/SSL, Rev. George Turner, Mālua, 16 April 1869.

7   Submission by the descendants of Mālietoa Mōlī *(LC 853)*.

8   LMS/SSL, Ella to Tidman, Upolu, 20 July 1853.

9   LMS/SSL, Turner, jnr. to Mullens, Apia, 10 May 1873. In the first clash between the two sides from 26 to 28 March 1869, 14 members of the Talavou side and 17 on the Laupepa side were killed (*SR*, 1, February 1870).

10   Also *SR* – 1, February 1870; 17, January 1856; 18, January 1857.

11   LMS/SSL, King to Mullens, Malua, 22 July 1870; LMS/SSL, Murray to Mullens, Apia, 7 July 1870.

12   LMS/SSL, Murray to Mullens, Apia, 15 March 1870; LMS/SSL, Murray to Mullens, Apia, 7 July 1870; LMS/SSL, Murray to Mullens, Apia, 6 September, 1870.

13   LMS/SSL, Whitmee to Mullens, Apia 31 August 1870; Tupua (1994:69).

14   Tupua (1992:3, 1994:69); LMS/SSL, Whitmee to Mullens, Apia, 31 August 1870.

15   LMS/SSL, Whitmee to Mullens, Apia 7 July 1870; Whitmee to Mullens, Apia, 31 August 1870.

16   LMS/SSL, Whitmee to Mullen, Leulumoega, 5 January 1874.

17   LMS/SSL, Davies to Mullen, Malua, 15 January 1874.

18   British Consulate Apia (BCA), Consul J. C. Williams to Foreign Office (FO), 17 October 1873.

19   BCA, Consul J. C. Williams to FO, 27 November, 1873; Journal of Commodore Goodenough, p. 200.

20   An attitude which has persisted to the present.

22   Methodist Conference Records 1857-1913.

23   LMS/SSL, Nisbet to Mullens, Malua, 20 April 1875. In this letter Nisbet says Steinberger had returned to Sāmoa for the second time in April 1875: 'as resident commissioner from America, *professedly to assist our native rulers to form and carry on an independent government in friendly alliance with the United States* [my emphasis]' (*ibid.*)

24   LMS/SSL, Turner, Jnr. To Mullens, Apia, 5 January 1876 and LMS/SSL, Whitmee to Mullens, Sāmoa, 20 March 1876.

25 LMS/SSL, Whitmee to Mullens, Sāmoa, 20 March 1876; BCA, Minutes of meeting at Mulinu'u in 8 February 1876. Present at this meeting were King Mālietoa, *ta'imua* and *faipule*, Captain Stevens, British Consul (J. C. Williams), American Consul (Foster), and Turner Jr. (interpreter).

26 *Ta'imua* and *faipule* to Liardet, Mulinu'u, 30 May 1877; British Consulate, Apia (BCA)/(In-Letters) IL, Mālietoa Talavou and Mālietoa Laupepa to Liardet, Fasito'otai, 5 June 1877.

27 *ST*, 181, 19 March 1881: BCA/IL, *ta'imua* and *faipule* to Graves, Mulinu'u, 18 March 1881; BCA, Graves to Foreign Office (FO), 12 May 1881; BCA, Graves to FO, 6 June 1881.

28 *ST*, 163, 13 November 1880: BCA, Graves to FO, 22 January 1881.

29 BCA, Graves to FO, 12 May 1881; *ST*, 186, 23 April 1881; *ST*, 193, 11 June 1881; Tamasese Brandeis Papers (TBP), Father Didier in 1881 – re Tamasese and Bishop Lamaze's visit to Leulumoega. In early June, Tupua Tamasese Titimaea was brought to Mulinu'u by his supporters to be proclaimed king.

30 *ST*, 171, 8 January 1881; BCA/IL, Mālietoa Laupepa to Graves, Mulinu'u, 17 January 1881; BCA, Graves to FO, 22 January 1881.

31 BCA, 2 December 1882.

32 BCA, Chiefs of *Tūmua* to Churchward, 19 January 1885; BCA/IL, the four *Tūmua* to Churchward, Leulumoega, 5 February 1885); BCA/IL, Becker to pro-Consul Wilson, 24 August 1887; BCA/IL, Becker to Wilson, 25 August; TBP, Tupua Tamasese to 3 Consuls, Mulinu'u, 25 August 1887: BCA/IL, Minutes of a meeting between *Tūmua* and Weber, 7 January 188?; BCA/IL, Stuebel to Churchward, 23 January 1885 (Stuebel was the German Consul. He was succeeded by Becker).

33 BCA/IL, *Tūmua, Pule ma 'Āiga* to Coetlogan, Fale'ula, 9 September 1888.

34 BCA/IL, Meisake to Matā'afa, Governor of Ātua, Apia, 10 June 1887; Tui Ā'ana Tamasese to Tui Ātua Matā'afa, Leulumoega, 12 June 1887. Leota had been with the Tupua Tamasese government at Leulumoega at the beginning, He later defected to the supporters of Matā'afa Iosefo. Matā'afa had just been conferred the Mālietoa title, and Leota was a direct descendant of both Mālietoa Taulapapa and the Tui Ātua title. This was probably one of the main reasons for Leota's defection to the Matā'afa side.

35 TBP, Tui Ā'ana Tamasese to Tui Ātua Matā'afa, Leulumoega, 13 June 1887.

3 | Keeping the old in the new – the 1962 constitution

SĀMOA'S 1962 CONSTITUTION featured a number of compromises between democracy and Sāmoan custom. For example, there was to be a unicameral parliament which would elect the prime minister, but only *matai* could stand for parliament, and only *matai* could vote in elections. Furthermore, there would be an office of head of state, but it was stipulated that the office would, in the first instance, be held jointly by two of the *tama-a-'āiga*. In trying to reconcile the old and the new, the framers of the constitution included provisions which sometimes proved to be irreconcilable.

Given its status as a UN trusteeship under the scrutiny of the UN Committee for Decolonization, it was inevitable that the political system chosen for independent Sāmoa would be democratic. Given Sāmoa's long association with New Zealand, it was also likely that the political system would be modeled on the system most familiar to Sāmoan leaders, the Westminster parliamentary system. This chapter examines the positions taken by Sāmoan leaders on constitutional issues concerning their customs and traditions.

The constitutional conventions

Preparations for the drafting of Sāmoa's constitution were made during the 1957–60 sitting of parliament. In January 1959, the *fautua* and members of the executive council, formally decided to establish a working committee on self-government; it would discuss and make provisional decisions on all matters concerning the attainment of self-government. The committee was to comprise the *fautua* (as joint chairmen), the seven elected members of the executive council, and seven members nominated by the legislative assembly. Arrangements had already been made for the appointment of two constitutional advisers: Professor J. W. Davidson of the Australian National University, and Professor C. C. Aikman of the Victoria University of Wellington in New Zealand. The latter had previously been appointed constitutional adviser to the New Zealand government in relation to Sāmoan self-government. The committee held its meetings between 3 February 1959 and July 1960, during which time they completed the draft constitution.

Among the proposals recommended by the working committee was the holding of a constitutional convention to decide on a constitution for the future independent state of Western Sāmoa. Realistically, however, it was a convention to discuss the draft constitution that had already been prepared by the working committee. The proposal was enacted in the Constitutional Convention Ordinance 1960. The meetings of the constitutional convention took place between 16 August and 28 October 1960. Membership of the convention was intended to ensure that general public opinion was as widely represented as possible. It included the two *fautua* (Tupua Tamasese Mea'ole and Mālietoa Tanumafili II), another of the *tama-a-'āiga* who was not a member of the legislative assembly, Tuimaleali'ifano Suatipatipa II, three additional representatives of each Sāmoan constituency, and ten additional representatives of the part-Sāmoan or local European (as they were known) community. The *fautua* were named as the joint chairmen, and the prime minister was appointed deputy chairman – an arrangement that was intended both to serve the interests of practical convenience and to demonstrate the unity of the titular and the executive leadership of the country. Of the 174 members of the convention, all except the 15 representatives of the European community were *matai*.

Village government

The framers of the constitution tried to sidestep contentious issues of traditional political rights. The old political order of Sāmoa was based on a substructure of autonomous village polities linked by a genealogically sanctioned superstructure of chiefly connections; by the late 19th century, these were most prominently reflected in the institutions of *tama-a-'āiga* and *Tūmua ma Pule*. The constitution gave no formal legal recognition to village governments; however, the constitutional recognition of *matai* titles may be interpreted as an indirect recognition of village governments. For example, article 100 states that a *matai* title 'shall be held in accordance with Sāmoan custom and usage and with the law relating to Sāmoan custom and usage'. While the phrase 'custom and usage' is not defined anywhere in the constitution, a circuitous definition is provided in the *Land and Titles Act 1981:* 'the custom and usages of Western Sāmoa accepted as being in force at the relevant time', which include both the principles accepted 'by the people of Western Sāmoa in general' and the customs and usages accepted as being in force 'in respect of a particular place or matter'.

However, village governments might be seen as implicitly recognized in the constitution by the provision that a *matai* title is a prerequisite to stand for and vote in parliamentary elections – because village governments have the traditional right to either accept or refuse new titleholders into the village council of *matai*. Moreover, no *matai* title is legitimately conferred on anyone unless the conferral has been sanctioned by the village councils. The constitutional provisions which define eligibility to vote and stand as a member of parliament in the Sāmoan constituencies preserve *matai* traditional rights in general, although they do not distinguish between the foundation titleholders and holders of subordinate titles, or between non-*tama-a-'āiga* and *tama-a-'āiga* titleholders. These provisions implicitly ensure that all traditional rights associated with the conferral of new titles and ownership of customary lands associated with them are entrusted to *matai* and members of their respective families.

The issue of whether or not there should be formal constitutional recognition of village government was raised when the definition of the state was discussed under the first article for provisions on fundamental rights. In the discussion, concern was expressed that, if reference to *ali'i* (chiefs) and *faipule* (representatives, members of *fono*) were not included in the constitution, their authority would have no formal recognition. With this in mind, Toluono Lama moved an amendment to the effect that the *Pule* (authority) of *ali'i* and *faipule* be part of the definition of the state (CCD, 1960, Vol. I, p 74).[1] Toluono had been one of the members of the committee commissioned in 1950 by the high commissioner to inquire into and report upon the organization of district and village government in Western Sāmoa. Noting that the recommendations of the committee had not been given effect (CCD, Vol. I, p. 75) Toluono's resolution was that:

… the Constitutional Convention affirms its conviction that the well-being of the country be given to the *pule* of the *ali'i* and *faipule*. The

Convention further believes that the relationship between the central government and *ali'i* and *faipule* of the districts and villages must be placed upon a formal constitutional basis. (CCD, 1960, Vol. I, p 99).

Responding to Toluono's amendment, one of the advisors, J.W. Davidson, said that the working committee considered that the relationship of the authority of the *ali'i* and *faipule* to the law of the country was too complicated and that the committee did not feel it could be dealt with in the constitution itself. (CCD, 1960, Vol. I, p 74). Nonetheless, the members of the convention insisted that the authority of *ali'i* and *faipule* should be included in the definition of the state. The constitutional advisors were anxious to avoid this vexed issue and, after various delays, a 'Draft Resolution regarding the *pule* of the *ali'i* and *faipule*' was presented to the convention. It advocated that the recommendations of the 1950 commission and all other relevant evidence be studied, and that legislation be prepared and enacted to ensure that the authority of the *ali'i* and *faipule* is properly protected in the interests of the well-being of Western Sāmoa and its people. (*CCD*, Vol. I, p 99). In other words, the convention was asked to deal with the issue separately from the constitution.

This seemed like a diversionary move to many members of the convention. All the Sāmoans knew what the authority of *ali'i* and *faipule* encompassed; what they wanted was a guarantee that this authority was not to be undermined. However, the chairman, steering committee and the working committee knew that for Sāmoa to gain independence, they had produce a draft resolution that would be sufficiently democratic in its provisions to be acceptable to the Trusteeship Council. Formal legal acknowledgement of traditional hereditary authority could lead to delays in Sāmoa attaining independence. By accepting a resolution to deal with the matter outside the constitution, the advisors proposed a compromise.

And not everyone wanted the authority of *matai* to be formalized, seeing this as a limitation on their powers. For example, Nonoa told the convention that:

> ...we do not want the *pule* [authority] to be legalised and so limited....
> As a member of this Convention, I do not want anything to do with any laws touching upon our customs, and the rights we have to exercise them. I would like to see the customary rights treated with freedom (*CCD*, 1960, Vol. I, p 101-2).

Although they accepted the resolution to deal separately with the legal affirmation of *matai* authority, Sāmoan speakers made it clear that the authority of village government and of the associated authority of *ali'i* and *faipule* was a major concern.

District representation

In the traditional system of government, aristocratic lineages were kept in check by the power of 11 district-based coalitions of *tulafale* (spokesmen or orators) who controlled the paramount titles that confirmed aristocratic rank. These coalitions of *fale'upolu* or *Tūmua* and *Pule* had very specific powers to bestow their paramount titles upon the heads of lineages. These powers were not recognized in the constitution. The argument that won the day in the 1960 constitutional convention was that the traditional rights of the districts were implicitly preserved through the continued recognition of 41 district constituencies.

Nevertheless, there were those who argued for an explicit role for *Tūmua* and *Pule*. In discussions of the draft provision that the future heads of state should be elected by the legislative assembly, Semau Peleseuma argued that the head of state should be elected by the *Tūmua* and *Pule*, saying:

> In the olden times we understand that some of the Tama-a-'āiga had become the "Tafaifa", literally meaning he was holding the 4 paramount titles. Therefore, I suggest that he shall become the Tafaifa and that I feel will be the very point on which we shall be able to realise that the Government of Western Sāmoa shall be based on its traditions, and in order to fully deal with this matter in the proper manner (CCD, 1960, Vol. I, p 283).

Fiso Fasi, who represented Palauli, one of the *Pule* centres of Savai'i, supported this view but was countered by Fata Matua of the *Tūmua* of Afega, who argued that the head of state should be elected by both the legislative assembly as well as representatives of the 11 traditional political districts. He argued that the legislative assembly would not carry enough weight to make such a momentous choice (CCD, 1960, Vol. I, p 285). In countering the argument that *Tūmua* and *Pule* were truly represented through the 41 Sāmoan constituencies, Talamaivao Vaela'a of Va'a-o-Fonotī pointed out that *Tūmua* and *Pule* were marginal to the political system as it was at that time. However, these views were not upheld by the majority, and Semau's proposed amendment was lost in a division by 37 to 126 votes.

Toluono had one more try, moving that 'The State shall include the Head of State, Cabinet and Parliament, and *Pule* and *Tūmua*' (*CCD*, 1960, Vol. II, p. 781). Expressing concern that there were those in government who had not been elected in accordance with customs and traditions, Toluono sought to gain formal recognition of *Tūmua* and *Pule* in order to make sure no law could supersede customs and traditions, and to ensure that a representative of *Tūmua* and *Pule* would assist in the election of the future head of state.[2] In the ensuing discussion, supporters of Toluono's motion justified their claim on four main grounds: First, it was unfair that *'āiga*, through their sons (or *tama-a-'āiga*), were included in the constitution and that *Tūmua* and *Pule* were not; second, the future affairs of the state would be governed by the parliament, thereby disassociating *Tūmua* and *Pule* from central government politics; third, if the new constitution were to be based on customs and traditions, then *Tūmua* and *Pule* should legitimately be in it. The fourth, somewhat contradictory argument, that *Tūmua* and *Pule* would endure for all time, regardless of legal recognition (*CCD*, 1960, Vol. II, p. 782)[3] was, as Lei'ātaua Poai of 'Aiga-i-le-Tai put it, a 'bag of wind'.[4]

The counter-argument revolved around the same four points. It was mentioned that the constitution contained no specific recognition of *'āiga* despite the constitutional recognition proposed for *tama-a-'āiga* in relation to the office of head of state. Those who opposed explicit recognition of *Tūmua* and *Pule* accepted the notion that real power should belong to parliament. In their view, *Tūmua* and *Pule* were duly represented following the subdivision of the traditional districts into the current number of constituencies; and that, *Tūmua* and *Pule* political centres were merely promoting their own interests. Fata Matua of Sāgaga-le-Usoga, among the leading *tulafale* of one of the *Tūmua* political centres, opposed the motion saying, 'I say to you *Pule* and *Tūmua* – you should not try so hard in your striving to obtain and to materialize your wishes. You must realize that *Pule* and *Tūmua* .... really belong to Sāmoa. It is not ours alone' (*ibid.*:791). In the same spirit, Fāolotoi Momoe of Lepā pointed out 'this...Government is not a Sāmoan form of Government, it is a modern form of Government' (*ibid.*:799–80). Tēvaga Paletāsala of Gāgā'emauga No.1 constituency said, '...your recognized authority has not been put down on paper, it is a matter understood in the minds of dignities of chiefs and orators of this country. If the time comes to express your authority, nobody will dare to stop you from doing so' (*ibid.*:785). Towards the end of the debate, the prime minister, Māta'afa Fīamē Faumuinā Mulinu'ū II, pleaded for *Tūmua* and *Pule's* support in realizing the country's higher ideal of attaining its independence.[5] Moreover, before Toluono made his final speech towards the conclusion of the debate, the chairman, Tupua Tamasese Mea'ole, warned members that foreigners may take over the country in the future if Sāmoan leaders did not act in unity. Tulono lost the motion.

The *fono* (parliament) and suffrage

Under colonial rule the Sāmoans had had sixty years of more or less peaceful representative government. The colonial system had given increasing representation to the districts and formal recognition to the highest chiefs and, in particular, to the *tama-a-'āiga*. However, for most of the colonial period, traditional leadership had a very weak voice.

Sāmoa's constitution is built upon the established institution of a legislative assembly. It established a *fono* or national parliament, comprising the head of state and a legislative assembly, whose members would be known as members of parliament. The *fono* was to make laws for the whole country under the provision that a bill passed by the legislative assembly after its third reading would become law when assented to by the head of state. Members of parliament were to be elected every three years.[6] Members of parliament were to elect one of their number to be a speaker of the legislative assembly. Parliamentary decisions were to be made by majority vote, but the speaker, or the deputy speaker (or a delegate in the absence of both) may have a casting vote in the case of a tie. The prime minister, to be chosen from among the MPs, was to be appointed by the head of state. The prime minister was to choose a cabinet of eight members from the members of parliament, also to be appointed by the head of state. The constitution provided that only citizens of Sāmoa might stand for election and vote in parliamentary elections. Candidates for election must not be disqualified under any other provisions of the constitution. There were to be 41 seats (derived from the incremental subdivisions of the 11 traditional political districts). In these Sāmoan constituencies, only *matai* could vote and become candidates in parliamentary elections. To accommodate the part-Sāmoan community, the constitution provided for a second roll, the individual voters roll, whose members (the number of which is to be determined by an act of parliament) would elect one of their number.

The provisions on suffrage reflect the unanimous opinion of the 1954 and the 1960 constitutional conventions – that the position of *matai* should be upheld by reserving for them the right to vote and stand in parliamentary elections. (CCD, 1960, Vol.II, p. 499). The provision meant that, under the constitution, the political rights of Sāmoan citizens who are not *matai* are restricted to electing *matai* in their respective families. Even then, the selection process is usually confined to elders, so younger Sāmoans were effectively disenfranchised.

In the 1954 convention debates, only 14 members supported the entitlement of non-*matai* Sāmoans aged 21 years and over to elect from among *matai* the members of parliament for the Sāmoan constituencies. In the 1960 constitutional convention, Paitomaleifi Siaki of Faleālili moved that every Sāmoan citizen who had attained the age of 21 years should be given the right to vote, although eligibility to stand as parliamentary candidates in the Sāmoan constituencies would still be restricted to *matai*. Speaking on the motion Paitomaleifi said:

> My opinion is based from the fundamental rights of every human being as we know that some of the people in our country may be 40 to 60 years while they are still untitled and hence, it would mean that they would go down to their graves without ever having a say in selecting their representatives to the Legislative Assembly ....I really think that our dignified customs and traditions would not in any way be hampered if this amendment is approved. ...Furthermore, I wish to ask as to when are we going to put it into effect, to comply with the constant crying out of our children who are untitled and intending to leave the country? I mean local born who are still crying out to be recognized (*CCD*, 1960, Vol. II, p 486).

Paitomaleifi believed universal suffrage would do away with the need for two electoral rolls. Supporters of his motion argued that universal suffrage was a sign of political progress and enlightenment, even of the brotherly love prescribed by the churches (CCD, 1960, Vol. II, p. 489). This view was particularly strong among members of the European and part-Sāmoan community who argued that it would protect the *matai* system, by ensuring people had no grounds to rebel against it, and safeguard human rights (CCD, 1960, Vol. II, 491).[7]

Paitomaleifi linked the constitutional provision for freedom of expression with the issue of suffrage, saying that all Sāmoans were entitled to freedom of expression; Tūgaga also noted this connection. They both identified a conflict between the freedom of expression and the expectation that *matai* should exercise unquestioned authority. It was well known to the convention that, in village governments, criticisms of a *matai* could result in a heavy penalty.

In this respect the constitution contained a major contradiction. The incorporation of the provision on fundamental rights in the constitution introduced a set of values that was contradictory to that associated with village government, and to the indigenous socio-political structure in general. The advisers, as the 'minds behind the minds', had the responsibility to draft a constitution acceptable to the United Nations and the New Zealand parliament as well as to Sāmoans. To achieve this they had to push a substantial majority of the Sāmoans at the convention to the limit of their cultural ability to adapt their indigenous institutions, if not to surrender them. The advisers wanted to establish in the constitution the basis for the future progressive democratization of Sāmoa's indigenous institutions. So, because Sāmoa had been a Christian country for about 130 years, the constitutional advisers tried to associate the concept of fundamental rights with Christian values (that all people were equal in the eyes of God). They hoped that in this way the Sāmoans would readily accept the concept of fundamental rights.

Those defending the restricted suffrage included Mālietoa Tanumafili II. He argued that Sāmoan identity and culture were at stake; the Sāmoan system was democratic because the extended family chose the *matai*, and so the votes expressed family opinion (*CCD*, 1960, Vol. II, p. 495) (*CCD*, 1960, Vol. II, p. 95). Other's pointed to the danger that universal suffrage might pose to the traditional hierarchy. For example, Tēvaga Paletāsala told the convention:

> ....with due regard and respect to the Hon. *Tama-a-'āiga*, what I am afraid about is this, if we are to give the right to vote to those of 21 years old, we never know in future the people might change their minds and vote for an ordinary *matai* to become the Head of State and the supreme leader of this country. As long as he is elected to represent the interest of all those people, then he would be concerned in deliberating the fate of this country (*CCD*, Vol. II, p. 496).

Tēvaga's words show that he assumed that younger people would be less inclined to uphold customs and traditions and would elect those more interested in catering for the wishes of their voters than in safeguarding customs and traditions. He clearly saw the threat to customs and traditions posed by a parliament inclined to respond primarily to their electorates' wishes, even with the *matai* as the only candidates for parliamentary seats. Tēvaga's comment also noted that custom allows for a wide difference in the rank of titles. He not only implied that 'ordinary' *matai* are less interested in safeguarding customs and traditions, but that they should not be in parliament in the first place. Under customary processes, lesser-ranking *matai* participate but don't have much say in major decisions, regardless of their personal abilities. It was probably the expectation of most members of the convention that the Sāmoan *fono* would continue the practice of electing mainly high-ranking titleholders as members of the legislative assembly. Even under today's more formal democratic arrangements, the expectation that high-ranking *matai* are more entitled to high office continues. For example, a politician expressing satisfaction with his electoral victory in 1993 told the author that he defeated the 'tiny *matai*' (*tama'i matai*) referring to *matai* with no local standing or status. Although members of the convention clearly understood the distinction between categories of *matai*, there seems to have been an agreement not to highlight this fact. The then prime minister, Matā'afa Faumuinā Fiamē Mulinu'ū II, was an advocate of universal suffrage; picking up Tēvaga's point about 'ordinary *matai*' he said:

> I would like to say that there are a lot of big brains over there in the UN and they might be suspicious of our set-up and they might say, you want the *Matai* system, but what is this discrimination which appears here? (*CCD*, Vol. II, p. 498).

The chairman of the convention then intervened and asked that there be no further mention of discrimination between the rank of *matai*, and that all *matai* be referred to as though equal (*CCD*, 1960, Vol. II p. 498).

Arguments both for and against universal suffrage invoked the issue of upholding customs and traditions. Although Paitomaleifi had few supporters from among the Sāmoan leadership, he defended his minority opinion by explaining to the convention that it was not his intention to abolish Sāmoan custom, but to ensure that the talents of educated Sāmoans would be used in the development of the country. Even though

Paitomaleifi had argued a case for universal suffrage, he believed that there would be little contest for parliamentary seats because he assumed that the existing practice in which the village *fono* nominated the candidate would continue. He thought individual votes would only be resorted to when the *fono* could not achieve consensus. (*CCD*, 1960, Vol. II, p. 500). Paitomaleifi was convinced that *matai* control over political affairs would remain intact and by his motion he intended to preserve *matai* authority, not to lessen or undermine it.

A roll of 'individual voters' was proposed and eventually upheld in the constitution to allow representation of citizens outside the traditional system. This was legitimized by the provisions for political and legal rights stipulated under Part II of the constitution, on fundamental rights. In a report of its visit to Western Sāmoa in 1959, the United Nations mission insisted that a bill of rights be included in the constitution (Powles 1970:3). The Trusteeship Agreement of 1946 had also obliged New Zealand to encourage respect in Western Sāmoa for human rights and fundamental freedoms. Therefore, the concepts embodied in the provision for civil liberties in Western Sāmoa's constitution have been adapted from the United Nations Charter of human rights and fundamental freedoms. In 1960, Tupua Tamasese Mea'ole explained to the convention why 'individual voters' must have two seats. The idea was to provide representation for those citizens who are not members of Sāmoan *'āiga* and therefore cannot be said to be represented through a *matai*. He acknowledged that members of the working committee accepted that the *matai* system of electing representatives was appropriate, but reminded the convention that many people had had the right to a vote in the past, and would feel a justifiable sense of grievance should they lose this right. (CCD, 1960, Vol. II, pp. 506, 82) It was decided, therefore, on the basis of the number of 'individual voter' compared with the number of voters in Sāmoan constituencies, that there should be two seats for individual voters.

The provision defining eligibility to be enrolled as an individual voter was seen as a temporary measure. It was envisaged that eventually all citizens of Western Sāmoa would be fully absorbed into Sāmoan society (*CCD*, 1960, Vol. II, p 483). Then, anyone who had any privilege under Sāmoan custom, such as holding a *matai* title, being married to a *matai*, or using customary lands, would have his or her name taken off the individual voters roll. Once the right to be on that roll was lost, it could never be reclaimed – the only exception being for a woman who was previously an individual voter but who had divorced a Sāmoan elector. The roll was also intended to accommodate foreigners whom the government agreed to accept as Sāmoan citizens by naturalization.

A representative of the European community at the convention, H. J. Keil, complained that the number of seats allocated to individual voters was not enough. He pointed out that 41 seats were given to about 700 *matai*, the total number of *matai* in Sāmoa at the time of the convention, while only two seats were given to the 662 individual voters (*CCD*, 1960, Vol. II, p. 502). J.W. Davidson, an advisor to the convention, estimated that the number 662 should be multiplied by three to give a rough total of all people who were not entitled to privileges that could have been attained under the *matai* system. With 'foreigners' included, each seat for the individual voters would, thus, represent roughly 1,000 voters. The 700 *matai* represented not only *matai* but also all the members of their respective families. On the basis of population, therefore, a representative of each Sāmoan seat represented roughly the same number of people. However, Keil told the convention that he foresaw the number of individual voters decreasing, and the disenfranchisement of the part-European community. He moved to refer the issue of the number of seats back to the working committee but the motion was defeated by 120 to 41 votes.

Political parties

The constitution does not provide explicitly for the establishment of political parties and the issue did not come before the convention. That political parties were not explicitly provided for in the constitution, nor mentioned during the convention, suggests that the committee deliberately decided against the inclusion in the constitution of any provision for the establishment of political parties; that political parties were a controversial idea not to be mentioned in the convention; and, that the committee thought that such a provision would be rejected by the convention. However, the minutes of the working committee show that at least one of the constitutional advisors believed that a party system would eventually develop (*WCM*, 3 February 1959). This view was not shared by the Sāmoan members. Tuātagaloa Simaile of Faleālili was recorded as having expressed concern that the party system could prove disruptive to Sāmoan society. Tuātagaloa held the high *ali'i* titles from other villages (Leutele, Te'o and Sātele), so he had a duty to maintain unity not only in the families of which he held the titles, but also in the villages to which they belonged. Tuātagaloa probably saw the establishment of political parties as a potential threat to family and village unity, which, he, amongst others, was obligated to maintain. Moreover, the general Sāmoan ideology is that unity means strength, and that unity and strength earn respect.

The minutes of the working committee meeting on 5 February 1960 provide other clues about the general Sāmoan attitude towards political parties. When the committee discussed Article 13(b) – the right to assemble peacefully and without arms – Luamanuvae[8] asked the advisers what the case would be if such an assembly involved official discussion of government matters. Aikman explained that the clause would permit this. Luamanuvae then expressed his belief that this should not be permitted because riots and scheming against the government could occur if such discussions were discovered when it was too late. Aikman reassured him that the powers of the police could deal with this kind of situation. Luamanuvae then clarified his position, explaining that he did not object to the formation of political parties but was only concerned with sedition (*WCM*, 5 February 1960).

Luamanuvae and Tuātagaloa would understandably have equated political parties with divisiveness, which they would have regarded with suspicion and great caution. Both had been alive during the *Mau* resistance movement in the 1920s–1930s, but were born close enough to events of the last quarter of the 19th century to know about and understand the negative aspects of those struggles. The social divisions in those times was something that Sāmoan leaders did not want repeated. In the past, there had been party-like factions supporting rival candidates for the kingship – a situation that Sāmoans would rather forget. The proceedings of the convention indicate clearly that its members were well aware of the divisive issues, historical events and past discord over national leadership and honours, and were anxious to ensure that the sources of discord were not revived (*CCD*, 1960, Vol. I, p. 253).

The head of state

The constitution provides for the position of head of state to be held jointly for life in the first instance by two *tama-a-'āiga*, Mālietoa Tanumafili II and Tupua Tamasese Mea'ole. To accommodate the other two *tama-a-'āiga*, Matā'afa and Tuimaleali'ifano, a new office of council of deputies was created. After the death of one of the joint heads of state, the survivor will continue to hold that office. Upon the death of both of them, a new provision will then operate to decide future heads of state. The new provision empowers the legislative assembly to elect future heads of state every five years.

The future of the *tama-a-'āiga* was partly decided in the 1954 constitutional convention. This provision was one of the most difficult questions faced by the convention because members were aware that reference to history or tradition could cause a new eruption of old, dormant rivalries amongst the Sāmoan leaders present. It was agreed that the *tama-a-'āiga* should be eligible to hold the office of head of state. This resolution was expected, considering the kingship struggles in the 19th century in which the *tama-a-'āiga* were the candidates. Moreover, their socio-political status had been maintained up to this time through the *fautua* office. At the time of the convention, only two *tama-a-'āiga* held office as *fautua*. They were Mālietoa Tanumafili II and Tupua Tamasese Mea'ole. When the other *fautua*, Matā'afa F.F.Mulinu'ū I, had died in1948, the *fono* of *faipule* had recommended to the council of state that no new appointment of a *fautua* should be made, thus leaving Mālietoa Tanumafili II and Tupua Tamasese Mea'ole as the only *fautua* by 1954. A successor to the Matā'afa title was later elected but he was not appointed a *fautua*. Following the death in 1937 of Tuimaleali'ifano Si'u, no successor to the title was elected until 1948 – thus, this position was also affected by the earlier decision not to appoint any more *fautua*.

When the issue of head of state was due for discussion, the four *tama-a-'āiga* vacated their seats to ensure that the dignity of their titles was not offended in the course of the debate. After the discussion of this issue, the convention then recalled the *tama-a-'āiga* to its concluding session. The convention agreed that the two *fautua* should together be the first head of state. This decision was acceptable on the grounds that a representative from each of Sa Tupuā and Sa Mālietoā was to be associated with the top office of government, thus adhering to the general Sāmoan attitude on the kingship that had prevailed since 1873 (*CCD*, 1960, Vol. I, pp. 248, 253). However, the problem remained of whether or not this resolution was acceptable to the other two *tama-a-'āiga*, Matā'afa F.F.M. II and Tuimaleali'ifano Suatipatipa, and their respective *'āiga*.

That it was not acceptable was soon apparent. When the *tama-a-'āiga* resumed their seats, Matā'afa spoke, pointing out that, despite their rank, he and Tuimaleali'ifano had been given no place in the new political structure, an offense which might cause his family to refrain from participating in the future affairs of state. Representatives of *Tūmua* and *Pule* present pleaded with Matā'afa 'not to destroy Sāmoan unity when the long-cherished objective of self-government was on the point of being realized'. Several days after the convention, at a joint meeting of the legislative assembly and the *fono* of *faipule*, a member of *'Āiga* Sālevālasi, speaking on behalf of that *'āiga*, withdrew Matā'afa's objection. Because the issue of the association of *tama-a-'āiga* with the office of head of state proved to be so sensitive, the convention resolved to defer the issue, making provision only that parliament could decide how to fill future vacancies in the position of head of state.

Freedom of religion

In the debate on the clause concerning the freedom of religion, a number of members of the convention argued that the qualifier 'Christian' be inserted before the word 'religion', thereby preventing non-Christian religions from being introduced into Sāmoa. This was only logical, it was claimed, as the preamble of the constitution said that Sāmoa was to be founded on Christian principles. However, Davidson countered this argument, claiming it was unnecessary. Christianity was intricately bound up with the *matai* system. The Sāmoans had accepted the notion that Sāmoa had been appointed by God to be governed by the *matai*, as it was the *matai* with whom God's name had been shared. The Sāmoans regarded the Christian God as their heavenly *matai*. Likewise, the *matai* was the embodiment of God's earthly authority. In short, Christianity had been successfully moulded into the indigenous socio-political structure to the extent that it had helped maintain the indigenous system. Thus, although Christianity might have meant a number of things to the Sāmoans, one of the things it definitely did not mean was interference with the *matai* system. But, placing the *matai* as central to the whole system was tantamount to the rejection of the notion of individual rights, and likewise of democracy.

In the debate on the clause on the freedom of religion, 'Auali'itia Fa'a'ole'ole said 'Religion, we understand, is a good thing as it enables men to know the Will of God and also to worship God but on the other hand it is a bad thing as it tends to create tension and disputes amongst the people'

(*CCD*, 1960, Vol. I, p. 173). He strongly urged the chairman to include provision in the constitution to prevent further religions coming to Sāmoa, anticipating their potential for social divisions. Semau Peleseuma took up this point as well, commenting on H. J. Keil's proposed amendment to ensure that missionaries would have the freedom to come to Sāmoa. Semau said:

> Order and peace must be maintained in the villages or in communi-ties, and as we have seen today, that harmony and peace is hardly to be found in the villages today because of the present number of mis-sionaries that we have here, we can imagine the amount of commotion that could be created if an additional number or more missionaries were introduced ... The more missionaries and the more preaching in regard to their religious beliefs are concerned, the more difficult it is for us to maintain peace and order amongst our own people (*CCD*, 1960, Vol. I, 181).

Fa'amoetauloa Sasi of Gāgā'emauga No. 3 constituency also pointed to the potential for disharmony, saying that, unlike European society, in Sāmoan society there was no age limit to parental authority over their children. He stated:

> I therefore would like to suggest, Messrs. Chairmen, that the old custom be revived - that is the understanding that wherever the head of a family goes to worship, all his family members should be forced to go too (*CCD*, 1960, Vol. I, p. 169).

The concept of individual rights implied in the notion of freedom of religion was in conflict with the accepted traditional notion associated with the authority of the *matai* and *faipule* in general. Māta'utia Fetaui of Aleipata Itupā-i-lalo constituency argued:

> What I am not clear of is whether the right of the *Matai*s can apply in any matters of worship, like in the question of the illustration I have just put forward regarding the *Matai*s as being heads and controllers of families affairs who still uphold the old or original religion of the family and yet the members of the families still take up their own religion. In exercising this so-called right to worship by the members of a family, it might lead to something more complicated, that I, as a *Matai*, would not look upon with favour on what they would be doing and I might revert to drastic measures which would then be regarded as an offence against the law. I therefore merely wanted to put this

straight in my own mind with the understanding that I am a *Matai* and I am supposed to be responsible for all matters in my own immediate family (*CCD*, 1960, Vol. I, p. 170).

There was concern that, by supporting the provision for religious freedom, the members of the convention could be allowing the teachings of churches to interfere with their customary authority. Papāli'i Pēsāmino of Fa'asālele'aga No. 2 constituency noted that some churches in Sāmoa encouraged their members to disobey the *fono*, saying:

> I have noticed that some of the members of other religions are not acting in accordance with our customs and traditions. For instance, when the village council instructs something to be carried out, members of some of these religions claim that they do not take part in such affairs (*CCD*, 1960, Vol. I, p. 184).

Saumālū Tui of Aleipata Itupā-i-Luga constituency pointed to the prospect of conflicting authority between churches and *matai*, saying:

> .... if, I a *Matai*, and members of my family, had a difference of opinion over something, then the members of my family would not see eye to eye with me in regard to something and would just go out and get the missionary or a preacher of a different religion. They would even go as far as asking that these new missionaries would put up a house of worship on this land that I am supposed to be responsible for as a *Matai*. I am supposed to take the full responsibility of the family and I might have to instruct these people not to establish a new religious denomination in the family lands, because I am not in agreement with those steps. This is the reason why I rise to state that I believe there should be a right where the *Matai* should be entitled to maintain peace in his own family, that this question when the ordinary members of the family bring in a new form of religion altogether and also proceed to establish their house of worship on this very land where I, as *Matai*, should have full responsibility or authority for. They can worship any form of religion, but as long as they do not bring that Mission onto my land and ask me to put up a house for worship on my land. I know that some of the provisions should be based on customary understanding and I understand and believe that if one of the members of my family wish to worship another religion, there is no reason why he should not walk over to where that religion has its prayers, but not to bring that into our land if I do not agree to it. If I am agreeable, then that is a different question altogether (*CCD*, 1960, Vol. I, p. 180).

Leva'a Fofoa of 'Āiga-i-le-Tai constituency also pointed to this potential conflict, saying that 'all the religions which have been brought into Sāmoa came here long after the *Pule* of the *Ali'i ali'i* and *Faipule*' (*CCD*, 1960, Vol. I, p 188).

Whatever the substantial majority of the Sāmoan members of the convention meant by Christianity or religion, two things seemed to be certain. First, religion should not interfere with the authority of the *matai* vis-à-vis their family, or with the authority of the *ali'i* and *faipule* vis-à-vis the affairs of village governments. Second, the idea of individual rights implied the provisions for fundamental rights and thus was difficult to reconcile with Sāmoan custom and tradition.

The constitution attempted to be a legal document that allowed for the realization of democratic ideals by relegating customs and traditions to second place. However, the substantial majority of Sāmoan members of the convention insisted upon retaining customs and traditions. As a number of them often remarked, if customs and traditions were to form the basis of the constitution, that meant 'all aspects' of customs and traditions were to be protected in the constitution. The truth of the matter was pointed out by the New Zealand high commissioner when he opened the convention. He told the members that the constitution would provide 'a legal framework inside which Sāmoan customs and traditions will operate' (*CCD*, 1960, Vol. I, p. 7). The following chapters analyze the success or otherwise of this legal attempt to reconcile Sāmoan institutions and values with democracy in the years after independence.

Notes

1   Toluono Lama (Palauli constituency).
2   The secretary of the convention paraphrased Toluono's motion which then read: 'That Part II [of the Constitution] should read as follows: "The State" shall include the Head of State, Cabinet, Parliament, *Pule* and *Tūmua*, *Āiga-i-le-Tai*, Va'a-o-Fonoti and all other authorities in the country.
    'That means there should be a representative of the *Tūmua* and *Pule* in the election of the Head of State.
    'There should be a separate representative of the *Pule* and *Tūmua* in the Legislative Assembly' (*CCD*, 1960, Vol. II, p 782).
3   Afamasaga Maua (Ā'ana Ālofi No.3 constituency).
4   Lei'ātaua Poai ('Āiga-i-le-Tai constituency).
5   The prime minister told the convention:
    …our customs and traditions will still exist….all the powers and authority is

being vested in *the Legislative Assembly* who *is to find a recognised position for Tūmua and Pule* ....My expressions tonight Hon. Gentlemen, are not just mere words. I wish to inform Members that my words come right from the abundance of my heart, and I really mean it when I say that *the only thing that I treasure most heartily in my mind is the recognised authority of the Tūmua and Pule, because I do believe that with their protection and their over-ruling authority over the affairs of this country, it will surely safeguard all corners of this country* (*CCD*, 1960, Vol. II, p 803) [my emphasis].

6   The parliamentary term was increased to five years following the passing of a constitutional amendment to that effect in 1993.

7   P. L. M. Morgan, representative of the European community.

8   That Luamanuvae was the earlier title of Tofilau 'Eti Alesana (the late prime minister of Sāmoa). Tofilau 'Eti Alesana was a member of parliament in this parliamentary term under the title Luamanuvae.

4 | From consensus politics to party politics

From consensus politics to factions: 1962–1970

THE CONSTITUTION of the Independent State of Western Sāmoa was based on democratic institutions and practices – however, traditional modes of leadership selection persisted, including the institution of *tama-a-'āiga* (and its cross-cutting links to other key traditional institutions and practices inherent in the *matai* system). Political parties did not develop until 17 years after independence in 1962. Paradoxically, the establishment of the first political party was largely a reaction against the defeat of the incumbent prime minister, who was a *tama-a-'āiga*. The establishment of the first political party was not only a democratic innovation in itself, but one of the most important developments towards the realization of democracy.

A liberal-democratic notion of competition for all positions of power is implicit in Sāmoa's Westminster model of parliamentary government, whereby individuals are free to pursue their own political preferences. However, the constitution also recognized traditional institutions. Thus, it created an inherent conflict between indigenous collectivist ideals and individual political freedom.

Though slightly modified following political developments of the European post-contact and colonial periods, Sāmoan institutions, such as *tama-a-'āiga*, represented a continuation of a long tradition of district paramount titles. The need for parliamentarians to remain united following the realization of the country's independence in 1962 made the traditional position of *tama-a-'āiga* particularly important. Upon independence, two of the *tama-a-'āiga*, Tupua Tamasese Mea'ole and Mālietoa Tanumafili II, became joint heads of state for life. The third *tama-a-'āiga*, Tuimaleali'ifano Suatipatipa II, became the first holder of the office of council of deputies. The remaining *tama-a-'āiga*, Matā'afa F.F. Mulinu'ū II, entered parliament in the 1957 general election, and was elected by the legislative assembly in October 1959 as the first prime minister of Sāmoa.

The constitution opened political offices to all registered *matai*, but in the first decade of independence it was clear that Sāmoans' preferred their prime minister to be a *tama-a-'āiga*. A substantial majority of members of the working committee on self-government, which developed the draft constitution and the *Sāmoa Amendment Act 1959*, favoured a 'full-blooded Sāmoan' to be the country's first prime minister. By the time the act came into force on 1 October 1959, the legislative assembly had made its choice of prime minister (Davidson 1967:364). The three nominations for the prime ministership were Matā'afa Fiamē Faumuinā Mulinu'ū II (minister of agriculture – hereafter Matā'afa) and Tuālaulelei Mauri (former minister), who were 'full-blooded' Sāmoans, and Eugene Paul (minister of economic development and leader of government business), a 'half-Sāmoan' representative of the European community. In the first ballot, Matā'afa emerged as the leading contender, but he lacked an absolute majority. He was elected in the second ballot (*ibid*: 364–65).

Mulinu'ū II, Matā'afa's first name, entered parliament as an MP for Lotofaga constituency under his other title, Fiamē. However, the fact that he held the *tama-a-'āiga* title, Matā'afa, seemed to have greatly influenced his election as prime minister. As Tufuga Fatu pointed out to the working committee on self-government, 'even if *tama-a-'āiga* come to the legislative assembly as lesser titles, they still would be paid the respect due to them as *tama-a-'āiga* and would thus be still appointed to some office such as Prime Minister and would undoubtedly hold these positions for life'. In short, Matā'afa's election befitted his status as *tama-a-'āiga*, and was acceptable to the general public. J.W. Davidson, one of the advisors to the constitutional committees, aptly summed up the general public feeling upon Matā'afa's prime ministerial election in 1959:

> Superficially, the choice of Fiamē as the first Prime Minister was a surprising one in so conservative a society. He was only thirty-eight years of age and a comparative newcomer to politics. His actions five years earlier, as a member of the Constitutional Convention, when he had both advocated universal suffrage and threatened to maintain

a position of non-co-operation unless his status as the holder of the Matā'afa title was recognized, had created anxiety as to his ambitions, rather than confidence in his claims to leadership. Yet, at a deeper level, his choice was wholly in accord with Sāmoan ideas and values. He was a *tama-a-'āiga*. He had shown firmness and clarity of mind as Minister for Agriculture. Less tangibly, though of no less importance, he had created in the minds of members an image of himself as a traditional Sāmoan leader. Eloquent and allusive in speech, confident but unaggressive in action, aloof but not unfriendly in manner, he had gained the respect of all and avoided close association with any group or faction. He was a leader who, like a good *matai* in his relations with his family, kept in sensitive touch with the feelings and opinions of those who had entrusted him with authority. And his first decision after his nomination, in selecting the outgoing Ministers and his rivals for the Prime Ministership, as members of his Cabinet, confirmed this reputation. It showed that he was determined to maintain the unity of the country during the remainder of the transition to independence. (Davidson 1967:365)

Matā'afa was re-elected unopposed as prime minister following the general election at the end of 1960. The intention was for that parliamentary term to see the country through to independence in January 1962, thereby making Matā'afa the first prime minister of the Independent State of Sāmoa. However, Matā'afa was also re-elected unopposed as prime minister by both the 1964–66 and 1967–69 parliaments.

The constitution provided for the prime minister to appoint his own cabinet ministers. The issues of whether the ministers of cabinet should be selected by the prime minister or the legislative assembly, and – if the former – how the prime minister would select his cabinet ministers, were thoroughly debated in the constitutional committee meetings in 1959–1960. At that time, Tuālaulelei Mauri expressed fears that 'should the prime minister be allowed to select his own cabinet there may be uneven distribution of ministers amongst political districts and consequently there may be some weighty opposition from the House to cabinet proposals'. Tufuga Fatu held the same view, forecasting the potential instability of government if all political districts were not represented. Pilia'e Iuliano said that 'Any method of appointing ministers should be done on a basis which would not ignore Sāmoan traditions of the people'. Luamanuvae Eti argued that, while the prime minister should choose his own ministers, there should be three each from Upolu and Savai'i and a representative of the European community. To'omata Tua suggested a compromise, proposing that the prime minister should select his ministers on the understanding that the ministers were to be selected from the main political districts. These opinions, and the continuing importance of the political status of the districts seem to have influenced Matā'afa's selection of his cabinet ministers, and parliament's choices of speakers and deputy speakers.

Although there were small and generally disorganized factions in parliament, the more noticeable divisions were the government on one side, and the rest of parliament on the other. Immediately following the announcement of the cabinet, those not appointed as ministers became an unofficial opposition to the government. One of Matā'afa's tactics to maintain a consensus-based government was to appoint the more outspoken members of parliament to cabinet if they won a second term. This channeled their criticisms away from the public arena and directed them towards formulating national policies. Among such appointments were Matā'afa's minister of finance from 1961, Gustav Betham, and Ulualofaigā Talamaivao Vaela'a, and Laufili Time (ministers in the 1964–66 parliament), and Tuaopepe Tame (appointed to cabinet in the 1967–69 parliament).

To keep the ministerial aspirations of newcomers to politics alive, Matā'afa appointed at least one newcomer to cabinet – for example, Papāli'i Poumau in the 1964–66 Parliament.[1] Others were appointed to the various parliamentary committees, including Afoafouvale Misimoa, who was the chairman of the public accounts committee for two consecutive terms from 1961 to 1966. Dissent was not always suppressed by appointing critics to committees and, at times, such appointments hindered government's policy formulation process, as these critics often voted against the government. From the public's standpoint, however, co-opting the critics of government to cabinet and parliamentary committees enhanced Matā'afa's public image, as he was seen as a leader who tried to work cooperatively with members of the house for the good of the country.

The Betham budget

The first budget after independence was delivered by minister of finance Betham[2] when parliament held its first session on 29 March 1962. It received strong criticism from both the media and members of parliament. However, despite the members' criticisms of the government, and particularly, the minister of finance, members maintained unity and cooperation. The desire for a parliamentary consensus is illustrated by the words of Tofaeono Taulima, who told parliament:

> During this first year of our Independent State it is not proper for us to criticize one another but there is a need for us all to work hand-in-hand, and to do whatever will be possible for the best interests of our people; and I would say that the future welfare and prosperity of our new State is the prerogative of Honourable Members of this House.

Unity and cooperation did not necessarily mean that members were to refrain from criticizing the government's handling of the economy or its cautious approach to developmental programmes. Rather, it seemed to mean that criticisms of the government were welcome so long as they were not intended to overthrow the government. Of the 27 motions voted upon in parliament between independence in 1962 and the end of the three-year parliamentary term, only one was moved in the 1962 session. Of all the divisions moved within this period, the government won only 16 (59 per cent). The cabinet ministers voted together in all divisions. (*WSH-* 1962, Vol I; 1963, Vol II).

There were no motions of no-confidence moved against the government in this period, and the nearest parliament came to such a measure was during the 1967–69 parliamentary session. In response to the general pessimism reflected in MPs' speeches in parliament's first session after independence, the government initiated a survey of the country's economy. The resulting Stace-Lauterback Report was presented in 1963. Among its recommendations was the building of a new wharf at Āsau Village on Savai'i. In anticipation of the wharf, a timber industry to exploit large forest resources at Āsau was proposed to parliament. In December 1966, with parliament approving in principle, a plan to develop a timber industry on Savai'i was proposed by the large US firm Potlatch Forests Inc. The proposal was not universally popular among members, but in December 1968, after years of negotiation and sometimes bitter debate, parliament passed the Potlatch Bill without amendment. However, the paths of other bills relating to the establishment of the Potlatch company were also rough.

Potlatch became the first foreign company to make a major investment in Sāmoan development. Although some saw the enactment of the

Potlatch Bill as a big step forward in the development of Western Sāmoa, others had reservations. The arguments against the proposals, embodied in supplementary bills, reflected not so much opposition to foreign capital as such, as Sāmoan fears – based on their knowledge of events in Hawai'i, Tahiti, New Zealand, and to a lesser extent Fiji – that they might lose their land to outsiders. The prime minister argued that the development of this timber industry would be an ideal way of bettering the lot of the 'landed but penniless masses'. In the month before the legislation was passed, the acting chairman of the bills committee, Fuimaono Moasope, arguing that Sāmoan interests were at stake, introduced amendments to the original Forest Bill which, if passed, would have defeated the whole project. The prime minister could no longer maintain his composure; Fuimaono's remarks implied that he, Matā'afa, did not have Sāmoan interests at heart. He told the house that, if the amendments were passed, he would take it as a vote of no-confidence in himself and resign and ask the head of state to dissolve parliament. The speaker then called for an adjournment, and sought guidance from the Almighty in a prayer. The meeting resumed briefly and Fuimaono withdrew his amendments.

The first eight years after independence, during which Matā'afa was prime minister, were characterized by the absence of organized parliamentary factions, despite differences of opinions among parliamentarians on certain government policies. Aside from the parliamentarians' overwhelming desire to maintain unity amongst themselves in the early years of independence, Matā'afa's conservative approach to the appointment of cabinet ministers, and his leadership tactics of appointing critics of government to his cabinet, were also factors. Although some MPs were dissatisfied with Matā'afa's policies and appointments to parliamentary offices, there had been no determined attempt to unseat him. Perhaps the most important reason for this was Matā'afa's status as a *tama-a-'āiga*. As Leota Leulua'iali'i Itū'au Ale commented to the writer, alluding to the prime minister's status as a *tama-a-'āiga*, 'even though Matā'afa had entered parliament as an MP from the Lotofaga Territorial constituency under his other *matai* title, Fiamē, he was still Matā'afa'. Members felt constrained by Sāmoan protocol against challenging him for the prime ministership. The overall outcome was the characteristic feature of the first eight years after independence, consensus politics. It was not until the need arose to choose the next prime minister, when the results of the 1970 general election were known, that parliamentary opinion crystallized into recognized parliamentary factions.

The decline of consensus politics: The 1970–1972 parliament

The 1970 prime ministerial elections saw Matā'afa's prime ministership challenged in parliament for the first time since 1959. There were no major political divisions on issues, and the country was in good economic shape.[3] However, the commitment to unity and consensus was disappearing from parliamentary processes. The divisions can best be understood as a contest for the ministerial offices that the prime minister could bestow. The three nominations for the prime ministership were Matā'afa, Tupua Tamasese Lealofi IV (hereafter Tamasese) and Tupuola Efi (hereafter Tupuola). Significantly, the first two were *tama-a-'āiga* and the third, the son of a *tama-a-'āiga*. In the first ballot to decide a prime minister, Matā'afa, Tamasese and Tupuola polled 19, 17 and 10 votes respectively. Tupuola's name was then dropped, allowing a ballot for the prime ministership between Matā'afa and Tamasese. The result of the ballot was a draw. Matā'afa and Tamasese each polled 23 votes. The speaker then adjourned parliament until the next day and Tamasese was eventually elected by 25 votes to Matā'afa's 20. Māgele Ate retained the office of speaker, having polled 24 votes to Tuala Paulo's 22 in the second ballot. Tuala Paulo later became the deputy speaker when only one nomination was received for the position.

The new prime minister was a medical doctor by profession. In 1969, after the bestowal of his *tama-a-'āiga* titles, Tamasese was appointed by the Matā'afa government to the office of council of deputies, as the former holder of that office had recently passed away. However, shortly afterwards, he gave up his medical career, resigned as a member of the council of deputies and stood as a parliamentary candidate for Anoāma'a East Territorial constituency. He was elected unopposed. The constituency comprised the two main villages of Falefā and Lufilufi, the capital village of Ātua. Residing in Falefā were some of the prominent members of 'Āiga Sa Fenunu'ivao whose *tama-a-'āiga* was Tupua. Among those members were Leutele (*Tinā o Tupua;* the mother of Tupua), Leala'isalanoa (*Tei o Tupua* – the younger sister of Tupua), and Iuli and Moe'ono (the *Matua o* 'Āiga Sa Fenunu'ivao – the seniors or parent of 'Āiga Sa Fenunu'ivao).

It is not formally recorded which members supported the rival candidates, but there were factions behind each, despite the negative connotations of factionalism. Some indication of Tamasese's support may be deduced by examination of the MPs that Tamasese appointed to cabinet. Of the eight ministers in Tamasese's cabinet, two were newcomers to politics, one (Tupuola) had been an MP since the last half of the 1964–66 parliament, and five had retained their seats. In order to avoid giving offence, I do not use the actual names. Of the five who retained their seats, one (Mr A) had been an MP since 1958, two (Mr B and Mr C) had been MPs since 1964, and two (Mr D and Mr E) had been MPs since 1967. Mr A had been a deputy speaker in the 1958–60 parliament, and speaker in the 1961–63 and 1964–66 parliaments, but was without a parliamentary position in the 1967–69 parliament. Mr B held no parliamentary position in the 1964–66 parliament, but was a deputy speaker in the 1967–68 and at the beginning of the 1970–72 parliament, and was later appointed a minister of cabinet. Messrs C, D and E had never held a parliamentary position.

Mr B told the author (in September 1993) that there were other dimensions of support for the Tamasese faction. Tupua is a *tama-a-'āiga* title associated with 'Āiga Sa Tuala, 'Āiga Sa Fenunu'ivao and 'Āiga-o-Māvaega. Mr B described how Tamasese arrived at his house asking for his support in Tamasese's bid for the prime ministership. At the time, Mr B was one of the few Sāmoan businessmen, owning a night-club, a bar and a number of shops in Apia and in villages on Savai'i. He had first entered politics when he won his constituency's seat in the 1964 general election, and had since retained the seat.

However, it was not only Mr B's political experience and financial resources that Tamasese sought. The title Mr B held was the name of one of the members of the 'Āiga-o-Māvaega, founded by Tupua Tamasese Titimaea. Mr B indicated that one of the reasons why he supported Tamasese was because he was a member of 'Āiga-o-Māvaega. On the basis of Mr B's reasoning, it is interesting to note that of the other three ministers, one came from a village belonging to 'Āiga-o-Māvaega, one held a high-ranking *ali'i* title in 'Āiga Sa Fenunu'ivao and the third held a ranking *ali'i* title in 'Āiga Sa Tuala. If Mr B was right, a number of Tamasese supporters supported him on the basis of allegiance to traditional *'āiga*. Mr B's decision to support Tamasese was not an easy one to make. His elder brother was married to Matā'afa's sister. Moreover, Matā'afa was a close genealogical relation of his. Matā'afa (the person but not the title) was a descendant of the Sa Pesetā family in Savai'i. Pesetā, one of the sons of Tui Ā'ana Tamalelagi (who lived in the 1520s), had had two sons, one of whom was the person from whom both Matā'afa (the person but not the title) and Mr B descended. The fact that Mr B supported Tamasese despite his kinship with the incumbent prime minister further suggests that Mr. B's primary interest was not familial loyalty.

Considering the intense competition for parliamentary positions, particularly ministerial posts (as is still the case today), it is likely that the five MPs who retained their seats supported Tamasese because they sought ministerial posts. The appointment of the three political newcomers to cabinet was probably to reciprocate Tamasese's prime ministerial support from among the newly elected MPs. Among these newcomers was the prime minister's brother-in-law. As J W Davidson commented, Tamasese 'owed his election ... to support from newly elected ... MPs ... and older members who felt they had no hope of high office with Matā'afa still in power' (1970:51). Tamasese himself, following his prime ministerial victory but before he announced his cabinet, was reported in the local press as referring to the large number of people who wanted to be ministers. In parliament, one of the newly elected MPs told the house that whoever was going to win the prime ministerial contest between the two *tama-a-'āiga* must make sure that cabinet ministers were selected from among both the old and the young MPs. Commenting on the day the cabinet was announced, the *Sāmoa Times* editorial said that the reading out of the names of ministers must be like the day of judgment, where people would be told whether to proceed to heaven or hell. Just before the prime ministerial election, the *Sāmoa Times* made the observation that, whoever was going to be nominated for the top job, would quickly have seekers of cabinet positions rallying behind them, as the election was not fought on issues. When he eventually announced his cabinet, Tamasese apologized to parliament that he could not choose all who wanted posts, and that he had made his choice with some difficulty.

Those who backed Tupuola included Leota Itū'au 'Ale, who told the author of his involvement in the 1970 prime ministerial election as follows:

> In 1970, when I first entered Parliament, we young and new members in the like of Le Tagaloa Pita (Leota then), A'e'au Tāulupo'o, Leilua Manuao, Le'aumoana Fereti, Tautī Fuatau and Tiatia Lokeni secretly met at the old Casino Hotel to back Tupuola 'Efi for the top post.

Leota Itū'au was one of the select Sāmoan students who had been sent for university education in New Zealand. Leota Pita, a university graduate, also entering politics for the first time, had been acting principle of the Alafua Agricultural Campus (in Sāmoa) of the University of the South Pacific before he entered politics. The Tupuola faction, therefore, comprised mainly young, newly elected *matai*, with relatively high education levels. Tupuola himself had undertaken law studies at Victoria University in Wellington, New Zealand, before returning to Sāmoa upon the death of his father and late joint head of state, Tupua Tamasese Mea'ole, in April 1963. In the mid-1960s, he had unsuccessfully contested in the Land and Titles Court the *Tupua* and *Tamasese* titles against his first cousin and successful prime ministerial nominee, Tamasese. Not long after Tupuola's unsuccessful bid for these titles, Leulumoega conferred the Tui Ā'ana title upon him, to honour him and to give him national recognition. However, after objection from other parties, Tupuola withdrew his claim. At 32 years of age he was much younger than Matā'afa and Tamasese who were aged 50 and 49, respectively; Tupuola was relatively young, but ambitious.

Matā'afa was presumably supported by his eight former cabinet ministers and the speaker, who were among the 24 MPs from the previous parliament who had retained their seats. Two of the MPs who retained their seats, other than those whom Tamasese appointed to his cabinet, nominated and seconded Tupuola's prime ministerial nomination. The election demonstrates that, aside from the competition among parliamentarians for ministerial posts, the support behind prime ministerial nominees relied heavily on personal and traditional connections. In this election, issues were never a serious consideration for supporting one prime ministerial candidate over another.

An interesting development in this prime ministerial election was the general tendency among newly elected MPs, including younger, overseas-educated *matai*, to challenge their elders in parliament. Apart from the emergence of overt factions, the 1970 prime ministerial election was also important on other counts. Among them was the revision in 1972 of the standing orders that governed the election of a prime minister. It stipulated how a majority of MPs, when electing a new prime minister, was to be determined. It stipulated that, to be elected, a prime minister would need to have the majority support – demonstrated by a vote – rather than 'the confidence' of MPs.

Of Tamasese's cabinet, six of his eight ministers came from Upolu constituencies: three from Ātua district, one from Tuamāsaga and two from Ā'ana. The other two ministers, the speaker and the deputy speaker came from different Savai'i constituencies. Compared with Matā'afa's cabinets in the previous four governments, the emerging pattern of ministerial appointments clearly reflected the developing existence of factional support. Matā'afa had appeared to consider the concerns about district representation in cabinet, but this no longer seemed to be such an important consideration. For example, both the speaker and deputy speaker were MPs of Savai'i constituencies. J.W. Davidson speculated that 'the omission of all the former ministers from the new cabinet may well lead to the crystallization of something like a party system in the new parliament' (1970:51). None of the ministers in the new cabinet had ministerial experience: two of them and the deputy speaker were newcomers to politics. Tupuola was appointed to cabinet as minister for works, marine and civil aviation, acknowledging the support given to Tamasese by his faction once Tupuola withdrew defeated from the prime ministerial contest. Ranging from 27 to 64, the average age of ministers in the new cabinet was 42; the average age of ministers in Matā'afa's Cabinet was 54. The new ministry included well-educated men, men who had travelled and lived abroad, and men who were known to support universal suffrage. It seemed to be a government of change and modernization – however, if this were so, the government's accelerated rate of economic and political development did not seem to be acceptable to the majority of the public.

Although the government had succeeded in preventing a possible public servant outcry against its economic measures – by granting them a 5 per cent salary increase in 1972 – in the same year, parliamentarians awarded themselves a 50 per cent salary increase. But large numbers of the population were very dissatisfied with wages and the cost of living. A number of articles criticizing the government appeared in local newspapers. In early August, a public meeting attracted 500 people. The meeting discussed sending a delegation to parliament to petition for removal of import duty increases, which were felt to have been responsible for the latest rise in living costs. The petition was rejected. The government's liberal economic policies, accelerated development programs, and departure from consensus politics (in terms of districts from which ministers came) cost it the 1973 general election.

Efforts to rebuild consensus politics: The 1973–1975 parliament

The March 1973 general election saw 31 newcomers to parliament (66 per cent of the house), with one previous member (Leota Pita) regaining his seat in July in a by-election following a successful petition against the winner. Among those who lost their seats were the speaker and four ministers, including the minister of finance, Tofa Siaosi. Parliament met on 14 March to elect a new speaker, deputy speaker and prime minister. Of the three nominations for the speaker, Tole'afoa Talitimu won by 28 votes; the former deputy speaker, Le'aupepe Faimaala, received 12; and Te'o Fetu, six. In the contest for deputy speaker, Te'o Fetū won by 27 votes to Le'aupepe Faimaala's 18. As in the previous parliament, three nominations were put forward for the prime ministership. On the first ballot, Matā'afa was re-elected for his fifth term, with 23 votes. Tupuola came second with thirteen votes, and Tamasese came last with nine votes.

When contesting the prime ministership, Tupuola was conscious of the fact that the title he held was not of *tama-a-'āiga* rank. When the unsuccessful prime ministerial candidates made their speeches to congratulate the winner, Tupuola speaking after Tamasese, said in his concluding remarks, '...although I am rather small in stature and my *matai* title is not very important, however, I feel that I am duty-bound to say a few words as one of the candidates for the election to the office of prime minister'. Tupuola's remarks showed how much not only he but the MPs and the general public were conscious of the special status of the *tama-a-'āiga*, not only in parliament but within Sāmoan society.

Three distinct factions emerged in parliament. Of the sixteen MPs who retained their seats, 11 could be identified (on the basis of support in previous parliaments) as belonging to factions which supported each of the three prime ministerial nominees. Tamasese had three supporters. They were three of the four ministers in the previous cabinet who had been re-elected (the fourth minister who retained his seat being Tupuola). Matā'afa had three supporters. Tupuola had four supporters. On the basis of future support for the same prime ministerial nominees, two would have supported Tupuola and one each for Matā'afa and Tamasese, leaving five MP whose support could not be identified. This information, and the number of votes the three prime ministerial candidates polled, give some idea of the kind of support for each faction: The major difference in the vote for the prime ministership came from the votes of new members, who supported Matā'afa, with 20 votes out of 33.

Support for Matā'afa among the newcomers to politics probably reflected the public antagonism to the Tamasese government. Seven of the ministers in Matā'afa's new cabinet had no previous ministerial experience. The most experienced of them was Lesātele Rapi, an MP from Vaisigano No.2 constituency since 1959, and one of the ministers in Matā'afa's 1967–69 cabinet. Of the others, Seiuli Taulafo had been an MP in the previous parliament, but the other five were newcomers. Considering that Tamasese had been the prime minister in the previous government, and yet had managed only nine votes in the prime ministerial ballot, his inclusion in Matā'afa's cabinet was rather surprising. His inclusion was both a reflection of Matā'afa's conservatism (wisdom, from the majority of Sāmoans' point of view) and his leadership tactics. Matā'afa gained the respect of the majority of the Sāmoans for having included in his cabinet the only other *tama-a-'āiga* in the house. It showed that he, as a *tama-a-'āiga*, had respect for the other *tama-a-'āiga*, as any Sāmoan should. As one of the strongest supporters of Tamasese, Polataivao (minister of works in Tamasese's cabinet), said 'We were happy that our Prime Minister had been selected by Matā'afa as a member of his Cabinet, and we thanked Matā'afa for it' (Pers. comm. September 1993). The inclusion of Tamasese in the cabinet was also an important way of establishing a consensus between the ruling factions and as many of Tamasese's supporters as could be won over to support the government.

Matā'afa re-established his principle of fair representation in cabinet of MPs from amongst the political districts of Savai'i and Upolu. Of the three ministers from Upolu constituencies, one came from Ātua district, one from Va'a-o-Fonotī and the other from Tuamāsaga. The three ministers from Savai'i constituencies were also from different political districts. The other two ministers were the two MPs representing the 'individual voters'. The speaker and deputy speaker were from constituencies in Savai'i and Upolu, respectively. Although there had been opposition factions in all previous parliaments following independence, they had not organized themselves into a single parliamentary opposition, nor were they able to rally under a single leadership. However, despite Matā'afa's inclination towards consensus politics, the notion of government and opposition began to become more firmly established. When asked whether he was the recognized leader of the current parliamentary opposition, Tupuola's response was:

> To a large degree this is true. The reason for this I think, was that I was the only one to be nominated for prime minister, besides the two *tama-a-'āiga* (Matā'afa and Tupua Tamasese) ... Matā'afa is now the prime minister, and Tamasese a cabinet minister and I am the only one left, so I think it is quite natural for the other MPs to rally around me, (Va'a 1974a:29).

Tupuola and his supporters advocated progress and development, which had so far come at a high cost. The huge balance of payments deficit inherited from the previous government was largely a result of materials imported for development projects, such as the construction of roads, the airport, and the new legislative assembly building. While the previous government had given first priority to infrastructural development, the new government adopted the view that agriculture and industrial development had to be of prime importance because they would result in a quicker increase in national income.

In his budget statement, the new minister of finance, Sam Sa'ili, pointed out that:

> ' ...we are concerned that substantial quantities of development expenditure have been utilised for infrastructure projects, rather than in projects which are directly productive and which would have immediate impact on increasing the national income of the country ....'

Sam Saili adopted a policy of economic conservatism. He stressed the importance of cutting government spending to reduce the deficit – which in 1972 was ST420,000 – as quickly as possible. For example, he was committed to reducing by 90 per cent the import allocations for private importers for the period from July to December 1973. The differences in developmental emphasis and economic policies between the government and its predecessor were constantly challenged by the seemingly more organized opposition under Tupuola's leadership.

The opportunity for the opposition to show its strength and unity came in the second parliamentary session, which commenced on 20 November 1973. The occasion was the debate on the 1974 budget. In his budget statement the minister stressed that the 'emphasis must be placed on development of our productive sector, income from which will, of course, enable infrastructural development to take place at an increased rate over a long-term period'. The 'opposition', on the other hand, argued that:

> Creating a balance causes unnecessary hardships to the nation. Even if there was a deficit ... Western Sāmoa would not be in any danger as there were reserves to fall back on and loans could be got from the International Monetary Fund to help offset deficits. It wanted the purse strings loosened to maintain the present standard of living and to develop the country. It did not believe in creating a balance of payments for its own sake while people were out of jobs (Va'a 1974b:39).

Among the restrictive measures in the budget were the absence of any wage increase for 1974, the postponement of some of the programs initiated by the previous government (such as the Apia water supply, Apia sewage schemes, and Apia road projects), and the postponement of Western Sāmoa's application to the Asian Development Bank for a loan for the Apia water supply project. The reason for this last decision was that it would enable the government to 'attempt to increase our productive capacity as quickly as possible and…concentrate all possible resources in this direction'.

The debate was described as 'one of the fiercest since independence' (Va'a 1974c:39). Tempted to seize the opportunity to topple the government, Tupuola postponed a trip to Fiji. Tupuola had moved a motion of no-confidence in the government but, in anticipation of a positive outcome, he moved another motion that parliament not be dissolved. Instead, the prime minister should resign, leaving parliament to elect a new prime minister. The 'opposition' was certain that it had the numbers to defeat the appropriation bill in its second reading. This being the case, Tupuola's motion of no-confidence would then be moved. Unfortunately for Tupuola and his supporters, five of the opposition supporters had a change of heart – two did not turn up, and three voted for the government – giving the government an easy victory, 26 votes to 17. The bill went through without any further serious opposition.

Tupuola's motion of no-confidence showed how difficult it was to try and reconcile the principles of democracy, with custom and tradition, in trying to overthrow a government of which the leader and a cabinet minister were *tama-a-'āiga*. As Tupuola himself knew, any such motion would be seen by the majority of the Sāmoans as a deliberate attempt to undermine the traditional status of *tama-a-'āiga*. The attempt also gave the government a more solid sense of unity against an 'opposition' that had, for the first time, threatened to overthrow a government. Perhaps worse in the eyes of traditionalists, it was an opposition comprising mainly younger parliamentarians with European education and backgrounds. Tupuola's speech, when withdrawing his motion, was a reflection of the general public attitude towards the status of *tama-a-'āiga;* for a lower ranking *matai* to oppose, then attempt to depose, such a high-ranking leader was culturally indefensible.

Another member of the opposition faction, Leota Pita, had submitted a private member's motion which, like the motion of Tupuola, was later withdrawn. Leota's motion was that only *tama-a-'āiga* should be eligible to be head of state and, in future, *tama- a 'āiga* should not be eligible to be members of parliament. Although Leota never explained the reason for his motions and his intention, judging from the context of the proceedings in this parliamentary session, it was probably to lessen the shock of having the Matā'afa government overthrown should Tupuola's motion succeed. The motion also showed how having *tama-a-'āiga* as members of parliament created a feeling of uneasiness among their fellow members. The democratic process of parliamentary debate and competition was constrained by the cultural norms of deference to those of the highest ranks. Leota's motion did not necessarily mean that he lacked respect for the *tama-a-'āiga*. On the contrary, his respect for custom and tradition meant he opposed the humiliation of *tama-a-'āiga* when defeated as prime ministerial candidates, or deposed as prime ministers.

For the remainder of the 1973 parliamentary session, no other divisions were called. The threat of the no-confidence motion had probably helped unify support behind the government. All 16 motions for which divisions were called in the parliamentary sessions of the 1974 were declared in favour of the government. This 100 per cent record contrasted with the Matā'afa government's success rate of 59 per cent in the first two years following independence. Clearly, divisions in the house between the respective supporters of the government and the opposition were now more firmly established than ten years before. But still no political party had been established.

Custom overrides the constitution: Parliament 1975

Prime minister Matā'afa passed away unexpectedly on 20 May 1975. The following morning the head of state, rather than calling for a parliamentary vote, appointed Tamasese to succeed Matā'afa as prime minister. This controversial move indicated yet again the difficulty of reconciling democracy with custom and tradition. At the beginning of parliament's first session for 1975, Tamasese explained how difficult it was for the head of state to arrive at the decision to appoint him as Matā'afa's successor and for him to accept the appointment. In his concluding remarks Tamasese said, 'I pray therefore for your support and confirmation of my appointment as your Prime Minister in respect of the move made by the Head of State'. The reasons behind the head of state's decision were not revealed to parliament, but it was generally assumed that Tamasese was appointed because he was a *tama-a-'āiga*.

The first MP to respond to the prime minister's plea, Toluono Lama, was an acknowledged opponent of the government, but one whose title was that of one of the six *Pule* political centres in Savai'i. His age and title dictated that he put custom and tradition before parliamentary or constitutional procedures: Despite what he recognized as an illegal move by the head of state, he moved that parliament confirm Tamasese's appointment, and urged other MPs to support his motion. Another notable opponent of the government, Leota Pita, supported Toluono's motion. Leota said, '… we are aware of the reason why the Head of State made the appointment, but was it in compliance with the Constitution?' Leota drew parliament's attention to the provision in the constitution (Art. 32.2[a]) which requires that 'The Head of State shall appoint as Prime Minister … a Member of Parliament who commands the confidence of a majority of the Members of Parliament'. Although Leota reluctantly agreed with the prime minister's appointment, he was concerned that this sort of thing should not be repeated in the future. He told parliament, 'Supposing the present Prime Minister passes away, what is the procedure then? Will the Head of State once again step in and select the next Prime Minister with the confidence and importance of Members' support being regarded as secondary?' Muāgututi'a Lavilavi pointed out that articles 33.3[4], 26.1-2[5] or 105[6] of the constitution did not justify the head of state's appointment of the new prime minister. Nevertheless, he supported Toluono's motion. Another notable opponent of the government and strong supporter of Tupuola, Fuimaono Mimio, said:

> I myself am undecided as to which is justice in this matter. The actual purpose of our gathering here in this House is to develop the truth only.

> Our hearts desire our custom and traditions in respect of our relation-
> ship with the *Tama-a-'āiga*. ... Your Honour the *Tama-a-'āiga*, we are
> cautious because you are the apple of our eyes to our minds. You bear
> the post which is treasured by us all. In the Constitution and speaking
> directly, it is true that there is no such provision therein. If we consider
> fully the provisions in the Constitution, I would then agree, but since
> our term is almost at end, I am satisfied therefore in the appointment
> of the *Tama-a-'āiga* to be our Leader for the meantime ...

Fuimaono was undoubtedly sincere in his opposition to the manner
in which the constitution had been undermined. He was also among the
more prominent opponents of the government. However, by his own title,
and by implication, as a person, he was, in custom and tradition, the 'father'
of Tupua, the *tama-a-'āiga* title that the prime minister held. Despite opposition from some MPs, Toluono's motion was passed on the voices.
Some MPs argued strenuously against a vote to confirm Tamasese's prime
ministerial appointment, as it would imply that the members were divided
over Tamasese's appointment. The division in terms of supporters of the
government and opposition might have been a fact, but it was not to be
seen as such by the public, and more particularly so when it was to do with
the issue of support behind the *tama-a-'āiga*.

With a new vacancy in cabinet, Tamasese's supporters were hoping
that one of their number would be appointed to fill the position by their
'preferred' prime minister (according to Polataivao Fosi, pers. comm.
September 1993). Tamasese, perhaps trying to form an alliance with
Tupuola's supporters, appointed one of Tupuola's strong supporters to take
charge of his former justice and land and titles portfolios. Before his seven
months as interim prime minister were over, Tamasese had sacked the
minister of finance and the minister of agriculture for undisclosed reasons.
The two replacement ministers had not been supporters of Matā'afa. They
continued as ministers in Tupuola's first cabinet after the election of the
following year. One was a known supporter of Tupuola, and the other was
Tupuola's brother-in-law.

In taking over the prime ministership, Tamasese had more closely associated himself with the criticisms previously leveled at the Matā'afa
government, which helped to boost Tupuola's prime ministerial prospects.
Following Matā'afa's death, there was already public speculation on the
chance of a non-*tama-a-'āiga* titleholder becoming prime minister.
Although there were other prospective prime ministerial candidates in the

parliament, Tupuola seemed to be in the strongest position. Despite the fact that Tamasese was in poor health, the former supporters of Matā'afa tipped him as the next prime minister, their reasoning being that the respective supporters of Matā'afa and Tamasese would unite behind him against any other challenge for the prime ministership (Va'a 1975:15).

The 1976–1978 parliament

When the results of the 1976 general election were known, four nominations seemed likely for the position of prime minister: the incumbent prime minister (Tamasese); the recognized leader of the opposition faction (Tupuola); and the veteran politicians, Va'ai Kolone and Tofilau 'Eti. Eventually, the choice of candidates narrowed down to Tamasese and Tupuola. Tupuola was elected prime minister and became the first non-*tama-a-'āiga* titleholder to achieve this office, winning by 30 votes against his first cousin and *tama-a-'āiga* titleholder, Tamasese, who polled 16 votes. The election for the speaker reflected the same divide and the polarization of the house into two distinct factions. Leota Itū'au became speaker, with 33 votes to Salā Suivai's 14. The deputy speakership was won by Tuimaseve Fa'asalafa with 33 votes against Le'aupepetele Taoipu's 13.

Tupuola's cabinet included three ministers from the previous cabinet. Although they had been appointed to the previous cabinet by Tamasese, following the death of Matā'afa and the sacking of the other two ministers by Tamasese, they had been known supporters of Tupuola. The other two former ministers who retained their seats, Laumea Matolu II and Lesātele Rapi, were both recognized supporters of Matā'afa, and were not appointed to cabinet by Tupuola. The other five ministers chosen were in cabinet for the first time. All except one had been in previous parliaments. An observer classified four of the Ministers as 'conservatives' and four as 'progressives' (Va'a 1976a:10). This reflected Tupuola's attempt to maintain a balance among his supporters between modernity and tradition (in terms of age, political experience, Western education, and traditional standing). Of the eight ministers of cabinet, five came from Upolu constituencies (two from different constituencies in Ātua political district, two from different constituencies in Tuamāsaga district and one from the constituency comprising the Va'a-o-Fonotī political district). Tupuola's title is from Ā'ana district, and the other three ministers were from different political districts of Savai'i. The speaker and deputy speaker were from constituencies in

Upolu and Savai'i, respectively. It seemed therefore that the manner in which Tupuola appointed the ministers to his first cabinet was similar to that adopted by Matā'afa.

Conscious of the prime ministerial defeat of the *tama-a-'āiga*, Tupuola, in his first speech to parliament as prime minister, said:

> ... Please do not regard the result of the ballot this morning as an illustration of Sāmoa turning her back to the *Tama-a-'āiga*, neither is Sāmoa losing due allegiance to the apple of her eye. In simple terms actually Sāmoa is searching for remedies to her multi-problems while the dignity and sacredness of the *Tama-a-'āiga* have continued to be jealously guarded, and the position of *Tama-a-'āiga* has continued to be given precedence by the nation; and some of these days you shall actually see the material implication of what I am saying now (*WSH*, 1976, Vol I, p 11).

Tamasese was promptly nominated by Tupuola as a member of the council of deputies, the position Tamasese had held before he became a politician.

Responding to Tupuola, Tofilau 'Eti said:

> ... there is no secret to the country that there were two distinct parties, those who supported the orator Tupuola Efi the Prime Minister Elect and those who gave their support to the Honourable Tupua Tamasese...

Despite Tupuola's attempts to explain the issue of the difference between the status of the *tama-a-'āiga* in Sāmoa's traditional political structure and the prime ministership in a democratic state, a number of MPs did not see it that way. It was a situation which Tupuola's opponents were subsequently to use effectively against him. Defeating the only *tama-a-'āiga* currently in parliament did not necessarily mean that Tupuola was 'losing due allegiance to the apple of [his] eye': The deeper issue was the difficulty of reconciling operational principles of democracy and custom and tradition.

Even Tamasese, who was regarded a 'liberal' (when compared with Matā'afa's personality, policies and leadership style), did not take his defeat very well. In his response to Tupuola's first prime ministerial speech, Tamasese drew parliament's attention to the tale of the Arab and the camel: After many unceasing attempts, the camel finally succeeded in occupying the tent, and forcing the Arab out. Tamasese then told parliament to interpret the parable as they wished. Exactly what Tamasese intended his parable to mean will never be known. The editor of the *Sāmoa Times* (19 March 1976) took the view that Tamasese was probably alluding to rumours that Tupuola had used his family wealth to buy prime ministerial votes. In stating this opinion, the editor of the *Sāmoa Times* implied that modern campaign tactics were not consistent with traditional ones. Others thought that Tamasese was comparing the camel to the non-*tama-a-'āiga* titleholder who had now ousted the *tama-a-'āiga* from the prime ministerial office. Given the many speeches by MPs in parliament concerning the status of *tama-a-'āiga*, the prime ministerial race among the same three candidates that began in 1970, and the fact that Tupuola and Tamasese contested the Tupua and Tamasese titles in the Land and Titles Court in 1965, it was more likely that the second explanation fitted Tamasese's analogy. Furthermore, Tamasese seemed to be implying that the office of prime minister should be reserved for *tama-a-'āiga* titleholders. Responding to Tupuola's recommendation that Tamasese be appointed a member of the council of deputies, Tofilau 'Eti moved a motion that 'only *tama-a-'āiga* be eligible to be Members of the council of deputies'. Although the motion was lost, it nevertheless showed the persistence of the sentiment embodied in Leota Pita's withdrawn motion of 11 December 1973. The defeat of Tofilau's motion also reflected the polarization of parliament into the respective supporters of Tamasese and Tupuola, and not necessarily a lack of respect and support for the institution of *tama-a-'āiga*.

Tupuola was determined to promote development, and his first speech as prime minister indicated his attitude to development. He said:

> ... property rights is the subject of unceasing family disputes while 90 per cent of the land remains uncultivated. Sixty per cent of our national revenue is being wasted in buying our daily livelihood from overseas while our soil is very fertile. We are proud of the beauty of Sāmoa while our sons and daughters are looking for their future in New Zealand or America.... If you really love this country; if you are a real Sāmoan aspiring after the good of the people, give me your hand – this is mine – let us work together.

The government stepped up the rate of development programs. For the 1978 financial year it budgeted ST15.9 million, representing 47 per cent of the government's total expenditure, an increase from that of 1976. Western Sāmoa's *Third Five Year Development Plan* launched in November

1975 had estimated expenditure of ST44.4 million over a five-year period. By the end of 1977, the government had already spent 83 per cent of that amount. While the value of imported goods had increased, exports had declined from ST11.5 million to STS9.5 million the following year, following an increase from ST4 million in 1973 to its 1977 level.

A number of national projects embodied fashionable development theories of the time and, in general, these were not successful. Having analyzed the first budget statement of the new minister of finance, Va'a (1976b:19) came to the conclusion that the country was no better off and that 'the government is ... bleeding the people white'. Comments like these were made in the new government's first year of office and worse was to come. In the debate on the appropriation bill in mid-1978, one MP told parliament:

> There are no improved standards at all here, but thousands of *tala* in loans have been granted to individuals in the country ... monies have been used for purposes other than those of developments ... check up on agricultural developments and ensure that the money is not being used to buy furniture and car batteries, or to pay for passengers' air fares to New Zealand or America.

The government was also ostensibly aiming to combat bribery and corruption, in the hope of improving efficiency. Commissions of inquiry were conducted and led to the dismissal of senior public servants. Among them were the director of the lands and survey department, the controller of customs, the secretary for health, the accountant of the health department, and the commissioner and superintendent of police. Though the findings of these commissions of inquiry might have been valid, some members of the public were suspicious about the government's motives in setting them up:

> Some people are still asking whether the firing of the commissioner [of police] represented a private vendetta by Talamaivao Niko, the Minister of Police, who years ago resigned from the police force over a disagreement with the fired commissioner (Va'a 1977:12).

Thus, in his first three years as prime minister, Tupuola made a lot of enemies. His accelerated development programs and his attempts to improve efficiency in the public service alienated many. The fact that he was comparatively young (he was 38 in 1976) in a generally conservative society that placed so much value on age, did not help him either. However, had he been a *tama-a-'āiga* titleholder, he may still have had the majority of the public's traditional respect and support.

The birth of political parties: The 1979 general election

The prime ministerial election following the 1979 general election, saw, for the first time, a contest for that office between two non-*tama-a-'āiga* titleholders. Seven people had been tipped as having good chances of becoming the next prime minister.[7]

Eventually, however, the list was reduced to two names, Tupuola and Va'ai Kolone. As in 1976, Tupuola had organized his supporters at his home at Tua'efu. Similarly, the opposition faction held their meeting at the Paradise of Entertainment tourist resort (which belonged to one of their members, Salā Suivai) and agreed on Va'ai Kolone as their candidate for the prime ministerial election. Among the successful parliamentary candidates at this meeting were some of the senior MPs in the previous parliaments and Leota Itū'au, the former speaker of the house, who had now defected to Va'ai's faction. The meeting also agreed on their candidate to contest the office of speaker. Va'ai, as the leader of the opposition faction, and his supporters tried unsuccessfully to recruit his brother, Lesātele Rapi (who had been a notable supporter of Matā'afa, but had been a member of Tupuola's cabinet).

Tupuola narrowly won the prime ministership with 24 votes to Va'ai's 23. In the speech complementing Tupuola on his second prime ministerial victory, a disappointed Va'ai said ' … the injury is inflicted, my own brother'. Va'ai's brother was re-appointed by Tupuola to his new cabinet. The election of the speaker saw a Tupuola supporter, Tu'u'u Faletoese, with 24 votes, defeating the Va'ai supporters' candidate by one vote.

Immediately after this prime ministerial election, Va'ai and his supporters founded the first post-independence parliamentary political party, the Human Rights Protection Party (HRPP). For the first time in Sāmoa, a faction sought to institutionalize itself publicly. The development of the HRPP and the subsequent establishment of other political parties are discussed in the next chapter.

Events after independence fulfilled the predictions of constitutional advisors Aikman and Davidson that a party system would eventually evolve in Sāmoa as different political interest groups emerged. What were the factors that took that evolution 17 years to occur? They were more than differences of opinion – these had existed during Matā'afa's prime ministership from 1959 to 1969, yet no political party had been established then. Only after Tamasese entered parliament was Matā'afa's prime ministership challenged, yet still no political parties were established. As long as the two *tama-a-'āiga* were in parliament, they continued to hold the prime ministership. The prime ministerial office had been held continuously by *tama-a-'āiga* since independence, but that status quo changed when the prime ministership was contested between two men of remarkable political skills but relatively minor rank.

The issue of accelerated economic development had been in the background since the mid-1960s, and the intensive competition for ministerial posts had been a feature of parliament since the early 1960s. The establishment of the first political party owes more to the conservative parliamentarians' reaction against the marginalization of *tama-a-'āiga* from parliamentary politics than to any change in policies – against Tupuola's usurpation of what was perceived to be an office to be held only by *tama-a-'āiga*. The speaker in Tupuola's first government had said, 'I, among others, advised Tupuola to form a party straight away, now that Fiamē [Matā'afa] and Tamasese were out' (Ale 1990:10). Ale's claim emphasizes the fact that the presence in parliament of *tama-a-'āiga* had been the main factor behind the non-establishment of political parties. Herein lies the contradiction between individual freedom to contest all positions of power (implicit in liberal-democratic ideals) and collectivist ideals (among others) considered important in indigenous institutions. Somewhat ironically, then, it was the conservative reaction, aimed at maintaining the traditionally exclusive right of the *tama-a-'āiga* to the prime ministership, that lead to the modern concept of political parties – which are an inevitable part of representative democracy: The reaction could be seen as a blessing in disguise in that it hastened the development of a democratic parliamentary system.

However, given that politics is a quest for power, perhaps the issue of tradition *versus* non-tradition is irrelevant. Power, which had been obtained and perpetuated through tradition, can also be obtained through 'modern' political parties. In this sense, the quest for power is a cross-cultural phenomenon. For the ardent traditionalists, it would be a political bonus if, having obtained power through modern political parties, that power could also be utilized to perpetuate aspects of the traditional order that would benefit them most not only in their political careers, but also in day-to-day traditional practices. Through endless competition between political parties for power, the public is also drawn into the political elite's game, because the latter need support, which is the merit of liberal democracy.

Notes

1. There were four new appointments in the 1961–63 cabinet to replace the four ministers in the previous cabinet who had resigned. Luamanuvae 'Eti had resigned from politics at the end of the 1958–60 parliamentary term. He re-entered politics in the 1967 election, and was appointed to the cabinet.

2. Betham was one of the five representatives of the 'individual voters'. A parliamentary legislation reduced from five to two the number of representatives of the individual voters as from the 1964 parliamentary term.

3. In the 1969 budget, the government recorded a surplus of $464,000 with total overseas government funds at $1.1 million. By the end of the same year, the government and the Bank of Western Sāmoa's overseas funds stood at $3.8 million, which was considered sufficient to pay for six months of the country's imports. These funds had increased by over a $1 million in 1969.

4. This article states that 'The office of any other Minister shall become vacant if the appointment of the Prime Minister has been terminated ...'

5. This states that 'the Head of State in the performance of his functions shall act on the advice of Cabinet, the Prime Minister or the appropriate Minister, as the case may be'.

6. This provision provides for the proclamation of a state of emergency.

7. They were Va'ai Kolone, Tofilau 'Eti, Leota Itū'au Ale, Fa'aso'otauloa Sam Saili, Fa'amatuāinu Tala Mailei, Polataivao Fosi and Tupuola 'Efi. All except Tupuola 'Efi were members of the group that eventually supported Va'ai as their prime ministerial candidate (*ST*, 16 February 1979).

5 | The development of political parties

THE COMPLEX and seemingly paradoxical nature of party politics allowed for the mixing of tradition and democracy. Modern political parties, developed in Europe and America in the 19th century, coincided with industrialization and the rise of capitalism, both of which greatly influenced liberal-democratic ideals – in particular, ideals associated with competition. The idea that political parties were, in a sense, comparable with business firms, but providing political rather than commercial goods for the consumers, reflects liberal-democratic notions of competition. Among ideas associated with 'political enterprise theory' is the impersonal nature of the relationship between the firm and the consumer. The consumer can be the voter – to whom the party sells its goods – or the members comprising the party. In either case it is the political goods and the impersonal nature of the relationship between the firm and the consumer that determines the nature of the political market. It is the latter idea – the impersonal nature of the relationship between the firm, in this case the politician, and the customer, or voter – that is the major theme of this chapter.

In contrast to political enterprise theory, 'clientelistic' explanations of competition place emphases on a personal relationship between patron and client, and on a system of mutual benefits upholding the relationship. Clientelism is a phenomenon which is generally practised in traditional societies. However, given the desire of political actors to obtain personal power, political enterprise and clientelistic theories are both means to the same end. The difference is that liberal-democracy usually implies certain notions about the nature of party competition.

This chapter provides an overview of the political history of Sāmoa as background for the detailed examination of democracy in Sāmoa in the following four chapters. This chapter also examines the nature of competition amongst political parties in Sāmoa since 1979 – in particular, the tactics used by parties and their leaders to obtain and maintain power.

The founding of the Human Rights Protection Party: The 1979–1981 parliament

When they established a political party in May 1979, the supporters of Va'ai Kolone suggested names and then selected one by vote. The name Human Rights Protection Party (HRPP) which narrowly won the vote, was suggested by Tofilau 'Eti Alesana and Lā'ulu Fetauimalemau (Ale 1990:12). HRPP's members drew up its constitution, elected its office-holders and developed its organizational structure (Va'a 1989:9). Though officially established in May 1979, the HRPP was only legally registered in late 1985. Its certificate of incorporation (No. 174) was issued in January 1986. The seven official objectives of the HRPP, as stated in its constitution, are very general, being:

1. To foster political education and provide leadership necessary to safeguard the rights, liberties, privileges and freedoms of the Sāmoan people and individuals; to protect their interests and to secure to them peace, security and prosperity in their native land; and to provide institutions which promote and guarantee to them economic, social and political welfare

2. To uphold the constitution of Sāmoa

3. To encourage and foster amongst the Sāmoans collectively and individually the spirit of independence, self-reliance, industry, assertiveness and acquisitiveness

4. To demand and guarantee the protection of the vital Sāmoan interests by means of appropriate constitutional safeguards in the constitution of Sāmoa or any future constitution of any government to be established in Sāmoa

5. To devise the means of informing the Samoan people by means of political education or otherwise about the international or local body politics, and finer and worthy aspects of other cultures, arts, music, philosophy, economics and other disciplines

6. To promote and encourage the means of improving the living standards of the people of Sāmoa

7. To do all such other lawful things as are incidental or conducive to the attainment of the foregoing objects.

The party was well organized, and wives of party members established a women's group to fund-raise for the party and to help win the support of elected MPs and intending candidates through their wives.[1] The HRPP's constitution established the party's organizational structures and functions. Elected every year at the party's annual general meeting (AGM), the executive committee comprises the president (the leader of the parliamentary caucus), vice-president (caucus member), secretary (not a caucus member), treasurer (caucus member), six members appointed by caucus, one non-caucus member each from Upolu and Savai'i elected annually at the AGM, and one representative of women. All party policies are formulated by the executive committee but have to be approved at the AGM.

The founders of the HRPP had no evident shared ideology or common goal beyond defeating the government. They comprised people of different age groups, work and educational backgrounds. Aside from family connections among some of them, the broad objections that seem to have united them against the Tupuola government were personal animosity to Tupuola (as well as objections to his leadership style), to some of the members of his government, and to the policies associated with it, such as the development programs.

The immediate aim of the party was to win government from Tupuola Efi and his supporters. Its long-term aim, according to an interview with one former prominent HRPP MP, was to prevent Tupuola from ever again becoming the prime minister of Sāmoa. Although the majority of the MPs that voted for Tamasese in 1976 were senior parliamentarians who, in previous parliaments, had been supporters of either Matā'afa or Tamasese, the unexpected victory of Tupuola came to be seen as flouting traditional rank precedence. For the first time since independence, a non-*tama-a-'āiga* titleholder held the prime ministership. Ironically, the modern innovation of political parties was initiated by a number of current and former HRPP MPs who thought Tupuola opposed political leadership by *tama-a-'āiga*. Added to this characterization of Tupuola was the underlying traditional cultural rivalry between orator groups and the *tama-a-'āiga* over questions of traditional authority. Considering that the Tupuola title was an important *tulafale* title from one of the two original *Tūmua*, Tupuola's prime ministerial success was seen by some of his critics as a victory of the orator groups against the *tama-a-'āiga* titleholders and the institution of *tama-a-'āiga* in general.

When Tupuola became prime minister, Tofilau 'Eti was a strong supporter of Matā'afa, and, after Matā'afa's death, he threw his support behind Tamasese. Referring to the contest for the prime ministership, his comments to parliament suggested that he felt traditional rank should be upheld. He said, 'there ... were two distinct parties, those who supported the orator Tupuola Efi ... and those who gave their support to the honourable Tupua Tamasese'. One ardent supporter of Tamasese told the author that, 'following the defeat of our candidate in the 1976 prime ministerial election, we, the senior MPs, started to look for ways whereby we could unite the public behind us'.

Nonetheless, the founders of the party sought a modern rather than a traditional ideological justification for the establishment of their party, as reflected in the name chosen by its members. However, while the first of the seven objectives of the party is to protect human rights, which seems to reflect general international trends, the name did not really reflect the point of view held by most of its members. For example, when asked by the author how the name of the party came to be chosen, one senior HRPP MP said that it reflected the perception that the Tupuola government was undermining the rights of the people – whereas, Tofilau has stated that the establishment of the HRPP was directly related to the Tupuola government's infringement of rights, especially 'the rights of *public servants*' (Rampell 1988:46).

The fact that Tupuola defeated his cousin and incumbent prime minister, the then Tupua Tamasese Lealofioā'ana IV, for the top political post in 1976, may have led many to feel that Tupuola was reaching above his traditional Sāmoan status – a status defined by his title rather than his other attributes – in a manner unacceptable to Sāmoan custom and values. Although the son of a *tama-a-'āiga*, Tupuola was also kin to prominent part-European business families – the Nelsons and Merediths – on his mother's side. Like his famous grandfather, Taisi Olaf Nelson, Tupuola had a foot in both the modern commercial and traditional chiefly worlds of Sāmoa. The editor of the government newspaper, *Sāvali*, referring to Tupuola by another of his titles, Tufuga, commented that, in a conservative society, he:

> ... was looked at by many people as a bright young political star in the firmament. Young, ambitious, and somehow too modern in his approach to the politics of the day, and too eager to change things quickly, Tufuga

Efi ... seemed to be a young man in a hurry in a conservative Sāmoa in a world undergoing fast changes at the end of the colonial era. Tufuga Efi wanted to develop and modernize Sāmoa in a hurry.

Of the 23 MPs in the 1976 parliament who regained their seats in the 1979 general election, eight were HRPP supporters. Among them, three were strong supporters of Matā'afa. They were Tofilau 'Eti (previously a minister in Matā'afa's cabinets of 1959–60 and 1967–69), Fa'aso'otauloa Semu Pualagi (in Matā'afa's 1973–75 cabinet) and Ulugia Suivai (a strong supporter of Matā'afa in the 1970 prime ministerial election). A fourth MP, Va'ai Kolone, had been a strong supporter of Tamasese. He had successfully contested the seat of Vaisigano No. 1 against Tupuola (then Tufuga) in the 1967 general election. A fifth MP, Fa'amatuāinu Tala, had succeeded Tamasese in early 1976 when the latter became a member of the council of deputies. A sixth was Taliaoa Maoama, and a seventh, Leota Itū'au, was a previous speaker of the house.

Of the 24 newcomers to politics in the 1979 parliament, 15 were HRPP supporters. Six came from Savai'i constituencies, seven from Upolu, one from 'Āiga-i-le-Tai district and one was elected by 'individual voters'. The newcomers, therefore, were representative of all the constituencies. Their ages, work and education backgrounds also varied. HRPP supporters did not represent any particular interest group, though generally they were older than those who supported Tupuola, and were fairly representative of the country's 11 political districts. Eleven of them met at Salā Suivai's resort and elected Va'ai and Leota Itū'au as their leader and deputy leader, and as their candidates for prime minister and speaker respectively. Of the 11, three were newly elected MPs, although one, Lā'ulu Fetauimalemau – the wife of the late Matā'afa – had had a long association with politics through her husband. A by-election following Matā'afa's death in 1975 saw Lā'ulu winning her husband's old seat of Lotofaga. She had lost at the 1976 general election, but regained her seat in 1979. Among the senior MPs was the speaker of the house under Tupuola's previous government.

Among the newcomers to politics who supported the HRPP were those who claimed to have been unfairly treated under the first Tupuola government, and those who were closely related to them. The best known in the latter group were members of the Pētaia family. They included Tofilau 'Eti, Lā'ulu Fetauimalemau and Nonumalo Sōfara. Nonumalo's wife, 'Eni, was Lā'ulu's sister. They and Tofilau were second cousins and great-grandchildren of Pētaia.

Also among the new members was the former commissioner of police who had been dismissed by the Tupuola government following the 1977 commission of inquiry into the police department. At the time, some heads of government departments considered that there was nothing in the commission's report that specifically required that the police commissioner and the chief superintendent be dismissed; it was felt by many senior officials that personalities were involved, and that the minister of police had instigated a commission of inquiry because, as a former senior police officer, he had clashed with the police commissioner.

Tupuola's political faction

Tupuola, modernist though he was, did not form a party of his supporters during his two terms in office, which began in 1976. This was a source of regret to some, such as Leota Itū'au Ale, the speaker in Tupuola's first government, who told the author that he had advised Tupuola to form a political party, modelled on those of New Zealand, and believed that Tupuola had missed a golden opportunity by not doing so. A party was needed, Leota thought, because:

> more and more ambitious politicians will aspire for the top executive post, and voters (*matai* suffrage) were beginning to appreciate the fact that "you scratch my back, I'll scratch yours" is often said in this political game. The voters give their vote to get something in return – recognition for high office or promotion in public and civil service (Ale 1990:10-11).

Of the 23 MPs who regained their seats, 16 were Tupuola supporters. Among them were the six ministers in the previous cabinet who had regained their seats. Another two, Le'aupepetele Taoipu and Fuimaono Mimio, were members of the traditional Sa Tuala and Sa Fenunu'ivao families, respectively. Another MP who voted for Tupuola in 1976 was Va'afusu'aga Poutoa. Although he held the Lefaga seat under that title, he also held the other title of Falefā village, Leutele, the 'mother of Tupua' and was a founding member of 'Āiga Sa Fenunu'ivao. The general public perception, that the Tupuola faction was anti-*tama-a-'aiga*, therefore, seems to be falsified by these traditional alliances. It seems more likely that the Tupuola supporters in the 1976 prime ministerial election opted for Tupuola as prime minister because they thought he would do a better job than his cousin Tamasese. As J.W. Davidson had told members of the working committee on self-government, 'the time would come when the ability of the person would be the major factor in determining who would be appointed prime minister' (WCM, 21 March 1960).

Tofilau's inference that the Tupuola faction in the 1976 prime ministerial election, was a party of orators was not totally correct either, as, among the Tamasese supporters, was Taliaoa Maoama, a high ranking *tulafale* from the *Tūmua* of Afega (or Tuisāmau). Perhaps Tofilau saw it that way because those who moved and seconded the motion that Tupuola be the next prime minister were high-ranking *tulafale* of *Pule* and *Tūmua*, respectively.

Against this background, the objection of Tofilau and the Tamasese's supporters to Tupuola's prime ministerial victory in 1976 can be interpreted as that of the generally older MPs, who had served in previous parliaments and had supported either Matā'afa or Tamasese but were now losing their influence in parliamentary politics to younger men entering politics. However, like the HRPP, the Tupuola faction comprised MPs of varying ages, work and education backgrounds, and, as with some of the core members of the HRPP, some of them are closely related. For example, Tofaeono Tile, a medical doctor by profession and minister of health in Tupuola's first government, was Tupuola's brother-in-law. Ulualofaigā Talamaivao Niko, a previous cabinet minister, was a relative of Tupuola. Tu'u'u Faleto'ese, the new speaker, was Lā'ulu and Eni's first cousin (in the influential Pētaia family) and his wife was Tupuola's wife's first cousin. Faumuinā Anapapa, one of the ministers in the new cabinet, was Matā'afa's first cousin. A minister in the 1996 HRPP government told the author how disappointed she had been when her father's cousin joined the Tupuola faction rather than the HRPP, to which her mother belonged.

In the case of Lesātele Rapi, political allegiance also proved stronger than kinship; he was the older brother of one of the HRPP founders, Va'ai Kolone, a minister in Matā'afa's 1973–75 cabinet, and in Tupuola's new cabinet. But Lesātele's son-in-law, George Lober, one of the two MPs for the individual voters, was one of the nine newcomers to politics in the Tupuola faction. Other members of Tupuola's faction included long-time friends, like Asi Aikeni, also a minister in the previous cabinet. A pattern was emerging whereby family connections and friendships influenced an MP's choice of party/faction. However, where MPs had relatives in the rival faction/party, they were usually appointed to parliamentary positions. Ale's claim (quoted above) that voters 'give their votes to get something in return' seems also to be true when MPs vote for prime ministerial candidates.

Overall, there was no evidence that the theoretical notion of political enterprise and the impersonal nature of political competition was operating. The rewards of political office were more evidently related to patron-client relations; and connections through kinship ties and personal friendship were evident in political groupings. However, despite the status associated with traditional *'āiga* such as Sa Fenunuivao and others, members of these *'āiga* did not necessarily join their traditionally allied candidate. Tradition became mixed with elements of the new order. The shift of leadership focus away from *tama-a-'āiga* towards charismatic and politically astute individuals is likely to have been the outcome of modern education and increasing links between Sāmoa and the outside world.

Three prime ministers: Party politics and the 1982–1984 parliament

The 1982 election was a major test for HRPP. Of the 24 MPs who regained their seats in the parliament, 13 were HRPP members and 11 were from the Tupuola faction. Of the 23 newly elected MPs (including some from earlier parliaments), 13 were HRPP members and 10 were Tupuola supporters. Following the election on 13 April, parliament elected Va'ai Kolone as the new prime minister by a narrow majority of 24 votes against Tupuola Efi's 23. Va'ai thus became the country's second prime minister with a non-*tama-a-'āiga* title. Nonumalo Sōfara, also of the HRPP, was elected speaker with the same margin of votes.

Among the HRPP MPs who regained their seats were senior members, such as Va'ai and Tofilau, as well as relatively junior members. Of the 13 HRPP members returned, nine had been first-time MPs in the 1979 parliament, one was a third-term MP, another a fourth-term MP and one – Va'ai Kolone – now held his seat for the sixth time in a row. Tofilau 'Eti was now elected to his seventh term since 1957. However, compared with members of the Tupuola faction, the majority of HRPP MPs who regained their seats were relatively junior in terms of parliamentary experience. The former commissioner of police regained his seat and was now joined by his younger brother who, for the first time since 1964, lost his seat in the

1976 general election. Nonumalo Sōfara, the new speaker, was now joined by another sister of his wife and former superintendent (later director) at the National Hospital in Apia, Matatūmua Maimoaga. Matatūmua's older sister, Lā'ulu, wife of the late Matā'afa, lost her seat. Thus, as in the previous parliament, there were two members of the Pētaia family as MPs, as well as Nonumalo, related to the Pētaia family by marriage. Four other MPs among those who regained their seats were closely related.

Among the 11 Tupuola supporters who regained their seats were six who had been ministers in the previous cabinet. Four were elected for the first time in 1979, while four were elected for the third time, one now held his seat for the fourth time, and two – Tupuola and Fuimaono Mimio – now had held their seats in five elections. Among those who lost their seats was the former speaker of the house, Tu'u'u Faleto'ese. His brother, 'Asi Sāgaga, joined the Tupuola faction despite the fact that most of his fellow Pētaia family members were in the HRPP. As the Tupuola faction candidate for speaker, he competed for the position against Nonumalo, the husband of his first cousin. Among the newly elected MPs were the son of the head of state, a former director of the Electric Power Cooperation, an accountant, and a high-ranking *matai* who had no employment experience but who had secondary school education. Thus, like the HRPP, Tupuola supporters did not comprise a specific interest group; instead their allegiance was mainly due to personal affiliations.

Following the 1982 election, about 14 election petitions were lodged with the Supreme Court. One, against Va'ai, was upheld by the court in early May following the decision that he had breached the 1963 Electoral Act. With Va'ai's seat being declared void by the court after he had served five months as prime minister, the head of state invited Tupuola to form a government. The HRPP believed that the head of state's appointment of Tupuola as prime minister was unconstitutional – because both parties at that time had 22 seats each in addition to the speaker, who was an HRPP member – and that he was repeating his 1975 action when he had appointed Tamasese to succeed Mata'afa. Consequently, the HRPP not only refused to participate in any coalition government, but also decided to boycott the swearing-in ceremony for Tupuola's new government. Tofilau 'Eti and Le Māmea Rōpati, both ministers under Va'ai, turned down offers of ministerial posts in the new government. On 6 October 1982, in Va'ai's absence, the HRPP elected Tofilau 'Eti as its new leader. With Tofilau at the political helm, the party suggested to Va'ai, after he regained his seat in a by-election on 9 January 1983, that he become a member of the council of deputies, a position that had previously been reserved for *tama-a-'āiga*. Va'ai declined, but accepted the chairmanship of the Western Sāmoa Trust Estate Corporation (WSTEC) board of directors. By early December, the HRPP and the government had 23 and 22 seats respectively, and both sides were keenly awaiting the results of the Sālega constituency by-election to be held on 4 December. Originally won by a Tupuola supporter in the general election, the seat was later declared void following the result of an election petition by an HRPP supporter, who eventually won the seat in the by-election by 215 votes to 123, giving the HRPP a one-seat majority in the parliament.

Tupuola's government once again became the opposition. Immediately after the Sālega by-election, HRPP's 24 caucus members signed a letter to the head of state petitioning him to call a session of parliament in order to elect a new prime minister; the head of state complied. On 21 December, Tupuola's budget was rejected by 23 to 22 votes, and on 30 December, Tofilau was sworn in by the head of state as the country's third prime minister in 12 months; he was the second HRPP MP to have been elected prime minister, and the third non-*tama-a-'āiga* to have held the country's top executive post.

Solidarity within HRPP placed Tofilau in the seat of prime minister; although, had he not been the head of the party, the office might have been contested by others. The HRPP members were united in asking the head of state to recall parliament and in rejecting the proposal for a coalition government. However, a new issue emerged; soon after the rejection of Tupuola's budget, one of Tupuola's supporters, Papāli'i Laupepa, a son of the head of state, declared himself an independent, allied with neither faction nor party. (This was to become an increasing, if short-lived, move by candidates in future elections.) Papāli'i later formed his own party, Sāmoa ua Tasi (Sāmoa United). However, sadly, he passed away at the end of the parliamentary term and the new party did not survive him.

On 7 February 1985, 15 days before the general election, Tupuola and his supporters established the second post-independence political party, the Christian Democratic Party (CDP). Given the timing of its establishment, the CDP seems to have been intended as a way of organizing support for Tupuola in the forthcoming election. Among those present at its establishment was Leota Itū'au, who claims to have chosen the name of the party. The CDP does not appear to have drawn up a constitution. However, it did publish a manifesto. An editorial in the *Sāmoa Observer* (13 February 1988) commented that the manifesto made no philosophical commitment, but comprised pragmatic proposals directed toward the weaknesses that the CDP perceived in the economy and national management. Tupuola supporters may have sought, by formalizing themselves as a political party, to keep their faction united and enhance their chance of winning government in the 1985 election – but the move was unsuccessful.

The 1985–1987 parliament

The HRPP won a landslide victory in the 1985 election; with 31 seats against the CDP's 16. Tofilau 'Eti was returned with a record majority of 326 votes. Of the 33 MPs who regained their seats, 20 were HRPP members and 13 were CDP members. Of the 15 newly elected MPs, 10 were HRPP members and four were CDP supporters. Compared with the previous election, the HRPP had increased its majority by seven seats. The 20 HRPP MPs who retained their seats included all the 13 who had retained their seats in the previous parliament. Of the other seven, all except Polataivao Fosi – who was now an MP for the seventh time in a row with the exception of his loss in 1976 – were now MPs for the second time in a row. The other two, 'Asi Aikeni and George Lober, were now in their fourth and second terms respectively, but had both lost their seats in 1982.

As in previous parliaments, both parties included people with family connections to other parliamentarians. Among the newly elected MPs were 'Ai'ono Fanaafi, wife of Le Tagaloa Pita (a third term HRPP MP), and Māta'utia Sae, the prime minister's brother in-law. A by-election in late 1985 saw Matā'afa's daughter and a Pētaia kin through her mother, Fiamē Nāomi, elected to parliament as an HRPP MP. Fiamē's aunt, Matatūmua, lost her seat, but Tofilau and Nonumalo Sōfara retained theirs, thus keeping at three the number of Pētaia family MPs in parliament, as had been the case in the previous two parliaments.

Friendship was also a factor in political alliances. Of the four newly elected CDP MPs, one told the author in an interview that he joined the CDP because a lot of people he grew up with and others who had been his friends for several years were in that party. He considered that the majority of MPs chose the parties they did because of personal affiliations. A notable development in this 1985–87 parliament was the crossing-over of MPs to the other party, most noticeably from the losing to the winning side. For example, To'ī Aukuso switched to the HRPP, having voted for Tupuola in the previous prime ministerial election.

From the moment of its victory, HRPP's solidarity was threatened by intra-party competition for the leadership. On 26 February 1985, four days after the election, the HRPP caucus met at government house at Malae-o-Matagofie to elect its leader and prime minister for the next three years. The leadership meeting followed an HRPP caucus decision the year before to defer choosing a leader until after a general election. The caucus voted that the leader should be chosen by the traditional method of consensus. The three nominations put forward were the prime minister (Tofilau 'Eti), Va'ai, and the former finance minister under Matā'afa's prime ministership, Fa'aso'otauloa Semu Pualagi. Fa'aso'otauloa later withdrew his nomination when it became clear that he did not have enough support to win. Towards the end of the meeting, Va'ai also withdrew his bid for the leadership – and on 7 March, in the presence of Tofilau and 10 other HRPP MPs, Va'ai officially resigned from the HRPP. In a press statement the following day, he told reporters that he had dissociated himself from the party, referring to his belief that the party was no longer conscious of its original ideals and objectives.

Immediately after Va'ai quit the HRPP, another prominent HRPP MP, Le Tagaloa Pita, and his wife, 'Ai'ono Fanaafi, also left the party. In a press statement, Le Tagaloa referred to what he considered to be the arrogant treatment of the party caucus by cabinet in the previous two years of government, and the cabinet's lack of consultation with caucus on major policy issues. Le Tagaloa had not been a cabinet minister in the previous HRPP government. However, as a qualified economist and senior parliamentarian he chaired a parliamentary sub-committee that coordinated tenders by local business people, attempting to control imports and thus regulate foreign exchange. In a speech at the HRPP's leadership meeting, Le Tagaloa expressed regret that he had not been considered as a leadership candidate, an omission which he felt overlooked the high rank of his title, as well as his qualifications.

Prior to the first session of parliament it was rumoured that Va'ai had the support of 11 HRPP MPs who, if they formed a coalition with the CDP's 16, could form a coalition government. In parliament, Fa'aso'otauloa nominated Tofilau as the HRPP's prime ministerial candidate. A senior

CDP MP nominated Va'ai as their prime ministerial candidate, but Va'ai declined the nomination, thereby allowing Tofilau to be elected unopposed for his second prime ministerial term. The HRPP's candidates for speaker and deputy speaker were also elected unopposed. Tofilau's new cabinet, announced in parliament on 26 March, comprised only two ministers from the previous cabinet. Among the new ministers was Toī 'Aukuso, who had voted for Tupuola in the prime ministerial election on 13 April 1982 but had defected to the HRPP.

Tofilau won unopposed because a number of issues concerning the composition of the proposed coalition were unresolved between the CDP and the Va'ai faction. The CDP argued that, because they had 16 MPs compared with Va'ai's apparent 11 supporters, they should lead the coalition leadership and have five cabinet positions. The Va'ai faction, on the other hand, wanted all these issues left to Va'ai's personal discretion. The two sides met four times but could not arrive at an acceptable settlement.

Eventually, the CDP conceded four ministerial posts to Va'ai but insisted that Tupuola become the prime minister and minister of finance. (Va'ai and Tupuola were old rivals; Va'ai had defeated Tupuola – who held the seat under his title Tufuga – in the 1967 general election). By the time of the prime ministerial election, the negotiators for the two sides had still not come to an agreement. HRPP, suspecting that at least eight of its members intended to leave the party, was reported to have taken measures to prevent this from happening before parliament met. Reported tactics included assigning loyal supporters as guards, monitoring phone calls, screening visitors to the parties headquarters, and sending observers to the CDP headquarters. Consequently, except for the defections of Va'ai, Le Tagaloa and 'Ai'ono, the 31 successful HRPP parliamentary candidates were still united when parliament met to elect a new prime minister.

Based on the numbers, a no-confidence motion was expected from CDP, Va'ai and other factions, when Tofilau convened parliament for its normal June/July session in 1985. However, his party had devised a strategy. Its senior members would occupy the floor for the whole two-hour session, to take advantage of the fact that Samoans generally give respect to their elders. The session was devoted to the discussion of reports, blocking efforts by the opposing party and factions to take the floor. When, at the end of the discussion, the anticipated motion of no-confidence was moved, it was not seconded within the two hours required by statutes[2] –

although Le Tagaloa tried unsuccessfully to postpone the adjournment of this parliamentary sitting until the next day. It was reported that 27 MPs had informed the speaker of the intention to move the motion before the session officially opened.

However, nine months later, the Tofilau government's budget for 1986 was rejected in parliament by 27 votes to 19; Tofilau resigned as prime minister the following week. In the meantime, there was heated debate in which Tofilau referred to the anger of his electorate towards his opponents who had defeated his government. During that week Tofilau also advised the head of state to dissolve parliament and call an election in order to ascertain the true feeling of the public, but his advice was rejected.

A coalition government was formed between the CDP and the Va'ai faction, with Va'ai as prime minister. The four cabinet ministers from the Va'ai faction were Le Tagaloa, Fa'aso'otauloa, Le Māmea Rōpati and Toe-sulusulu Si'ueva (whose former HRPP affiliation had been based on his support for Va'ai). Among the 11 MPs in the coalition who supported HRPP was Fepulea'i Semi, whose victory in the by-election on 4 December 1982 had given the HRPP its one-vote majority.

The coalition's path towards the next general election in 1988 was not smooth sailing. By late June 1986, there were moves within the coalition to have Va'ai removed as prime minister. Va'ai had resisted moves by some influential members within the coalition to set up in Sāmoa the Chinese-based Superlandlord's Logging Company. Some of these coalition members were former HRPP colleagues who had switched allegiance to support him as prime minister. However, to make sure that this was in the best interest of Sāmoa, Va'ai set up a commission of inquiry into the likely impact of the logging operation on the country (*Observer*, 25 June 1986).

Not long after Le Tagaloa and his wife, 'Ai'ono Fanaafi, left the HRPP in 1985 – by which time Tofilau's HRPP was in government – the speaker, Nonumalo Sōfara, charged them under the *Electoral Act 1963* for being 'guilty of conduct unbecoming a Member of Parliament' because, he alleged, they were not validly married. The act furher stipulates that, if such a charge is denied by an MP, the speaker must refer the matter to the Supreme Court. Le Tagaloa and 'Ai'ono denied the charge and Nonumalo duly referred the matter. However, before the charge was heard in the Supreme Court, evidence was found that the two MPs were validly married. Although the speaker then withdrew his charge, the *accused* tabled motions in the Supreme Court to disqualify the *speaker* for 'behaviour unbecoming of a Member of Parliament' – the same offence with which the speaker had charged them – and to sue Tofilau's HRPP government for S$6 million in damages for defamation of character. Because the speaker was involved, the deputy speaker, Ati'ifale Fiso (also voted in by the HRPP to this position), in accordance with the Electoral Act, had to refer the matter to the Supreme Court; but he refused to obey the law. On 15 January 1987, acting chief justice Denis Pain of the Supreme Court struck out the motions by Le Tagaloa (now minister of economic affairs under the coalition government) and 'Ai'ono because they were not filed according to the law.

The uneasiness surrounding these legal challenges arose out of the fact that, had Le Tagaloa and 'Ai'ono succeeded in disqualifying the speaker, parliament would have had to elect a new speaker. On the other hand, had the speaker succeeded in his motion, the coalition would have lost two seats, thereby reducing its majority to 25 seats.

In January 1987, a row in cabinet between Tupuola Efi, deputy prime minister and minister of public works, and the minister of economic development and the post office, Le Tagaloa Pita, was reported in the media. The deputy prime minister took offence at the manner in which the minister of post office had dealt with the chief architect in the public works department, Hank Ward. Le Tagaloa was unhappy with the long delays in getting the plans for the new post office drawn up, which he believed was the chief architect's fault. When Le Tagaloa invited a local private architect to draw up the plans, he received strong criticism from the public service commission, which is responsible for all public servants, and the office of the attorney general. They questioned the minister's right to consult a private architect without their knowledge and approval. In the end, the minister had his way (*ST*, 30 January 1987).

Probably because of political considerations, the coalition government only tabled its 1987 supplementary budget together with the 1988 budget during parliament's last session for 1987, in December. Two of the controversial items in the budget were the drastic cuts to the National University of Sāmoa and the overspending on the post office project. The cost of the new post office was S$3–4 million – a blow out in the budget way over the one per cent allowed under the law. Post office expenditure and the substantial overspending on the independence celebration in June were some of the major concerns stated in the public accounts committee's report to parliament on the 1987 supplementary budget. According to the committee, cabinet had abused its power in approving these huge amounts without the approval of parliament. Overspending over and above the one per cent unauthorized expenditure allowed under the law was such a serious issue that the speaker of parliament and the attorney general were considering taking this matter to the Supreme Court for clarification. Although cabinet had sought the approval of the head of state for the the additional expenses, the legally required contract had not been laid before parliament. Money to recover this expenditure was being sought in the supplementary budget now before parliament (*ST,* 11, 18 December 1987).

The ST300,000 cut in the university vote in the 1986 budget was restored in the 1987 supplementary budget. In 1986, the coalition government had decided to close down Avele College, one of the government schools established in 1924, to make room for the relocation away from its temporary site of the two-year old National University of Sāmoa. The closure of Avele College became such a politically controversial issue that the recommendation by the parliament's public petitions committee to close the school was lost in a division by 22 votes to 12. The HRPP and four members of the coalition opposed the recommendation. As an old boy of Avele College and one of its strongest supporters, the prime minister, Va'ai Kolone, must have found it extremely hard to vote for the closure of his old school. The other old boy of Avele College, a member of the coalition government, Fepulea'i Semi, dropped his political affiliation in favour of his old school. Thus, the Avele College issue divided not just the country but also the coalition government (*ST,* 29 January 1988).

Other major events of 1987 that added to already existing tension in the coalition ranks were three legal issues heard in the Land and Titles Court. They related to the authority to confer the *tama-a-āiga* title, Tupua Tamasese; the authority over the traditional seat of the Tui Ātua title; and the authority to confer the Tui Ātua *pāpā*. The new socio-political loyalties manifested in modern political parties had to give way to the old loyalties inherent in traditional lineages and alliances. After three separate hearings to decide these highly sensitive traditional issues, Tupuola Efi, deputy prime minister in the coalition government, emerged victorious. The conferral on him of the *tama-a-'āiga* title, Tupua Tamasese, by 'Āiga Sa Fenunuivao on 11 December 1986 was confirmed by the Court on 29 August 1987. That authority over the Tui Ātua *pāpā* resided with Lufilufi village, which had conferred the *pāpā* honour on Tupuola Efi, was also confirmed. The authority over the traditional residence of the Tui Ātua title was also awarded to the petitioning party that Tupuola had supported.

Among members of parliament in the coalition government who were opponents of Tupuola in those hearings were Fepulea'i Semi and 'Ai'ono Fanaafi, both former HRPP members who had switched allegiance to form the coalition. One of the strongest opponents of Tupuola in the hearings was Fiamē Nāomi Matā'afa, a member of the HRPP opposition. The HRPP leader, Tofilau 'Eti Alesana, by virtue of that title was a member of the traditional Sa Levālasi lineage, which was led in these hearings by Fiamē Nāomi Matā'afa. Thus parliamentary politics had found another avenue, the Land and Titles Court of Sāmoa, in which to play itself out. The result of these Land and Titles Court hearings was probably more politically beneficial to the HRPP than to the coalition government.

Thus, even before the 1988 general election was held, there had been important developments that would affect the future of the coalition. The Tupua Tamasese title was bestowed upon Tupuola. The Tui Ātua title, which had also been held by his late cousin, was also conferred on him in 1986 and confirmed by the Land and Titles Court in 1987. As was the case with the former holder of these titles, pressure was placed on Tupuola (now Tui Ātua Tupua Tamasese 'Efi – hereafter referred to as Tupua) to stand for the constituency of Ānoāma'a East in the 1988 election.[3]

Tupua's succession to these titles had a direct effect on his new constituency's choice of parliamentary candidate. The incumbent MP (for the period 1985–88), Fa'amatuāinu Tala Mailei, stood down, allowing Tupua to be the candidate. Fa'amatuāinu was one of the six members of the Lufilufi orator group, and also one of the 11 HRPP MPs who had defected to form the coalition government. 'Āiga Sa Fenunu'ivao, in a collective statement over national radio, informed the country that its parliamentary candidate was Tui Ātua Tupua Tamasese 'Efi, despite the fact that Iuli Sefo, another nominee for the candidacy, was a founding member of HRPP and a high-ranking titleholder of both Falefā village and 'Āiga Sa Fenunu'ivao. Iuli eventually succumbed to traditional pressure and withdrew his nomination. As was the case with his predecessor, Tui Ātua Tupua Tamasese 'Efi was elected unopposed in the 1988 general election. In opting to stand as a candidate for the Ānoāma'a East constituency, Tupua had to leave the Ā'ana Ālofi No. 2 constituency, which he had represented since 1970.

The 1988–1990 parliament

The fact that both Tupua and Va'ai were elected unopposed probably influenced the coalition's decision not to elect its leader before the 1988 general election. As well as waiting to see whether the coalition or the HRPP won the most seats, the two coalition factions were probably also waiting to see which *faction* won the most seats, as this would determine the prime ministerial candidacy and ministerial selections.

The results of the general election of 26 February 1988 gave the HRPP 25 seats. Of the 11 MPs who had defected to the coalition government, three did not seek nomination again, while only three retained their seats. However, after official recounts, the HRPP majority was reduced by two seats and the election for a third seat was found to be a tie; this was later won by the coalition candidate following a recount. Thus, the number of HRPP seats fell to 22. Among the successful candidates were the three who, immediately the election results were known, founded a new party, the Sāmoa National Party or SNP. SNP's spokesman was Leota (the former speaker of the House, who had defected to form the HRPP in early 1979 and who was re-elected following his earlier defeats in 1982 and 1985). Three members of his political party had not been offered support, nor been approached for their support, by the HRPP, and so SNP decided to support the coalition. The SNP's three members gave the coalition 23 seats.

There were also three independents who won seats in 1988; two of them were Sagapolutele Sipaia and Misa Telefoni. They were courted for their support by all parties. Sagapolutele eventually joined the HRPP, giving it 23 seats. There were unsubstantiated rumours that Tupua had offered him a new car, the justice portfolio and $5,000 for his allegiance.

Although Misa had campaigned as an independent, the previous coalition government had appointed him attorney general. Moreover, he was Tupua's maternal first cousin, so it seemed likely that he would eventually support the coalition. Before the general election, Misa's constituency informed both camps that a decision as to which political party Misa would join would be made after the results of the election were known, which would undoubtedly reflect Misa's own preference. He eventually gave his support to the coalition, giving it a one-vote majority.

Not long after the results of the general election were known, during which time the HRPP had seemed assured of a parliamentary majority, the coalition leadership changed. Va'ai handed over leadership to Tupua, reversing their former positions as leader and deputy leader. Va'ai was reported as saying that he gave the leadership to Tupua in reciprocation for Tupua's respect for him in the previous government.

On the night of 4 April, with parliament due to meet on 6 April to elect a new government, Tanuvasa decided to withdraw his support for the coalition and join the HRPP; the one-seat majority changed hands. His nomination of Tofilau as the HRPP's prime ministerial candidate, was seconded by Sagapolutele. Having won the prime ministership, Tofilau appointed Tanuvasa minister of economic affairs and development, tourism and trade. Sagapolutele was appointed chairman of the *Pulenu'u* (village mayors) committee. In a speech formally accepting Tanuvasa into the HRPP, Tofilau mentioned that Tanuvasa was his distant relative. Although Tanuvasa had stood as the candidate for Tupua's old constituency of Ā'ana Ālofi No.2, against the HRPP-supported candidate, and with implied support for Tupua, his leaning toward the HRPP was known; he had twice stood unsuccessfully against Tupua in previous elections. Tanuvasa's defection was felt bitterly by the coalition partners.

The continuous election of some MPs – among them Tofilau, Va'ai, Tupua Tamasese 'Efi, Polataivao, Fuimaono Mimio – in both parties had been a feature of their political career dating back to the period before political parties. However, even if their affiliation to political parties did not affect their chances of being re-elected, it certainly helped their chances of getting ministerial posts and other political positions. Party loyalties and the rewards of office could prove stronger than kinship. For example, Tafa'ese Uili, now an MP for the first time, had long supported Tupua in previous elections but now switched to the HRPP: Tafa'ese Uili was given a parliamentary under-secretary post. Lei'ātaua Vaiao and Le Tagaloa Pita were brothers, now members of opposing parties, since Le Tagaloa and 'Ai'ono had left the HRPP. Lei'ātaua was appointed minister of justice in Tofilau's cabinet.

On 8 April 1988, two days after their defeat, the coalition named itself the Sāmoa National Development Party or SNDP. It has since remained the main opposition party in the house. Its 23 MPs pledged their loyalty to the party in a signed public notice in the press. Not long after, their number was reduced to 20. Election petitions declared two seats void, and one member's *matai* title was stripped by the Land and Titles Court, thereby rendering him unable to hold a seat. Despite the loyalty pledge, later in the parliamentary term a member of the original three-member SNP declared himself an independent, as did Le Tagaloa. Thus, by the end of the parliamentary term, the number of parliamentary members of the SNDP was reduced from 23 to 18.

Having acquired the numbers to form a government, Tofilau had to judiciously select members for his new cabinet, weighing the question of allegiance with qualifications. Of the eight members of the current HRPP caucus who retained their seats, only two had not held ministerial posts in the previous HRPP governments, although one of them had been a cabinet minister in Tamasese's government (1970–72). Of the other 16, one was a cabinet minister in the 1982 HRPP government, two held PhD degrees, one had a Masters degree and was a former chairman of the PSC, one was an Australian-qualified electrical engineer, and a number of others had held high-ranking positions in the private and the public sectors. In a caucus meeting to ascertain MPs' feelings on the possible candidates for ministerial posts, one MP – a minister in the previous government – argued that the 'newcomers' should give way to those with ministerial experience. The matter was debated heatedly in caucus. Older, experienced members found themselves pitted against younger, more formally qualified members who reportedly threatened to withdraw their support. To'ī Aukuso was said to have saved the day. A former supporter of Tupua, who later in 1982 decided to switch his allegiance to the HRPP, To'ī was a member of Tofilau's short-lived cabinet in 1985. To'ī voluntarily withdrew as a possible ministerial candidate, thereby creating an opening for another ministerial aspirant – it was To'ī's company which soon after won the contract to put up power lines throughout the country in the HRPP government's rural electrification program. One of the two MPs with PhD degrees was appointed as Sāmoa's ambassador to the United Nations. The other became the vice chancellor of the National University of Sāmoa in 1992, having decided not to seek parliamentary nomination in the 1991 general election. Tofilau's new cabinet included three MPs with no previous ministerial experience. Of these, one was a member in the two previous HRPP governments and two were newcomers to politics. The two newcomers were

Tanuvasa and Lei'ātaua Vaiao, the latter had been Sāmoa's first chairman of the public service commission in the 1960s.

Two important developments during this parliamentary term that helped shore up support for the HRPP were the introduction of the HRPP pledge – which made it difficult, but not impossible, for members selected by the party to switch political allegiance – and the passing of the *Parliamentary Under-Secretaries Act 1988*. The Parliamentary Under-Secretary Bill was tabled in parliament on 31 May 1988, the first session of parliament since the prime ministerial election on April 6. The intention of the bill was to allow the government to appoint from among the MPs, nine parliamentary under-secretaries. In tabling the bill, the prime minister argued that the measure would maintain the smooth running of the government. Compared with the 1960s, the ministers' workloads had increased by about 75 per cent. Moreover, ministers were not able to meet the growing demands of their constituents. He pointed out that the practice of appointing parliamentary under-secretaries had grown in overseas parliaments, and Western Sāmoa was now in a financial position to cater for such a development. The other option was to increase the number of ministers in cabinet, which could not be done without amendment to the constitution. Having parliamentary under-secretaries would provide the public with an alternative

The opposition, opposing the bill, pointed out that Western Sāmoa had more MPs and cabinet ministers per capita than New Zealand. Opposition members argued that the expense was unreasonable for a developing country and that the bill threatened the principle of the separation of powers between executive and legislative, as a number of the current members of parliamentary committees who would be appointed parliamentary under-secretaries would become more closely associated with the executive arm of government. As some MPs bluntly put it, the whole purpose of the bill was to compensate those who did not get ministerial posts. Notwithstanding, the bill was passed into law, and the government appointed nine parliamentary under-secretaries from among the HRPP MPs.

The third major political development was the *Public Service (Special Posts) Act 1989*, which empowered cabinet to appoint heads of departments on two-year contracts. A prominent SNDP MP told the author that the effect of the act was to ensure that public servants would toe the party line. The passing

of the act was the culmination of a long and vexed relationship between the
PSC and the government on one hand, and the individual ministers and
public servants on the other. The constitution states that:

> In the performance of its functions, the Public Service Commission
> shall have regard to the general policy of Cabinet relating to the Public
> Service, and shall give effect to any decision of Cabinet defining that
> policy conveyed to the Commission in writing by the Prime Minister
> (Art. 87.3).

Nevertheless, various ministers at different times had complained about
their inability to exert influence upon their respective departments, and
in particular on the heads of departments. In early 1983, Tofilau told the
heads of departments that he wanted neither the heads of departments nor
their deputies to be involved in politics; alluding to the fact that heads and
deputy heads of departments who supported MPs in the opposition were,
in general, noticeably uncooperative with their respective ministers and the
government of the day. The effect of politicizing the executive meant that
heads of departments might have to place political considerations ahead of
their professional judgment if they wanted their contracts renewed.

The 1991–1996 parliament

The 1991 general election, the first to be conducted under universal
suffrage, gave the HRPP a comfortable win. The HRPP held 27 seats to
the SNDP's 15. When parliament met on 7 May to elect a new prime
minister, Tofilau was elected for his fourth term (by 30 votes to Va'ai's 15).
All the four independents and one SNDP MP (Tole'afoa Fa'afisi), who
had switched allegiance to HRPP, voted for Tofilau. One MP, presumably
Misa because he left the house at the time of the prime ministerial ballot,
did not cast a vote. Tole'afoa was elected deputy speaker. Of the five independents, Pa'u Sālea'ula and Fuataga Ioane were known to be supporters of the HRPP. Both had campaigned as independents because HRPP
policy gave priority to sitting MPs. Of the other three, one (Nonumalo L.
Sōfara) had been the HRPP-elected speaker of the house in the 1982–84
and the 1985–87 parliaments, but lost his seat in 1988. Another (Matai'a
Visesio) was Tupua's paternal first cousin. Mataia's only opponent was the
sitting SNDP MP, Faumuinā Anapapa. The fifth independent MP was
Le Tagaloa.

As in previous parliaments, most candidates who stood as independents in the end joined the party with the most seats; MPs who retained their seats remained loyal to their parties. Of the 31 votes that Tofilau polled in the prime ministerial election, 27 came from HRPP MPs, three (Pau, Fuataga and Nonumalo) from independents and one (Tole'afoa Fa'afisi) was an SNDP MP. Of the 19 MPs who retained their seats, 10 were members of the previous parliament, one was in his third term, two in their fourth term, three in their fifth, and Polataivao and Tofilau in their ninth and tenth terms respectively. Members with family connections generally joined the same party. Those who changed party affiliation tended to do so for a reward.

Among the SNDP candidates who lost their seats was Tupua Tamasese 'Efi, who, in the previous general election, had been elected unopposed from his Ānoāma'a East constituency. Following the confirmation of his defeat by 27 votes (after recounts), Tupua asked Va'ai to take over as leader of the opposition. Misa Telefoni resigned from the SNDP in April 1991, explaining to the press that his conscience was at stake, and that his reason for changing allegiance was due to Va'ai's leadership. Misa added that he did not think that Tupua had a mandate from his party to pass the leadership to Va'ai and suggested that an agreement had been made between the two that Tupua would resume party leadership if he were re-elected in the future.

Tofilau's new cabinet contained only two ministers from the previous cabinet. Among the other six were To'ī Aukuso (who was a minister for seven months in 1985, and had voluntarily declined nomination as a possible ministerial candidate at an HRPP caucus meeting after the 1988 general election), one newcomer to politics and four members who had retained their seats. Five ministers of the previous government who had retained their seats but were overlooked this time by the prime minister were discontented. One of them said that, on the eve of announcing his cabinet, the prime minister had assured the ministers in the previous cabinet that they would all be re-appointed. The prime minister even asked them to help him encourage the HRPP MPs to remain in the party and to help encourage others to join the party (interview, 11 July 1993). But, though they felt cheated, the disappointed former ministers, and others who had aspired to ministerial posts, awaited another chance.

In the June/July 1991 parliamentary session, the prime minister tabled three constitutional amendment bills.[4] They included bills to increase by four the number of ministers in cabinet, to increase from three to five the number of years for each parliamentary term, and for the addition of two more parliamentary seats (thereby increasing from 47 to 49 the number of seats in the house). The three constitutional amendments were passed by parliament on 21 November 1991. The bill to increase by four the number of ministers in the cabinet was passed by 32 votes to ten. The bill to increase from three to five the number of years per parliamentary term was passed by 34 votes to eight. The bill to add two more parliamentary seats was passed by 41 votes to one.

The prime minister announced his four additional ministers on 14 August 1992; they were sworn-in by the head of state six days later. Among them was Misa, two MPs who had served as ministers under the previous government, and one newcomer to politics. Of the two ministers in the previous government who were re-appointed, one had been the chairman of the bills committee and the other had been the chairman of the public accounts committee (PAC). The chairman of the PAC was replaced by another minister in the previous government, while the chairman of the bills committee was replaced by one of the four independents, a medical doctor by career. The other independent, Nonumalo Leulumoega Sōfara, was appointed to the public accounts committee to replace the newly elected MP who had now been appointed to cabinet. With 12 ministers and the prime minister in cabinet, together with 13 parliamentary under-secretaries, the HRPP enjoyed the guaranteed support of 26 members of the 49-seat parliament.

By the June/July 1993 session of parliament there had been a number of important political developments. Two by-elections had seen two addition-al HRPP MPs. Tupua had eventually regained his seat and was sworn in during parliament's mid-year session in 1992. In parliament on 17 August 1992, as Misa had anticipated, Va'ai announced that he was relinquishing the leadership of the SNDP to its former leader. In early April of that year, for the first time since its establishment, the HRPP had elected a deputy leader during a parliamentary term, and not immediately after the general election; the elected deputy was Tuila'epa Sa'ilele. Tuila'epa had served as minister of finance under Tofilau since he became prime minister in late 1982. As deputy leader, Tuila'epa was also the deputy prime minister and it was expected that he would succeed to the prime ministership should Tofilau decide to bow out of politics.

Among the 13 parliamentary under-secretaries was another SNDP member, working under Misa's portfolio. During the period in which Tupua was absent from parliament, another SNDP MP (Amiatu Sio) had switched allegiance to the HRPP. Amiatu became the parliamentary under-secretary of education and a member of the public accounts committee.

When Misa joined the HRPP, but before he was appointed to cabinet, he suggested that the party endorse the concept of specialized groups. The proposal was accepted by the prime minister and other members. A specialized group (the FRG) was formed to raise funds for the future use of HRPP members. While no cabinet ministers were in it, it did include two of the three ministers in the previous cabinet who had missed out on ministerial posts this time around. The third member had been appointed parliamentary under-secretary to the prime minister. The HRPP fundraising group was led informally by one of the oldest HRPP MPs, who was in his first parliamentary term, having been elected unopposed by his constituency.

The group concept soon backfired on the HRPP. By the June/July 1993 session of parliament, the fund-raising group claimed to have more than 10 members, which, if combined with the opposition, would have given the 26 votes needed to defeat the government. Among the group's members were all six members of the PAC, whose chairman had been a minister in the previous HRPP government but had been overlooked by Tofilau in the appointment of his new twelve-member team. At this time, the PAC had decided to move a motion in the house to have a budgetary item reduced.[5] Members of the specialized group had met frequently and had decided to support the PAC recommendation when the motion was tabled. Opposition MPs had been informed about these developments, as they were used as a tactic eventually to defeat the government, and a paper had been circulated among opposition MPs and the FRG to be signed by their respective members. Among other things, it stipulated an agreement on who would be the PM and cabinet ministers should the intended strategy succeed.

In parliament, the chair of the PAC moved the acceptance of the report. In a division, 19 voted for it while 26 voted against. The 19 who supported the report included all 13 SNDP MPs, four members of the PAC, and the two independents, Le Tagaloa and Matai'a.[6] The other two members of the PAC told parliament that they had informed their chairman that they were not supporting the motion after they had listened to an explanation by the minister of finance in parliament as to why the item (among others) was included in the budget.[7] One of these two members held the same title as the PM (and was therefore a relative of the PM); he was in his first parliamentary term, having been elected, along with the PM, from a constituency which, because of its population size, provided two seats. Most of the alleged members of the FRG voted with the government. The only one who did not sign the agreement between it and the opposition MPs refused to do so because the opposition had agreed to Tupua being the PM without first consulting FRG members. Moreover, he suspected that one of their members was with them 'in body only but not in spirit'. This particular member had recently been offered a consultancy job and a vehicle for his personal use by the government, on top of his initial appointment as parliamentary under-secretary for post office and telecommunication. As it turned out, the PM knew about the signed agreement between the two groups. In parliament, the PM accused the leader of the opposition of political scheming and trying to induce the HRPP MPs to gang up with him.[8] As a direct result of the unsuccessful plan to defeat the government, three HRPP MPs of the PAC who were directly involved in the signed agreement were expelled from the party. One of them later lost his seat following a court decision that upheld the complainant's suit for criminal offence. A subsequent by-election, in which he stood, was won by an HRPP-endorsed candidate.

The FRG's unsuccessful attempt to overthrow the government in mid-1993 was the first serious test of HRPP solidarity since the defection of its 11 members in 1985. The victory of the HRPP in the 1996 general election and the subsequent prime ministerial election of Tofilau, who polled 34 votes to Tupua Tamasese Efi's 14, was further evidence of not only the continued existence of political parties but also of the electoral success of the HRPP as an organization (see So'o 2005 for an update on post-1991 political parties).

The 1996–2000 parliament

The 1996 general election saw the HRPP winning 25 seats, the SNDP 12, Samoa Labour Party (SLP) one; 12 independent candidates were elected. However, by the time of the prime ministerial election, the HRPP had secured the support of 10 independents to win comfortably, thereby giving Tofilau 'Eti Alesana the majority to form another government and resume the prime ministership. Of the 27 who retained their seats, 19 were HRPP MPs, seven SNDP and there was one independent. Tofilau's cabinet included five newcomers to politics. When Tofilau passed away in 1998, Tuila'epa Sa'ilele Malielegaoi, minister of finance and deputy prime minister, took over as prime minister.

The lead-up to this general election saw several political parties being established (see So'o 2005). With the exception of the HRPP and SNDP, the only new political party that was able to win a seat was the Samoa Labour Party; it was won by its leader, To'alepai Toesulusulu Si'ueva, one of the 11 HRPP MPs who had defected to form the coalition in 1985. He had lost his seat in the 1988 general election and was unsuccessful again in the 1991 general election. However, his electoral victory in 1996 was short-lived. His election was declared void following an election petition, and his seat was won by an HRPP candidate in the ensuing by-election.

The 2001–2005 parliament

The results of the 2001 general election saw the HRPP winning again, this time by 25 seats. The SNDP won 10 seats, independents 13 and the Samoa All People's Party (SAPP) one. In the first meeting of parliament, Tuila'epa Sa'ilele Malielegaoi was re-elected prime minister. The HRPP, therefore, had a renewed mandate to govern the country for another five years. One of the independents joined the HRPP before the first meeting of parliament. Another independent candidate joined the HRPP after successfully defending her election-night win against a petition lodged against her. Three more HRPP candidates were elected in by-elections following court rulings of election petitions that declared void some seats (one of them was the only seat won by the SAPP). Of the 23 MPs who retained their seats after the general election results were confirmed but before the results of election petitions were known, 15 were HRPP candidates and eight were SNDP supporters.

Tuila'epa's new cabinet included four of the five ministers from the previous cabinet who had retained their seats. One of the ministers in the previous cabinet did not contest his seat again because of ill-health. With Tuila'epa succeeding to the leadership when the late Tofilau 'Eti

Alesana passed away in 1998, Misa Telefoni was elected deputy leader by the party, and was, therefore, also the deputy prime minister. Tuila'epa dissociated himself from the minister of finance portfolio for the first time since his first appointment in 1983. Misa was given the portfolio. Given the fact that this was the first time that Tuila'epa had appointed ministers to cabinet, and that there had been no complaints amongst HRPP MPs who had missed out on ministerial appointments, either the party system had become firmly consolidated or the new prime minister's choice of ministers had the general support of his party. The lack of complaints could also have meant that the MPs who had missed out on ministerial posts were happy with their parliamentary under-secretary appointments. Regardless, the calm contributed to the consolidation of the party system and to its legitimacy, not only among party and caucus members but also among the public.

Immediately upon confirmation of all parliamentary seats but before the results of election petitions were known, the 'independents' organized themselves around Asiata Sāle'imoa Va'ai as their leader. Their grouping became known as the Samoa United Independents Party (SUIP), although it is not certain whether or not the party was registered. Although Asiata was a newcomer to politics, he is a seasoned lawyer, had graduated in 1997 with a PhD from the Australian National University and had been in touch with political developments in the country through his father, the late Va'ai Kolone, who had twice been prime minister.

After a long political career, Tui Ātua Tupua Tamasese Efi decided that he would relinquish the party leadership to Le Māmea Rōpati. Although one of the 11 HRPP MPs who had defected to form the coalition government in late 1985, Le Mamea was by now a devoted member of the SNDP. In 2004, Le Mamea's SNDP and Asiata Sāle'imoa's SUIP joined to form the Samoa Democratic United Party (SDUP), with Le Māmea Rōpati and Asiata Sāle'imoa as leader and deputy leader, respectively.

The 2006 – 2010 parliament

Nominations for candidates for the general election on 31 March 2006 closed two weeks before the election. Seventy-eight candidates registered for the HRPP, 49 for the Samoa Democratic United Party (SDUP), 22 for the Samoa Party (SP), five for the Christian Party (CP), and there were 56 independents. A total of 210 candidates, 16 of whom were women, registered, compared with 153 for the 2001 general election.[9] Among the independents were HRPP supporters who could not register themselves as official party candidates because of the HRPP party policy allowing the sitting MP the right to agree or not to having a new candidate endorsed as an official HRPP candidate from his/her constituency. The 2006 general election stood out because of the amount of media coverage of party campaigns. The SDUP in particular utilized to the utmost existing media organizations. In spite of its massive campaign effort, however, the result of the election was another HRPP landslide victory; it won 30 seats, with the SDUP managing only 10 and the independents 9 (Lesā 2006a:2–3).

Immediately after the election, two independents, Muāgututagata Pat Ah Heem of Sāgaga-le-Usoga constituency and Lāfaitele Patrick Lei'ātaualesā of Alataua West constituency, joined the HRPP, giving it 32 seats. By the first session of parliament, however, another three independents had joined the HRPP, giving it 35 seats and ensuring another HRPP term in government. After the election, but before the first session of parliament to elect a new government, the two parties had made their choices of leaders. The HRPP unanimously re-elected Tuila'epa. Misa, on the other hand, regained his deputy leadership position after a caucus ballot at which he won 19 votes compared with the other candidates, Faumuinā Līuga, Fiamē Nāomi and Leota Lu, who won 9, 4 and 1 votes, respectively (Lesa 2006b:4). Similarly, the SDUP unanimously re-elected Le Māmea Rōpati and 'Asiata Sāle'imoa as leader and deputy leader, respectively.

Applications by other independents to join the HRPP were turned down. Some of them had allegedly signed a memorandum of understanding to fight the general election as 'true' independents, which, according to the HRPP whip, Mulitalo Siāfausa, was the reason why his party did not accept their applications (Lesā 2006c:2). Tuila'epa's cabinet included five new faces. Of the ministers from the previous government, two were not re-appointed.

Results of by-elections after the first session of parliament elected two additional HRPP members, giving the party 37 seats. A by-election was held in the Āleipata Itupā i Luga seat after it was successfully petitioned; originally won by an SDUP candidate, it was claimed by the HRPP. And, when Sililoto passed away unexpectedly in early March 2007, a by-election for his seat saw an SDUP MP in the last parliament regaining his seat, though under the HRPP banner.

SDUP's parliamentary leverage went from bad to worse. Party infighting over the leadership became public in August. Assured of the support of four members, 'Asiata announced to media reporters that he had taken over the leadership from Māmea who had the support of only three members of the SDUP's nine-member caucus. Māmea and one of his supporters, Sililoto Tolo, refused to accept the new leader and resigned from the party but remained as independents, thereby reducing the number of SDUP members from 9 to 7, one less than the number that would allow it to be recognized as a party in parliament. 'Asiata's efforts to reduce the statutory number of members in a party from 8 to 7 in order for his party to be recognized were of no avail. Although numerically a very weak voice in parliament, Asiata continued to stand up against the mighty HRPP. The rest of the HRPP members who were not appointed to Tuila'epa's 13-member cabinet were appointed associate ministers after a bill tabled in parliament in June 2006 changed the title parliamentary under-secretary to associate minister. Tuila'epa argued that parliamentary under-secretaries deserved more respect because of the amount and nature of work they do, thus the new title. It was also a way to use the talents of those HRPP MPs for the development of the country. It was a 'disgusting' bill according to Asiata, who argued that the move had not only rewarded the HRPP MPs not appointed to cabinet but, worse still, given Tuila'epa and his cabinet excessive executive power over a mere rubber-stamping parliament (Lesa 2007a:2). Tuila'epa's counter-argument was that associate ministers do not sit in cabinet meetings.

The impetus for and performance of the party political system

This era of political parties saw the structural strengthening of the HRPP, and the establishment of the CDP, and later the SNDP and SDUP. The parties were primarily directed towards attaining power – in this respect the HRPP was the most successful. When asked by Fa'alogo what the status of Sāmoan political parties was, Tupua said, 'I think by and large that if you were to seek a historic parallel we are still probably in the (first) Elizabethan period, where it was more personality rather than ideology'. To a large extent this is still true. Nevertheless, despite the fact that party unity has been maintained – through personal affiliations, the offer of ministerial posts and other incentives – political parties have, generally very successfully, performed one of their important democratic functions – organizing the 'chaotic public will' (Neumann 1956:396), thereby ensuring majority government. This success has been achieved amidst intra-party factional rivalries and intense competition for parliamentary positions. Three pieces of legislation, passed by parliament at different times, have contributed to the progressive consolidation of the party system. The *Electoral Amendment Act 1995* requires MPs to identify on ballot papers the political parties they support (Clause 2). The *Electoral Amendment Act 2000* provides for the registration of political parties (Part IIA). The *Electoral Amendment Act 2005* adds Section F to Part IIA and requires MPs to stay with the party they had chosen to be a member of prior to the taking of the oath of allegiance. Switching parties after that point would result in MPs losing their seats and the subsequent calling of by-elections to fill those seats.

The origin of political parties in Sāmoa cannot be put down to just one of the three theories of party formation – institutional, crisis or modernization. Rather, elements of all three have been evident. An example of the crisis theory is the claim by some founders of the HRPP that Tupuola had usurped the tradition of having only *tama-a-'āiga* as prime ministers (even though it was a misconception) and that this helped the HRPP to win support from among the conservative Sāmoans. In that sense, Tupuola's critics saw the change of prime minister from *tama-a-'āiga* to a non-*tama-a-'āiga* titleholder as a cultural crisis.

Among the original Tamasese and Tupuola factions were the generally younger politicians with tertiary education, business backgrounds and a generally modern outlook of life, who contributed to Tupuola's prime ministerial victory in 1976. Others later became members of the HRPP. Thus, events in Sāmoa showed aspects of the political modernization theory of the origin of political parties.

Finally, as political parties in Sāmoa emerged after the establishment of parliament, and as a direct consequence of parliamentary politics, their formation adheres to Duverger's (1954:xxiv) institutional account of the parliamentary origin or parties.

Clientelism has been the main means by which party support among MPs has been obtained. It has been the tendency among party leaders to reward prime ministerial support through the promise and offer of ministerial posts and other political positions. Such practices have been mainly dictated by the personality-bound nature of Sāmoan society implicit in this collectivist orientation towards family and village unity. Herein lies the contradiction between political parties (as political enterprises), whose ideological connection to liberal-democracy implies notions of the impersonal nature of the political marker, and individualism, operating in a traditional society still heavily oriented to collectivist values.

The impersonal and individualistic nature of a political party (in the context of the political marker theory of political parties) implies three basic ideals. First, that the customer (voter) freely chooses the party with the policies he/she prefers. Second, that in deciding his/her choice of party, the consumer does not take into consideration kinship, church, village, and other collectivist affiliations. Third, that in deciding the political goods (policies) he/she prefers, the consumer's choice is dictated primarily by what he/she considers best for him/her.

These liberal-democratic values are considered foreign in a society whose custom and tradition place more emphasis on the group (kinship, village, church and other affiliations) than on the individual. As such, the customer usually chooses his/her family member, village member, etc. ahead of party policies come parliamentary election time. Conversely, in cases where adherence to collectivist values is threatened (as in the cases where village councils have agreed on their preferred candidate before the day of the election), village voters are coerced into casting their votes for the 'village's candidate'.

The impact of traditional institutions on parties has been both positive and negative. The positive impact has been the use of family and friendship connections to obtain and maintain governing majorities. The negative impact has been when party members with such affiliations leave the party, thereby leaving the voting public who elected MPs to their preferred party in the cold.

The negative implication of parties (as outgrowths of democracy in the liberal-democratic sense) is its divisive impact on institutions associated with collectivist values. Such has been the case in Sāmoa. However, as politicians often have their own political agendas to live out, the temptation towards the party system, with its personal rewards, has often been stronger than the desire to uphold traditional collectivist ideals.

Strains of both the old and the new order have combined to propel the establishment and consolidation of the party system. If the desire for power is the driving force behind all kinds of competition, and, if such drive for power in the context of party competition leads to soliciting public support in the political elites' power game, then the voting public will also gain. Voters may be able to influence their politicians to cater for their interests in reward for their support, the main benefit of liberal democracy and the party system whose roots have already been planted in Sāmoa.

Notes

1 Galumlemana Nētina Schmidt, wife of Lavea Lio, told the author that she always accompanied her husband to the HRPP's caucus meetings at Vaivase and, becoming tired of waiting outside for her husband, she and the wives of the other MPs decided to organize the women's section of the party. At the time, she was reading the book of Papua New Guinea's Chief Minister, Michael Somare, *Sana: an Autobiography of Michael Somare*, on how he had organized the Pangu Party. Somare's book gave her and the other women ideas on how to strengthen the organization of the HRPP.

2 Article 42.2 of the standing orders of the legislative assembly states that: 'The mover of any motion may speak on the principle and merits of his motion before formally moving, but if it is not seconded it shall lapse forthwith'. Article 58.4 states that: 'The debate on a Private Member's motion shall not exceed two hours duration and shall lapse upon the adjournment of the sitting'.

3 This constituency comprised the two main villages of Lufilufi and Falefā. The traditional residence of the Tui Ātua title is in Lufilufi; and it is the traditional responsibility of the Lufilufi orator group to care for the holder of the Tui Ātua *pāpā*. Falefā village comprised two of the main settlements of the 'Āiga Sa Fenunu'ivao.

4 Any amendment to the constitution requires that a bill for any such purpose is supported at its third reading by the votes of not less than two-thirds of the total number of members of parliament (including vacancies) and if not fewer than ninety days elapse between the second and the third readings of that bill (Art. 109.1).

5 The reduction would have affected the appointment of a government officer in Wellington to monitor the progress of Sāmoan scholarship students in New Zealand.

6 Personal observation, 23 June 1993.

7 Personal observation, 23 June 1993.

8 Personal observation, 23 June 1993.

9 *General Election Report 2006 & Annual Report 2005-2006*, Office of the Electoral Commissioner, pp. 6, 20.

6 | Campaign strategies

DESPITE THE MODERN trappings of emergent political parties in Sāmoa, the tactics used by politicians to win votes continued to appeal to indigenous values and practices. In terms of traditional values, the most challenging aspect of democratic processes in the period following independence was competition for office. Initially, traditional consensus and reference to high rank predominated in the choice of political representatives. The first elections to the reformed legislative assembly, on 15 November 1957, saw 31 members for the 41 Sāmoan seats elected unopposed. However, in the other 10 seats, the candidates, who were among the highest-ranking *matai*, and the village councils in these constituencies could not agree on their representative. The next general election, in 1961, saw the number of members elected unopposed reduced from 31 to 23. The number of MPs elected unopposed continued to decline in the years after independence until 1985, when all 45 Sāmoan seats in the 47-seat parliament were contested. It is against this brief historical background that the campaign strategies deployed by candidates in parliamentary elections are discussed.

Unopposed nominations

Normally, a *matai* who aspired to be elected to parliament made his request known to his village *fono*. When formally making his wish known, the candidate normally provided a feast, and other gifts for the *fono*. Throughout the parliamentary term, an MP usually remained closely attached to the villages that made up his constituency, to the extent that he was involved in and contributed substantially to local projects, such as the construction of church and school buildings.

An MP could be elected unopposed in two ways. Either the *matai* of all the villages comprising a constituency unanimously agreed upon one of their number being their MP, or the villages comprising the constituency came to an agreement whereby every village would have a turn in electing one of their number to be the constituency's MP for one term.

An example of an MP elected under the first procedure was Lesātele Rapi, who represented the constituency of Vaisigano No. 2 from 1958 until he died on 14 December 1979. He was elected unopposed for eight consecutive terms. Lesātele was the holder of one of the highest-ranking *ali'i* titles in the constituency, and, as a successful businessman, he was in a financial position to live up to what the constituency expected of him in his positions as a high-ranking titleholder and as a politician. Another MP who was elected unopposed several times by his constituency was Polataivao Fosi. Polataivao was successful when he first contested his constituency's seat in the 1964 general election. He polled 41 votes (53.2 per cent) against his only rival's 36 votes. He was elected unopposed in the next three general elections. Like Lesātele, Polataivao was a holder of one of his village's and his constituency's highest-ranking *ali'i* titles, and was also in a financial position to maintain the support of his constituency. A well-known boxer in Sāmoa, Polataivao later turned businessman, before entering politics.

> Politics is a hard life. Perhaps in my political career there is no other politician who can be compared to me regarding the manner in which I have looked after my constituency. That is why I have been in parliament for over 30 years. Had I neglected my constituency I would have been out of parliament. I have given everything I had to my constituency. I have taken care of my constituency better than I have taken care of anything else in my life. In doing so I must have spent about four million dollars of my own money. I have lost all my shops. I must have had over a billion dollars [*sic*] Credit in the Bank at one point which have now all been spent. I am now in debt. (Interview, 30 September 1993).[1]

Lesātele and Polataivao are examples of politicians who not only held high-ranking titles but also looked after their respective constituencies, using money from their own pockets. The support they had earned from their respective constituencies was not necessarily because of their performances as statesmen in the central government policies: Instead, it was associated with their socio-political status in their respective villages and constituencies, and the material resources they had at their disposal that enabled them to maintain political support.

The second means by which an MP could be elected unopposed – rotation – satisfied a number of traditional cultural values. First, it put every village comprising a constituency on an equal footing, as every village had a turn to elect an MP for the constituency from among its *matai* population. Moreover, it gave every village the right to elect a *matai* of their choice. In most cases, the villages' choices of candidate were the holders of their high-ranking titles. As inter-village competitions were avoided by means of rotation, harmony in the villages or in the constituency as a whole was not at risk. As control over the elected candidates rested solely with the *matai* comprising the village council in general and the influential *matai* in the council in particular, village custom and traditions and those of the traditional district in general were maintained. Because of the change in MP every three years, each serving member did not have to carry as much economic responsibility as those elected by the entire constituency.

Among the Sāmoan constituencies that persistently adhered to this method of election were Sāgaga-le-Usoga and Faleata East. The Sāgaga-le-Usoga constituency comprised the three villages of Tuana'i, Afega and Malie. In the 1958 election, Luafatāsaga Kalapu, the holder of a high-ranking title of Tuana'i village, was elected unopposed as the constituency's MP. In the next general election, in 1961, the MP was Le'apaitausili'inu'u Sefo, the holder of a high-ranking *tulafale* title in Malie. In the general elections in 1964, 1967 and 1970 respectively, the constituency's MPs – who were all elected unopposed – were Savea Toso from Afega, Sā'ena Sa'imoa from Tuana'i and Seiuli Taulafo from Malie. Similarly, those elected unopposed as Faleata East's MPs from 1958 to 1973 respectively were Matai'a Europa from Vaimoso village, Vaitagutu Siaki from Lepea village, 'Une Sefo from Vaimoso village, Leteletaneolevao Siaosi from Lepea village, Matai'a Europa, and Vaitagutu Siaki. (The constituency comprised the two main villages of Vaimoso and Lepea.) All the MPs were holders of high-ranking titles in these villages.

In unopposed elections, rank was important but parliamentary candidates also needed sufficient economic resources to reciprocate, in keeping with Sāmoan ideology, the support of the *matai*, villages and constituency.

Second, unopposed elections generally satisfied the traditional preference for high-ranking titleholders to represent the constituency. Candidates were required to satisfy the village *matai*, particularly those *matai* who were influential in village government affairs, usually those of the highest rank.

Unopposed elections limited democratic competition, but preserved traditional political norms. The erosion of the practice began when some of the villages comprising a constituency broke the tradition of selecting only the holders of their high-ranking titles. For example, Ala'ilima and Ala'ilima (1966) document the case of the constituency of 'Āiga-i-le-Tai in the period leading up to the 1964 general election. The constituency comprised the settlements in the traditional political district of 'Āiga-i-le-Tai. They included the villages on Manono, Apolima and the subvillages of Mulifanua. The latter settlement was on the northwestern end of Upolu. A series of meetings among the representatives of these settlements resolved that, from 1964, the constituency's MP would be elected on the basis of rotation among the three settlements. Representatives of Mulifanua made it absolutely clear that their acceptance of the resolution was based on the understanding that, among other things, a holder of the Lei'ātaua title, the highest-ranking title in the district, whose traditional residence was in Faleū village on Manono, would have the first turn. The two contenders for the seat from Faleū village were a holder of the Lei'ātaua title and a lower titleholder of the same family. Eventually, the Lei'ātaua family decided unanimously to support the lower-ranking titleholder, following the Lei'ātaua titleholder's decision to withdraw his candidacy when he saw that his supporters in the family were in the minority. A high-ranking *tulafale* titleholder from another village of Manono had withdrawn his candidacy following Faleū village's unanimous decision to support the lower-ranking candidate. However, the *matai* of Mulifanua were concerned that Manono had endorsed the candidacy of a lower-ranking titleholder; so they encouraged the holder of the Lei'ātaua title to stand. The results of the ballot suggested that all the *matai* of Mulifanua voted for Lei'ātaua. Of the constituency's 174 *matai*, only 154 voted. Six ballots were disqualified. Of the 148 valid ballots, the lower-ranking titleholder polled 97 votes (64.2 per cent) to the Lei'ātaua titleholder's 51 (36.7 per cent). The total number of *matai* in Mulifanua was 51, thus suggesting that all the Mulifanua *matai* voted for Lei'ātaua. The *Electoral Act 1963* provided that a candidate for parliamentary election had to be formally nominated by at least two *matai* of the constituency. One of the two *matai* who nominated Lei'ātaua was one of the senior holders of the same title. After the election, the latter Lei'ātaua was suspended from participation in village affairs by Sālua village because he had defied the village's unanimous choice of a lower-ranking titleholder. As *matai* status is traditionally recognized not only by the family but, most importantly, also by the village (through its council), the suspension was an effective punishment, especially for as senior a high-ranking titleholder as Lei'ātaua. Since then, the 'Āiga-i-le-Tai seat has been contested in all general elections. It was only in the 1988 and 1991 general elections that the seat was held by one person for consecutive terms (that person was the Lei'ātaua titleholder who lost the election in 1964).

The end of unopposed election gradually eroded the traditional influence of high-ranking *matai*.[2] For the candidates, support can no longer be guaranteed from other high-ranking *matai*. Furthermore, because the high-ranking titles are held by relatively few *matai* in comparison with the *matai* population of a constituency, candidates have to look to other means of support – leading to new titles being created specifically for the ballot and conferred on family members.

Bloc-voting

As the practice of unopposed election gradually disappeared, bloc-voting developed. Under this system, before the constituency went ahead with the election, its constituent villages came to an agreement whereby they took turns to nominate the constituency's parliamentary candidate from among their *matai* population. This method of election gave every village a chance to have one of their *matai* as the constituency's MP. It also gave the voters in the constituency a chance to decide their MP from among the candidates their own village had nominated. Theoretically, it would also give every *matai* in the constituency a chance to be nominated by their respective village as a candidate for parliamentary election.

One of the constituencies that adopted this method of electing its MPs was Palauli West. Since the first (November 1957) general election, to fill seats in the newly reformed legislative assembly, Palauli West's MPs had been elected unopposed on the basis of rotation among its three constituent villages, Sala'ilua, Gāgā'emalae and Taga. The agreement established a tradition in the constituency that held until the 1976 general election. Following his unopposed election in the 1973 general election, Vaovasamānaia Filipo successfully contested the seat in 1976, making him the first person to hold the constituency's seat for two consecutive terms. A practising lawyer before he entered politics, Vaovasamānaia was appointed minister of finance in his second parliamentary term in Tupuola 'Efi's first government. He was again elected unopposed in the 1979 general election and was re-appointed to the same portfolio in Tupuola's second government. He successfully contested the same seat yet again in the 1982 general election. When the HRPP government under Va'ai Kolone's prime ministership lost its majority in mid-1982, Tupuola took over as the new prime minister, and Vaovasamānaia was again appointed minister of finance. The HRPP government, under Tofilau 'Eti's prime minister- ship, regained office in late 1982. In early 1983, the HRPP government appointed Vaovasamānaia as Sāmoa's first chief justice. His replacement was Faiumu Eteuati, a high-ranking *tulafale* of Taga village.

Before the 1985 general election, the three villages of Palauli West con- stituency re-established their old 'tradition' of rotation, only this time all the *matai* in all three villages would vote for the candidate they supported in the village whose turn it was to nominate candidates from among its *matai* population. It was further agreed that Sala'ilua village would have the first turn, hence the election in 1985 of Mulipola Fiatau. Tau'ialo Lanumoana Palepoi of Gāgā'emalae village was elected in 1988. Tamala Uilisone of Taga village was elected in 1991. The system dictated that a *matai* from Sala'ilua village would be the constituency's 1996 MP, as indeed it was.[3] However, out of turn, Tamala Uilisone of Taga won the 2001 general election.

The constituency's MP in the 1988–90 parliamentary term explained to the author the events in the constituency leading up to the 1988 general election (interview, 29 September 1993). As it was the turn of Gāgā'emalae village to nominate a candidate, or candidates, for the constituency's seat, it was its right to choose whatever method it considered appropriate to decide her candidate(s). Gāgā'emalae comprised the three subvillages of Sātuiātua, Fuālalo and Fuāluga. The three subvillages agreed to rotate among them- selves the right to nominate candidates from among their respective *matai*. Fuālalo agreed that it would have its turn in the future, leaving Sātuiātua and Fuāluga to decide who was to have the present turn. As no agreement was forthcoming, Fuāluga then nominated Tau'ialo Lanu Pālepoi, the candidate who eventually won the constituency's seat in 1988.

Likewise, Sātuiātua nominated one of its own *matai* as its parliamentary candidate. Eventually, two other candidates from Fuāluga were nominated by their respective supporters. However, this situation was not a serious problem as the other candidates were also from a subvillage of Gāgāʻemalae village. What was more serious was that Taga village defied the constituency's 'tradition' and nominated its own candidate, who polled 78 votes (26 per cent). The winner, Tauʻialo Lanu Pālepoi of Fuāluga, polled 111 votes (38 per cent), Sātuiātua subvillage's candidate 62 (21 per cent), and the other two Fuāluga candidates 33 (11 per cent) and 11 votes (4 per cent) (*WSG* 22[4], 10 March 1988). Despite the intervention of Taga, it was still, as rotation dictated, a candidate from Gāgāʻemalae who was appointed.

In the 1991 general election, it was a candidate from Salaʻilua who defied the constituency's tradition, because it was supposed to be Taga's turn to nominate candidates. The two Taga candidates polled 444 (35 per cent) and 143 votes (11 per cent), while the Salaʻilua candidate polled 444 (35 per cent) (*ibid.* 25[5], 22 April 1991). The man who eventually won the seat in 1991 was the same Taga person who had defied the constituency's tradition in the 1988 general election.

Thus, even though candidates in some villages have defied the constituency's tradition, those who eventually won the seat have generally been the candidates nominated by the villages in their rightful turns. For example, in the 1988 election, 76 per cent of the votes cast were won by the four Gāgāʻemalae candidates, and, in the 1991 election, 65 per cent of the votes cast were won by the two Taga candidates. However, in 2001, 35 per cent of the valid votes cast went to the winning candidate from Taga village, Tamala Uilisone. As 12 per cent of the votes went to the other Taga candidate, Taulapapa Siaosi, Taga village, therefore, polled a total of 47 per cent of the constituency's valid votes cast. The Gāgāʻemalae candidate, Tauavamea Lanu Palepoi, won 27 per cent of the votes and the Salaʻilua candidate, Lealaʻitafea Tauʻave, 26 per cent. In accordance with the rotational principle, a Gāgāʻemalae candidate should have won the seat. At least two conclusions can be drawn from these results. First, Taga has usurped Gāgāʻemalae's turn, which means, that the rotational principle has again lapsed as it did during Vaovasamānaia Filipo's four consecutive terms from 1973 to 1982; second, Tamala Uilisone was clearly the most popular candidate as he also beat the other candidate from his village.

In the 2006 general election, five candidates contested the seat, two from Sala'ilua, two from Taga, and one from Gāgā'emalae. The two Sala'ilua candidates together polled 52 per cent of the votes, the two Taga candidates together 40 per cent and the Gāgā'emalae candidate 8 per cent. Taua Falaimo of Sala'ilua won the contest having polled 38 per cent of the valid votes cast. Given that a Taga candidate won the previous general election when it was the turn of Gāgā'emalae, and a Sala'ilua candidate won the 2006 election, it seems clear that the contest is now between Sala'ilua and Taga to the demise of Gāgā'emalae. Again, the rotational principle seems to have been abandoned.

Bloc-voting satisfies such traditional values as maintaining title and village ranks, as well as guaranteeing support for certain candidates. However, the fact that, in most cases, village councils predetermine and sanction candidates defeats the democratic purpose of appealing to other voters for support. While this situation is an advantage to candidates, the voters who might prefer rival candidates are denied a choice, thus losing the opportunity to exert pressure on their politician to respond to their interests.

Proliferation of *matai* titles

Over time, increasing competition for parliamentary seats has resulted not only in a decline in the number of MPs elected unopposed, but also in a sharp increase in the number of *matai*. As only *matai* could vote in the 41 Sāmoan constituencies, it was inevitable that a number of candidates and their respective supporters would resort to the tactic of splitting titles in order to increase the number of supportive *matai* in their respective constituencies. However, the increase in the number of *matai* has not only been ballot-driven. In many cases, titles are divided because families cannot agree on appointments. For example, on 10 September 1978, a village in Ālātaua West constituency conferred more than 200 titles – and another 500 the following day.[4] Some villages are believed to have conferred titles on children.[5] The titles may be newly bestowed titles or currently recognized titles that have been split among several holders. Newly created titles may be derived from names in the families' genealogies. Although the creation of titles from time to time is not a new phenomenon, the sharp increase in the number of titles, and noticeably in the years immediately before general elections, was undoubtedly related to political goals. The population of Sāmoa increased by 65.7 per cent between 1957 (*matai* population – 5,473; national population – 97,327) and 1990 (*matai* population – 21, 649; national population – 161,298), the number of *matai* in the same period increased by 295.5 per cent. The number of *matai* increased from 5.6 per cent of the national population to 13.4 per cent within 33 years.

One of the constituencies to have deployed the tactic of increasing the number of *matai* for political purposes was Ā'ana Ālofi No 3. Three candidates contested the seat in the 1964 general election: Afamasaga Maua, Tago Alapati and Vā'ili Tātupu, polling 68, 6 and 70 votes respectively. The first candidate was a holder of the highest-ranking *ali'i* title in Fasito'otai village, while the last candidate was a holder of the highest-ranking *ali'i* title in Sātapuala village. The results of the general election were rendered invalid by successful petition, and in a by-election ten months later, Tago Alapati withdrew his name from the race. Afamasaga Maua won by 266 votes to Vā'ili Tātupu's 207. Considering that there were 167 *matai* who voted in the general election (twenty-three votes were rejected as ineligible) and 478 (five votes were rejected) in the by-election, the number of voters had increased by 186 per cent.

The 1967 general election was characterized by a sharp increase in the number of votes cast, as compared with 1964. However, in the 1970 general election, the rate of increase slowed down considerably because of more stringent measures applied by the Land and Titles Court for the registration of titles. Despite these measures, the rate of increase picked up again from the 1973 general election.

Aside from electoral considerations, village governments have other reasons for allowing the increase in the number of titles conferred. Of fundamental importance to the socio-political life and working of village governments is the continued recognition of respective ranking systems and of the socio-political structures and cultural values associated with them. As holders of high-ranking titles in villages had always exercised influence and power in the indigenous socio-political system, it was only natural that they extend this influence and power into the new political structures established under the country's constitution. If the constitution were to be based on custom and tradition, it logically followed that the holders of these titles should be the same people who held positions in the new independent state of Sāmoa. It was this line of thinking that initially sparked the practice of increasing the number of *matai* for political purposes. It was the same thinking that had prompted constituencies to opt for the practice of rotation.

The initiative to create new titles in Āʻana Ālofi No. 3 constituency came from the holders of high-ranking titles. The view of the holders of these titles and of the people associated with them was that, as in the pre-European period, titleholders have a legitimate role in all socio-political affairs affecting them. The substantial majority of Sāmoans continue to see political developments through cultural eyes. Consequently, the competitive aspect of politics introduced by the institution of the ballot recalls traditional political struggles, some of which had been fought several generations in the past. These political struggles are nevertheless still important, because they established the currently recognized socio-political system and the socio-political ranking that goes with it. Consider, for instance, the two main contestants for the Āʻana Ālofi No. 3 seat in the 1964 general election. The Vāʻili title is the highest-ranking *tulafale* in Sātapuala village. He is the traditional leader of that village's orator group, called *Faleāʻana*. Among the Vāʻili titleholder's traditional responsibilities is to look after the highest-ranking *aliʻi* titleholder in Sātapuala village, who is Toʻalepai. Next door to Sātapuala is Fasitoʻotai village, whose highest-ranking *aliʻi* title is Afamasaga. It was the holders of Vāʻili and Afamasaga titles who contested the seat.

A somewhat similar dispute over the issue of succession to the Tui Āʻana and Tui Ātua titles in approximately the 16th century culminated in a national war. In that case, the two sons of the previous holder of the titles who disputed the right to succession were Fonotī and Vaʻafusuʻaga. Fonotī married the daughter of the founder of the Toʻalepai title, while the founder of the Afamasaga title was a grandson of Vaʻafusuʻaga. In the war, Fonotī and his supporters defeated Vaʻafusuʻagaʻs sons and their respective supporters. As the main *tulafale* of Toʻaleapai, Vāʻili became the embodiment of the Toʻalepai title and of all the people associated with both the Vāʻili and Toʻalepai titles. In short, in the 1964 general election, Vāʻili was Toʻalepai and both of them were Sātapuala people. Likewise, as Afamasaga was the head of the traditional ʻĀiga Taulagi and the highest-ranking *aliʻi* title of Fasitoʻotai village, all the Fasitoʻotai people naturally threw their support behind the holder of the Afamasaga title. The clubs and spears of the war of the 1600s have been replaced by the number of *matai* either candidate conferred in order to gain the edge over the other in the symbolic war to maintain traditional rank and recognition in the new political structure. The speaker of parliament in the 1991–96 parliament was a holder of the Afamasaga title. He was in his second parliamentary term, having won the seat for the Āʻana Ālofi No. 3 constituency in the 1988 and 1991 general elections. The constituency's MP in the two parliamentary terms before that was the holder of the Toʻalepai title.

Party campaign strategies

The formal establishment of political parties added another dimension to the strategies deployed in political campaigns. Sāmoans maintain several family connections at the same time, and *matai* may hold plural titles, meaning one *matai* may hold titles from several different family branches and electorates. Section 17.5 of the *Electoral Act 1963* provides that, 'Each plural titleholder may at any time choose in respect of which of his titles he will be registered as an elector, … a choice made and notified to the Registrar may be revoked, and a fresh choice be made and notified to the Registrar at any time'. That is, *matai* with multiple titles can only vote under one title. At family, village and constituency meetings from which the *other* titles were conferred, the *matai* would encourage his family members and their friends to vote and campaign for the person he or she preferred. Others would support the candidate whom they knew would support the party to which a member of their family belonged, regardless of which constituency the incumbent MP or candidate represented. Evidence of campaigning through family connections and friendships undertaken by successful parliamentary candidates has been discussed in the previous chapter.

In the 1982 general election the names and photographs of HRPP candidates were published in a party statement, thereby making it the first post-independence political party to utilize modern campaign tactics. For the first time, parliamentary candidates were made known to the public. In the statement, the HRPP declared that its aim was to change the government. As from 1985, the HRPP adopted the practice of including not only photographs of its candidates in its campaign statement, but also information on programs and projects the party intended to complete during its term (were it to win the election). Copies of this document are distributed throughout most parts of the country by the HRPP candidates and their supporters. The HRPP's general election manifesto in 1991 stated its policies for roads, water, the country's electrification program, wharves, communication, town beautification, agriculture, education, hospitals, environment, sports development, tourism and other revenue-earning industries, women, old-age pensions and reconstruction of houses damaged by Cyclone Ofa.

HRPP's rivals, CDP and SNDP, adopted the practice in 1985 and 1988; however, neither the CDP nor the SNDP included the photographs of its members in their party statements, perhaps due to lack of funds, or because of concerns that if HRPP were more popular among the people, identifying their candidates would not help the parties' cause. It is possible that lack of success by parties in the polls is due to the non-publicizing of their candidates, as a substantial majority of voters did not know who the parties' candidates were. In 1991, at the launching of its manifesto, the SNDP invited all its candidates who were present to line up in front of the hall so that members of the public could see who they were. About 400 people were present and most of them were SNDP supporters.

Selecting parliamentary candidates

The ideal candidate for any party is someone who holds a high-ranking title in at least one of the villages of the constituency, is well-known in his/her village and constituency (through local presence, contributions to local projects and involvement in church activities), and has a sound financial basis and good education. As the HRPP has so far proved the better-organized political party, its methods of selecting candidates and maintaining them once they are elected are described in more detail here.

HRPP candidates are selected by the executive committee (EC), comprising the current prime minister, minister of finance, three other ministers of the cabinet and three MPs plus one representative from Savai'i, one representative from Upolu, and a national representative of women. A person who wants to stand in an election as an HRPP party member is referred to the EC for approval, or decision if there is more than one candidate wanting to contest the same seat. Before the Sāfata by-election in 1992, the party's standing policy was that the incumbent MP got first priority as the party's candidate for a constituency.[6] Any other candidate who wanted to contest the seat would have to stand as an independent. That policy changed after the Sāfata by-election. Now, any number of candidates may contest a seat provided they have notified the party and obtained its approval. As explained in the previous chapter, every HRPP candidate has to sign a form pledging his/her loyalty to the party if elected. Until 1984, the candidate's nomination fee, paid to the chief returning officer, was ST10; in 1984 the fee was raised to ST100 (in 2000 it was further increased to ST300). The HRPP has paid its candidates' fees. Other procedures have remained unchanged.

Upon taking up the prime ministership, following the defeat of Tupuola's three-month-old government in late 1982, Tofilau, as prime minister and minister of finance, outlined in his budget, remedies for the country's economic situation. Tofilau told parliament that:

> the fundamental cause of [the country's economic problems] has been that for some years we have consumed more than we have produced …. Beyond our control are increases in oil prices and prices of our export commodities. Nevertheless, an inability to influence such developments does not remove the responsibility from government to make the appropriate policy adjustments. And for those adverse developments which were within the control of my predecessors there can be no excuses for failing to take the necessary corrective measures (*WSH*, Vol I, 4–5).[7]

One of the effects of the then current economic policy was that 'payment arrears have been allowed to climb to ST13 million, almost as much as total export earnings for 1982' (*ibid.*:9). Tofilau's economic remedies included curbing spending, raising taxes and custom duties, and devaluing the dollar by 10 per cent. Furthermore, the government decided not to table a supplementary budget in the 1983 mid-year session of parliament. HRPP's economic strategies were a success (see Table 1), and were probably reflected in its landslide victory in the 1985 general election.

Table 1: Sāmoa economic indices 1983–85

	1983	1984	1985
Real GDP (% change)	0.5	1.3	6.0
Net foreign assets (STm)	-1.3	1.2	6.4
Government overall deficit (STm)	1.4	- 6.0	- 0.3
Consumer price index (% change)	16.7	11.6	9.1

Source: *Report of the Department of Economic Development for the Year 1986*

Persistent public support for the HRPP was probably reflected in the defeat of six of the nine HRPP MPs in the coalition who had sought nomination in 1988, and in the HRPP's narrow victory in the 1988 prime ministerial election, despite the fact that they had been in opposition since late 1986. Explaining to *The Courier* reporter the reasons for the HRPP victory in 1991, Tofilau said it was mainly due to the introduction of universal suffrage because:

> If people had wished to express themselves this time on such issues as the improvement of infrastructure, we would not have had a chance to come back to power, because you have seen the state of the roads and of the water and electricity supply. They are all in a pretty bad shape (*The Courier*, No.128, July-August 1991).

Tofilau's claim that his party's victory was due to the introduction of universal suffrage might have been true. However, he forgot to mention other government developments that probably also contributed to the HRPP victory. The 1990 budget included money to pay for a pension of ST50 per month to all Sāmoan citizens aged 65 and over (*WSH*, 1989, Vol IIA, p. 3). A new building was also constructed to house the newly created ministry of women's affairs. While these policies, among others, might have been intended to win over to government the support of the conservatives who might object to the introduction of universal suffrage, they nevertheless contributed to the HRPP victory.

The 1991 manifestos of both parties show very little difference. For example, considering the importance of universal suffrage in this election, both parties were dedicated to the development of sporting facilities for youth, improvement of educational standards, and recognition of the invaluable contribution of women to society. A slight difference was in the recognition of women's affairs. While the HRPP saw women making known what help they might need from the government through the newly established department of women's affairs, the SNDP seemed to be implying that money allocated to help in women's development projects would be handed directly to respective women committees in villages and districts. Both parties also pledged to continue the old pension scheme that the HRPP had started in 1990. But, while the HRPP said it would continually review that policy to make sure that the pension did not abruptly stop after the election, the SNDP said it would reduce from 65 to 60 the age at which people were entitled to the pension. Hoping to exploit the controversial nature of the *Public Service (Special Posts) Act 1989* and the *Parliamentary Under-Secretaries Act 1988,* the SNDP promised that it would repeal both these Acts. Thus, both parties put forward policies that seemed attractive to voters. There is no evidence of either party having an identifiable ideological inclination.

The strategies of individual candidates

While political parties, such as the HRPP, select their candidates for the elections, pay their candidates nomination fees, and are collectively responsible for the party's manifesto, the bulk of the campaign is left to individual MPs. There are generally two phases in any party's campaign. The first, discussed above, involves the party as a whole. The second, discussed here, relies solely on the individual MP. As the competition for parliamentary seats intensified, the economic resources required by the high-ranking titleholders to reciprocate their traditional support became increasingly difficult to obtain. There had also been a gradual realization of the need to have people with formal education as the constituency's MP. These factors gave rise to the notion of accepting as candidates, lower-ranking titleholders with some formal education and economic resources for political campaigning. At the same time, the embarrassment of a high-ranking titleholder being defeated by a lower-ranking titleholder would be avoided, because, should the lower-ranking titleholder be successful, he or she, as a member of the family, would help maintain the traditional rank and recognition of the family's highest-ranking title within the village and constituency, as well as nationally. The political career of a parliamentarian whom I call Olo will be discussed in this context.

Olo's campaign

Olo's campaign strategies give insight into what is generally regarded as the common campaign tactics used by candidates in parliamentary election, into the roles played by the village councils and cultural aspects associated with village governments which the candidates have to take into consideration in their campaigns, and into the expenses incurred by parliamentary candidates in their quest for political success.

As a low-ranking titleholder and an outsider who lived outside his wife's village with her family, Olo could not rely on traditional means of obtaining support. He polled 34 votes out of the 175 votes cast in 1982 when he successfully contested a seat for the first time. Most, if not all, of his votes came from *matai* of his wife's family, whose titles had been bestowed in order to enhance his chance of winning. The fact that seven other candidates ran contributed to his win. Although Olo's previous job in a government department and his general performance in his first parliamentary term contributed to his victory in the next general election, his high campaign expenditure and the manner in which it was spent sheds light on the importance of village government in obtaining political support.

Of Olo's campaign expenditure in the 1985 general election, nearly ST16,000 was spent on presents (cartons of tinned fish, cash, a cow and other items) for the six villages of the constituency. This expenditure was an equivalent of seven year's salary including tax for a local government employee on ST2,300 per annum, the average annual salary in 1984. Despite laws forbidding 'treating and bribing' electors, the substantial majority of Sāmoans see it as proper for candidates contesting a parliamentary seat to channel all their campaign efforts through village councils, with associated generosity. As long as members of the village council are satisfied, there is a good chance that they will pass word to their family members and friends on the choice of candidate to support. In some cases, the village council makes a ruling, with sanctions attached, that all village members vote for a particular candidate. In this way, village councils are an important political asset for both incumbent and aspiring MPs. The party system should help eliminate the practice whereby politicians dish out food and cash to 'targeted voters' in the days leading up to election for the sole purpose of influencing voter support. However, in the context of Sāmoan values, gift-giving justifies the tendency of successful candidates to pursue their own interests – rather than those of the party – after being elected. The justification for this attitude is that one's political success had relied heavily on one's own financial effort.

Presents in the form of cash, liquor and other things have traditionally been helpful in ensuring that family members abide by the word of the family *matai* or the village council. Among other things, the introduction of universal suffrage has contributed to the erosion of these traditional values.

Universal suffrage

In theory, universal suffrage should have weakened the campaign strategies described so far. The 1991 general election was the first to be conducted
under universal suffrage, a change that added another dimension to candidates' campaign strategies. Returning, for illustration, to Olo's campaign:
Before the adoption of universal suffrage, Olo would visit the six villages
in his constituency and distribute the presents he had brought. The goods
were officially presented to the respective villages' councils of *matai*; it was
the village councils' responsibility to distribute the goods to the people by
whatever method they chose. Following the adoption of universal suffrage,
however, the procedure became more complicated – and more expensive
from the candidates' point of view. Not only would goods be presented
to the council of *matai*, who normally occupied one house, but also to
the rest of the sub-organizations in the village so that all would feel acknowledged by the candidates. This meant that the other organizations,
such as *faletua ma tausi* (wives of *ali'i* and *tulafale* respectively), *aualuma*
(ladies of the village, ie. unmarried village girls, widows and divorcees
belonging to village families), *taulele'a* (untitled men) and *āvā taulele'a*
(wives of untitled men) had to be presented with gifts as well.[8] Before the
adoption of universal suffrage, it was mainly the *matai* who came to the
candidates asking for things such as money for various cultural activities,
most noticeably in the period immediately before the elections. Following
the adoption of universal suffrage, it was the non-*matai* who seemed to
dominate the exercise of this rare political privilege.[9]

The Electoral Amendment Act 1990 not only introduced universal
suffrage but brought a number of changes in voting procedures. Among
these were provision for special voters, and the requirement that all voters
hold valid certificates of identity. The special voters provision enabled 'a
person who is qualified and registered to vote at any election in any constituency ... to cast his or her vote for that constituency ... as a special voter
at a polling place outside that constituency'. Previously, polling places were
located only in the constituencies and there was no requirement for voters
to have ID cards. In order to make sure of the prospective voters they had
transported to and from the registration offices (to have their names registered on the electoral rolls), some candidates and their campaign committees held on to the voters' ID cards until just before the voters cast their
ballots on election day. Candidates did not want 'their voters' won over to

rival candidates before the elections. The commission of inquiry into the *Electoral Act 1963* as amended, that sat after the 2001 general election, recommended that electoral ID cards be abolished. Instead, all electors/ voters would be photographed at the time of registration so that identification of voters will be by way of photographs and the use of invisible ink to prevent multiple voting.[10] The recommendation was accepted by parliament and put into effect in the 2006 general election. Another commission of inquiry into the Electoral Act that sat after the 2006 general election, endorsed the recommendation.[11]

Olo as an example

To use Olo's 1991 campaign as an example: On the day of the election, Olo joined the registration committee in his electorate. As in previous elections, Olo and the committee provided vehicles (three buses in 1991) for the transport of voters to the polling booths, provided the voters with food after they had cast their ballots, and transported them back to their places of residence. The same procedures applied to voters at villages both within and outside the constituency. Because of the distance that some voters had to travel, the task undertaken by the committee started the day before the election. Olo's guest house was set aside to accommodate voters on the eve of election day. Having transported about 200 voters to Olo's residence, members of Olo's family were responsible for providing food for them. Such ubiquitous campaign strategies are expensive in terms of time and financial resources – and have become increasingly so as competition among parliamentary candidates has intensified over the years since independence.

The competition for political support can be discussed in relation to the role of political parties, and in relation to its effects on both democracy and indigenous institutions. The competition for votes has involved strategies described in both the political enterprise and clientelistic theories. Evidence of the first approach – political enterprise – includes the publicizing of a party manifesto between general elections and before by-elections. The existence of indigenous institutions – such as village governments and the *matai* system in general, and the traditional values associated with them – have partly contributed to the use of various clientelistic practices.

The extent to which voters' choice of candidate is influenced by party policies, gifts, title rank or any other factor, is a complex issue. Although party policies may help create, among informed voters, a favourable impression of parties, a candidate's electoral success is ultimately determined by his individual campaign efforts and personal relationships with voters. One of the most experienced politicians and the leader of the Sāmoa Liberal Party in 1996, Nonumalo Sōfara, has said, 'The electorate will never vote on party lines, nor on issues. . . . I don't think we've reached the age where people will vote for a candidate because he's a HRPP or a SNDP member' (SNL, 4 February 1996). As the competition for parliamentary seats has intensified, so too has the cost of individual campaigns. It raises the question: Why do candidates stand?

As Max Weber explains, politicians get extrinsic and intrinsic benefits from their chosen careers. Extrinsically, a politician's electoral success enables him/her access to positions of influence and information that can be put to both personal use and the use of people associated with the politician, such as relatives, friends and villages. The electoral success of a Sāmoan politician brings pride to people associated with him/her, particularly his/her families, both immediate and those associated with the title that the politician holds. Intrinsically, satisfaction is associated with a sense of empowerment, personal recognition, increased status and prestige. For foundation titleholders and people associated with them, democratic competition has been another means of maintaining and enhancing their titles' traditional status.

Among the impacts of intensified competition for parliamentary seats is the disappearance of the practice of unopposed elections and the adoption of bloc-voting, though this latter too is gradually disappearing. Total disappearance of these practices removes from village councils the power they used to exercise in determining which parliamentary candidates village members should support. It also means that the role of traditional respect for title rank and village rank in the acquisition of political support now competes with other factors, such as education and wealth. Gifts and other incentives associated with competition have contributed to the weakening of traditional bonds between parents and children, *matai* and family members, and village councils and villages.

Although the incentives associated with competition are perceived as culturally degrading, they have nevertheless drawn into the political arena more members of the public. This too is not necessarily good from a traditional perspective. It is not easy for people used to tradition to accept competition from the newly enfranchised. The logic behind competition is for elites to earn support. To earn that support they have to appeal continuously to voters. In this way, voters exert pressure on politicians to cater for their interests. In this way, the erosion of tradition in order to earn support has been a democratic achievement. The generally negative attitude towards political parties will gradually diminish as political parties deliver the collective political goods of infrastructure and so on.

But the intensity of competition can also have a negative effect upon the successful candidates who put so much effort into their campaigns. Increasing competition for parliamentary seats partly explains the constant shifting of party allegiance among MPs. One of the most important factors, if not the most important factor, influencing the behaviour of successful candidates has been the cost of their campaigns – time, effort, family involvement and, most importantly, finance. To be appointed a minister of cabinet has been seen as the ultimate reward for the time, effort and money that have gone into the election campaign. Moreover, candidates generally feel that their election successes have been due mainly to their personal financial resources. At the end of the day, the election victory has been a personal victory, and not necessarily one for the voters who supported him/her. Consequently, the candidates argue, the issues of which political party the successful candidates join and which prospective prime minister they attach themselves to are their personal decisions, not those of their constituencies. Joining the 'right political party' or the 'right prime ministerial candidate' enhances the MPs chances of getting a ministerial post or another political position.

Notes

1   The interview was conducted in Sāmoan. The transcription quoted here is the present author's translation of what Polataivao said.
2   Appendix 7 gives other examples of traditional means of acquiring political support.
3   The election period had been increased from three to five years in 1991. A candidate from Sala'ilua won the 1996 election by 498 votes.
4   Report of the committee appointed by cabinet to consider the report of the 1975 committee which inquired into *matai* titles, customary lands and the Sāmoa Land and Title Court, *Parliamentary Paper No. 12*, Legislative Assembly of Western Sāmoa, p. 3.
5   *Parliamentary Paper No. 12*, p. 9. For more information on the proliferation of titles, see Meleiseā (1987a:201).
6   The by-elections in the Sāfata and Sālega constituencies followed the passing of

a constitutional amendment in late 1991, which provided for an additional seat.

7   Minister of Finance, Tofilau 'Eti Alesana, 'Economic policy statement, 28 June 1983', p 4.

8   The term *aumaga* could also have been used here instead of *taulele'a*. There are generally two ways in which the Sāmoan language is spoken. In ordinary usage (*gagana o aso uma*) the word *taulele'a* is used. When using the 'polite way' of speaking (*gagana fa'aaloalo*), the word *aumaga* is used. In the context of village politics, *aumaga* also refers to the most senior *taule'ale'a* (singular for *taulele'a*) of a foundation family, or a family that was established by a foundation titleholder (see, Chapter 1).

9   In some candidates' campaigns, uniforms and rugby balls were purchased for villages and districts' rugby teams. Sports teams were offered free beer at the end of the games in the periods leading up to elections. Other candidates offered huge donations to the church and, sometimes, to pastors of parishes in the constituency. Some young voters told the author about how cash ranging between ST5 and ST50 had been offered to them (which they willingly accepted) by some candidates on the night before the election.

10 Commission of Inquiry: *Report on the Electoral Act 1963 as amended,* 11 October 2001.

11 Commission of Inquiry Into Electoral Matters Following the 2006 General Elections, 30 October 2006.

7 | Competition and participation in Sāmoa's political system

COMPETITION AND PARTICIPATION are central to the democratic process and imply a levelling effect, in the sense that people who do not comprise political elites are brought into the political system. Competition upholds the notion that individuals should be free to pursue their own preferences in political affairs, and is associated with freedom of choice. This chapter examines the impact of competition in the political system on Sāmoa's indigenous institutions and its value system and practices.

Achievement and ascription

The Sāmoan saying, *O Sāmoa ua uma ona tofi* (Sāmoa is a land where all positions have been allocated) illustrates the tradition of ascribed social rank and political status. It is an ideology that permeates all aspects of the indigenous socio-political structure, ranging from its smallest unit, the immediate family, to the national level. Families of higher rank jealously guard their ascribed positions from those of lower rank, and, still today, infraction of traditional rights can result in violence.

Voters adhering to traditional values would prefer that their MPs were elected unopposed, and better still, under the rotation method discussed in the previous chapter. This method of political representation within a democratic framework satisfies a number of traditional values. The traditional value of consultation among all the political actors is maintained, be it villages as units or foundation titleholders as political actors in villages. In this way, everyone (implying the *matai*, but more particularly the foundation titleholders, who collectively represent members of their respective families in village governments) contributes to the selection of their parliamentary representative.

Furthermore, the traditional ranking systems among *matai* in respective villages, and among villages comprising the constituency, are maintained. In the unopposed and rotation electoral options, high-ranking titleholders are usually selected. Selecting politicians in this way avoids ill-feeling among foundation titleholders, or among the members of their respective families. Conversely, deciding parliamentary seats in contested elections may result in violence. For example, in the 1973 general elections at Ānoāma'a West constituency, in a contest between three high-ranking candidates, the elected member won by one vote; the announcement of the result was followed by an outbreak of violence as people expressed their rage at the loss of traditionally allocated recognition, dignity, and prestige.

As shown in previous chapters, MPs are increasingly being selected in contested elections and a greater number of low-ranking *matai* are now elected; this even extends to *matai* who are outsiders in their electorate, residing there through marriage ties. Traditionally, in-marrying spouses have low status relative to the members of the family into which they have married, but Sāmoan custom permits a family to bestow a title on an in-marrying spouse. However, when in-marrying spouses become MPs, traditional problems can arise in the villages of their titles' origin, and in the constituency in general. In every foundation village, every foundation title has associated with it certain traditions. These include a particular place at the meeting-house, the order in which titleholders speak, and the order in which one drinks kava in important ceremonies.

A holder of a title other than a foundation title has no place in the 'official' (or traditional) protocol of his/her village, subdistrict, and district. However, because of the villages' and constituency's respect for their MPs (even though they hold lesser titles), they are permitted to occupy, for the duration of their parliamentary term(s), a temporary position, which would normally be reserved for the titleholders of rank. After that, they revert back to the places of less (or no) traditional significance in the meeting-house.

Moreover, although traditionally all political positions would have been held by the high-ranking titleholders, that has not been the situation more recently. Sāmoan custom also allows for recognition of high personal rank through both ancestral connections and exceptional personal qualities, and there have been holders of lesser titles in public office as cabinet ministers and speakers. Thus, despite the emphasis on traditionally allocated positions, the traditional order accommodates new realities.

Vigorous defense of traditional privilege by high-ranking and highly educated political figures has been a recurrent theme in Sāmoa's politics. For example, Le Tagaloa Pita established the short-lived Temokalasi Sāmoa Fa'amatai political party to uphold Sāmoan customs and traditions, and the privileges and rights associated with the *matai* system (although when he lost his seat in the 2001 general election his political party ceased to exist). However, as we have seen in previous chapters, political competition has led to increasing disconnection between rank and high public office. Political parties have accelerated the disconnection of traditional rank and modern political leadership. The defeat of Tupua Tamasese, the last *tama-a-'āiga* prime minister, was followed by the establishment of the HRPP and the rise of non-*tama-a-'āiga* titleholders (Tupuola 'Efi, Va'ai Kolone, Tofilau 'Eti and Tuila'epa Sa'ilele) to the prime ministership. The operation of the political party system has also opened up competition for the political offices of head of state and council of deputies. The attempt by Tofilau 'Eti to legislate that only *tama-a-'āiga* could occupy the office of council of deputies was defeated in parliament, allowing Tofilau, years later in 1993, to legitimately and conveniently appoint a non-*tama-a-'āiga* title-holder, Va'ai Kolone, to the ceremonial, non-political council of deputies.

Whether or not the 'levelling' outcome of political competition and broader participation will eventually allow non-*matai* to become leaders remains to be seen. The historical trend has been in three phases: Events that led to the establishment and legitimacy of divine authority in the context of district governments in the pre-European contact era; the kingship wars in the 19th century that led to the elevation of district paramount titles to their current status as 'national titles'; and the marginalization of *tama-a-'āiga* titles in parliamentary politics. Competition established divinely sanctioned paramount authority; competition elevated district titles to their colonial and early post-colonial status; and competition marginalized them in parliamentary politics.

The status of one of Samoa's most accomplished leaders and longest-serving prime ministers, Tofilau 'Eti Alesana, illustrates the negotiation of traditional rank and leadership. 'Eti held at least four high-ranking titles. He first entered parliament in the 1957 general election under his first title, Luamanuvae. As a supporter of Matā'afa, he was appointed minister of health during that parliamentary term. The original person whose name was Luamanuvae was a direct descendant of the Sa Levalāsi family who lived in the 1770s. As long as 'Eti is known by his title Luamanuvae (the highest-ranking *ali'i* title at Sālelologa village in Fa'asalele'aga district on Savai'i), as he was when he first entered parliament, he is a member of the Sā Levālasi family. As Matā'afa is the *tama-a-'āiga* of Sa Levālasi family,[1] it was to be expected that Luamanuvae 'Eti would support Matā'afa F. Mulinu'ū II's prime ministership, as indeed he did right up to Matā'afa's death on 20 May 1975. The Tofilau title was originally an *ali'i* title. However, sometime later in the history of 'Iva village (in Fa'asalele'aga district), probably following the arrival in the village of other descendants of the Sa Levālasi family (who thereafter inherited the honour of being the highest-ranking *ali'i* in the village), Tofilau retained the *ali'i* socio-political status. But he could also become a high-ranking orator (thus assuming a more *tulafale*-like role[2]), one of the few *matai* of the exclusive group of speakers who could address a meeting of all Fa'asalele'aga when they meet at Sāfotulāfai, the district's political centre. Tofilau also became the spokesperson for Sa Levālasi in 'Iva village and one of the spokespersons in Fa'asalele'aga district.

'Eti also holds the Tua'ilemafua title, one of the four highest-ranking *ali'i* of Lefagaoali'i village in Sāfune-i-taoa traditional subdistrict on Savai'i island. As the original Tua'ilemafua was a direct descendant of both Pesetā and Lilomaiava, under this title 'Eti can be a member of either the traditional Sa Pesetā family or the Sa Lilomaiava family. 'Eti's other title is Nanai, one of the seven highest-ranking *ali'i* of the Tauā'ana family of Falelātai subdistrict. Following the wars of succession to kingship office in the 19th century, the Tauā'ana family, together with the traditional families of Sa Tunumafono and Taulagi, established the Tuimaleali'ifano title as their *tama-a-'āiga*. Thus, under the Nanai title, 'Eti is a member of the Tauā'ana family, whose *tama-a-'āiga* is Tuimaleali'ifano. Because of the close genealogical connections to both the Tui Ātua and Tui Ā'ana titles, as a holder of the Tua'ilemafua title, 'Eti could legitimately support either the *Tama-a-'āiga* Tupua (as successor to the Tui Ātua title) or the *Tama-a-'āiga* Tuimaleali'ifano (as successor to the Tui Ā'ana title). Following the death of Matā'afa F. Mulinu'ū II, Tofilau 'Eti and his supporters put forward Tupua Tamasese Lealofi IV as their prime ministerial candidate. When Tupuola 'Efi defeated Tupua Tamasese Lealofi IV in the 1976 prime ministerial election, Tofilau 'Eti, Va'ai Kolone and others established a faction, which later became the HRPP, to defeat Tupuola 'Efi's prime ministership in 1979 and 1982. Tupuola won in 1979 by one vote but lost to Va'ai in 1982 by the same margin.

Political parties and competition

One of the notions associated with modern political parties is that they provide a means whereby people organize themselves on the basis of common interests, whatever those might be, in their pursuit of the realization of those interests. As interests vary from time to time and differ between people, collective competition in this sense can be a threat to traditionally established alliances. The relationship of the Fuimaono title to 'Āiga Sa Fenunu'ivao provides an example of this dilemma in Sāmoan politics. One of the high-ranking titles (or members) of Sa Fenunu'ivao is Fuimaono[3], who is referred to as the father of Tupua. Because Tupua is Sa Fenunu'ivao's *tama-a-'āiga*, it is 'natural' that any holder of the Fuimaono title should side with any holder of the Tupua title. Although since 1964 the holder of one of the two seats for Faleālili constituency has always been a Fuimaono titleholder, the 'traditional guilt' of siding in parliament against a Tupua titleholder had been hidden from public in the absence of full-fledged political parties. Thus, from when Fuimaono Mimio first entered parliament in 1970 until his death, he always sided with Tupuola 'Efi, even though Tupua Tamasese Lealofi IV had contested the prime ministership against Tupuola 'Efi and Matā'afa F. F. Mulinu'ū II in 1970 and 1973. When only Tupuola and Tupua Tamasese contested the prime ministership in 1976, Fuimaono Mimio continued to support Tupuola.

But political circumstances change. Not only had Tupuola (or Tupua) lost the prime ministership to the HRPP in 1982, but also, following the 1988 general election, another holder of the Fuimaono title, Fuimaono Lotomau, won the second seat for Faleālili. Worse still from a traditional perspective, Fuimaono Lotomau was an HRPP supporter. He was appointed a minister of cabinet in the 1988–91 parliament. Traditionally, Lotomau is on 'the wrong side of the fence'. Very often, members of the public make the comment that Lotomau should have been in the SNDP, supporting Tupua Tamasese 'Efi.

Undoubtedly, Fuimaono Lotomau had some discomfort supporting the HRPP while Tupua was the leader of the opposition SNDP. Towards the end of the 1988–1990 parliament, he moved a motion to have Tupua Tamasese 'Efi appointed as a member of the council of deputies, which, at the time, had two vacancies. The motion was seconded by Ulualofaigā Talamaivao Niko, a member of the SNDP. It had already been discussed and approved by the HRPP caucus. In putting the motion, Fuimaono Lotomau was publicly signifying not only his Sa Fenunu'ivao identity but also, most importantly, his respect for the traditional honour, prestige and dignity associated with the Tupua title. He was expressing what had for some time been an opinion shared by a substantial majority of the public: That Tupua should be 'promoted' to the council of deputies, thereby removing him from the demeaning conduct of parliamentary politics, where personalities as well as policies can sometimes be ruthlessly scrutinized in a manner unbefitting the highest titleholders.

Fuimaono Lotomau's motion came in the run-up to the 1991 general election, and, understandably, both Tupua and the opposition saw it as a political move – regardless of Lotomau's motive. The SNDP opposition saw the motion as another HRPP tactic to divide and weaken it. (The SNDP comprised two main factions, the Tupua and Va'ai factions, and removing Tupua from parliament could have been detrimental to the SNDP; the Tupua faction would have had to elect another leader from among themselves, as the Va'ai faction comprised a minority in the SNDP, and, even if such a faction leader had been elected, it was not certain if Va'ai would accept him as the SNDP leader, considering that Va'ai was Tupua's deputy leader.) The leadership problem aside, Tupua was one of the few MPs who could counter the prime minister's outstanding political skills.

Tupua's perspective was that Fuimaono Lotomau should have consulted him about the potential appointment before the motion was put to parliament. Because he had not been consulted, Tupua declined the nomination – but, because the motion had been moved and seconded, it had to be tabled. However, after two hours of debate in the parliament, the motion lapsed, in accordance with standing orders.

If the motion had been formally put, the overall effect would have been a further weakening of the SNDP. Had the motion succeeded, the HRPP would have gained the sympathy of the traditional voting public, and Fuimaono Lotomau would have enhanced his chances of retaining his seat in the forthcoming general election. However, as it turned out, Fuimaono Lotomau retained his seat, the HRPP won the general election by another landslide majority, and Tupua lost his seat to an HRPP candidate – a relatively low-ranking *matai*.

Lotomau's concern about the relationship of his title to the Tupua title is a concern that is generally shared by not just other members of 'Āiga Sa Fenunu'ivao, but also by the general public. As Lotomau and Mimio supported different prime ministerial candidates when they first entered parliament, it was to be expected that they would remain loyal to the parties of the prime ministerial candidates they supported. In terms of breaking custom and tradition (in the sense that both of them should have supported any holder of the Tupua title in every prime ministerial election), it is not certain whether it is Mimio who is guilty (because he supported Tupuola against Tupua Tamasese Lealofi IV in 1976) or Lotomau (because he supported Tofilau against Tupua Tamasese 'Efi in 1988, 1991 and 1996). Implicit in these conclusions are two related issues: The loyalty of both Lotomau and Mimio to 'Āiga Sa Fenunu'ivao will continue as long as they hold those titles, though not necessarily inside parliament; and, their common relationship to 'Āiga Sa Fenunu'ivao has not prevented them from pursuing whatever other interests they have in the present political set-up. In short, it is another example of how traditions have adapted to modern conditions. The traditional dilemma discussed here was also experienced by members of other traditional *'āiga* such as 'Āiga Sa Tuala and 'Āiga-o-Māvaega, when members of these *'āiga* supported prime ministerial candidates who were not the *tama-a-'āiga* of their respective *'āiga*.

The indigenous socio-political status of the leaders of political parties established to date demonstrates the persistence of traditional values. Except for one leader of the SNDP, all leaders have been members of the HRPP. Although there have been a variety of reasons why they left the HRPP to form new parties, one reason is related to the traditional values associated with the titles they hold. Except for the specific traditional rights and responsibilities associated with all the high-ranking titles, be they *ali'i, tulafale* or *tulafale-ali'i,* all such titles in their own right are politically equal. Accordingly, as holders of such high-ranking titles, MPs do not easily accept others imposing decisions and political demands upon them. In the political structure established under the 1962 constitution, their roles were perceived through a traditional perspective. Although they did not have any traditional power, they were nevertheless looked upon with much respect because their rank was higher than the rest of the high-ranking titles. Thus, when Tupuola 'Efi defeated *tama-a-'āiga* Tupua Tamasese Lealofi IV in the 1976 prime ministerial election, there was no longer any reason why any of the other high-ranking titleholder-parliamentarians should not be prime minister – hence the establishment of the HRPP and subsequent establishment of other political parties. Because the leaders of all the political parties established thus far are holders of high-ranking titles, they have traditional appeal in their 'new' leadership roles as long as the voting public continues to uphold and perpetuate traditional values, and in particular those associated with the *matai* system.

The leadership issue was not brought up for discussion during the time Tupuola was leader of his parliamentary faction from 1970 to 1981, or when he was leader of the CDP in early 1985. Despite attempts by him and his supporters to retain him as prime minister in the coalition government when they joined those who had left the HRPP in late 1985, Tupuola eventually gave in to Va'ai, thereby relegating himself to deputy leader. The coalition government went to the 1988 general election leaderless, having decided not to elect its leader until the results of the election were known. In the period leading up to the 1988 prime ministerial election, when it became certain that the HRPP had the support of the majority of the newly elected parliament, Va'ai voluntarily handed the leadership to Tupua (formerly Tupuola) in order to reciprocate Tupua's support of him as prime minister in the previous coalition government (*Observer*, 19 August 1992). At this stage both the Va'ai and Tupua factions of the coalition seemed content with their respective leaders' decisions.

When Tupua lost his seat in the 1991 general election, Va'ai resumed the leadership. The party did not formally elect another leader through a ballot; instead, it seemed to accept Tupua's public statement that, because Va'ai was the deputy leader, then naturally he was to succeed to the leadership. It was this state of affairs that angered another SNDP MP and first maternal cousin of Tupua, Misa Foni, who thereafter left the party and joined the HRPP. When Tupua regained his seat in early 1992 he resumed the leadership and Va'ai again stepped down to be deputy leader. This was the situation when Va'ai accepted his appointment to the council of deputies. Leota replaced Va'ai as deputy leader, although it is not certain whether he was elected to that position through a ballot or whether the party unanimously agreed that he succeed Va'ai. Leota remained deputy leader until 26 June 1995, when he decided to form his own political party. Tupua continued as leader when the SNDP went into the general election in early 1996.

As the best organized of the currently recognized political parties, the HRPP also seems to be the most advanced in terms of the method by which its leaders have been selected. In government, the HRPP caucus unanimously elected Tofilau to succeed Va'ai as leader of the party when the latter lost his seat in mid-1982 following a successful petition. Va'ai returned to parliament in a by-election in early 1983. Like the SNDP in the 1988 general election, the HRPP in the 1985 general election had decided not to elect its leaders until the results were known. Both Va'ai and Tofilau regained their seats and the HRPP won a landslide majority. The new caucus eventually resolved to choose its leader through the traditional method of discussion, despite attempts by Va'ai's supporters to elect the leader by a secret ballot. Tofilau was elected to continue as leader of the HRPP, and thus to continue as prime minister. Va'ai left the party before the 1985 prime ministerial election, and was later followed by the majority of his supporters in the HRPP after Tofilau had announced his new cabinet.

Tofilau remained leader of the HRPP until the results of the 1988 general election were known. Before the 1988 prime ministerial election, an HRPP caucus meeting was held, at which Tofilau initiated a discussion about the party leadership. A vote was not necessary as the caucus unanimously agreed that Tofilau continue as leader, and therefore as prime minister. When the results of the 1991 general election were known, but before the prime ministerial election, Tofilau again initiated a caucus discussion on the party leadership. As in 1988, the caucus unanimously re-endorsed his leadership and thus another prime ministerial term.

Tofilau's standing policy has been that, when the prime minister is overseas, cabinet ministers would rotate among themselves the responsibility of deputy prime ministership. However, in April 1992, the caucus introduced a new practice when they decided to elect a 'formal' deputy leader of the party, who thereafter was also the deputy prime minister. The minister of finance, Tuila'epa Sa'ilele, won the ballot against three other senior caucus members and cabinet ministers, Pule Lāmeko, Toī Aukuso, and Polataivao Fosi.[4] Following the deputy leadership ballot, Tuila'epa was referred to as the deputy prime minister and carried out all the prime ministerial duties when the prime minister was overseas or ill. Tuila'epa's election as deputy leader has set a precedent for electing future deputy leaders, and leaders as well. Tuila'epa remained deputy leader until 1998 when he succeeded Tofilau 'Eti Alesana to the prime ministership when the latter resigned after serious long-term illness.[5] Tuila'epa Sa'ilele was re-elected prime minister by his party after the 2001 and 2006 general elections. Misa Telefoni was elected deputy leader.

The connection between high traditional status and national leadership ended when the HRPP opened up the competition for the leadership to younger members. Tuila'epa Sa'ilele was a younger man with no direct connection to the *tama-a-'āiga* titles. By adopting the ballot as a means of electing their leaders, HRPP and SNDP created the means to change the established political preference for – and deference to – seniority and high rank. The HRPP caucus also accepted the concept of factions within the parliamentary section of the party, which opened up the competition for all party positions – including the offices of prime minister, deputy prime minister, cabinet ministers, speaker, and deputy speaker – to all caucus members.

Parties and village politics

The competition fostered by the party system has challenged village governments. For example, in 1993, Leulumoega was divided into two subvillage councils. The division of a previously unified council came about because of a dispute traceable to the 1982 general election. Leulumoega and Nofoāli'i villages comprise Ā'ana Ālofi No. 2 constituency. The constituency's parliamentary seat was held by Tupuola 'Efi from 1970 until he switched to Ānoāma'a East constituency, from where he was elected unopposed in the 1988 general election. Tupuola successfully contested the seat for the first time in 1970. He and his only rival, 'Alipia Siaosi, polled 57 and 18 votes respectively. As prime minister in the 1970–72 parliament, Tamasese appointed Tupuola to the position of minister of works. Tupuola was elected unopposed in 1973, and again in 1976 when he subsequently won the prime ministership against Tamasese. With two distinct factions in parliament, Tupuola's parliamentary seat was contested for the first time in 1979. He won against Tanuvasa Livigisitone, a high-ranking *ali'i* of Nofoāli'i village, by 98 votes to 27. Thereafter, the seat has been contested at each election.

However, in 1982, Tupuola's only contestant was another high-ranking *tulafale* of Leulumoega village, Lepou Rōpati. Despite Leulumoega putting strong pressure on Lepou to have his candidacy withdrawn, in order that Tupuola be elected unopposed, Lepou would not give in. It was particularly embarrassing to Leulumoega that its own *matai* was opposing Tupuola because Nofoāli'i, which should have contested the seat, agreed not to put up its own candidate, thereby signifying that it had unanimously agreed to have Tupuola continue as the constituency's MP. Moreover, Tupuola had been the incumbent prime minister since 1976. Consequently, Lepou and his main supporter, Sāmoa Pita[6], were suspended from the village council.

The rift in Leulumoega arising from the 1982 general election persisted until it took another turn for the worse in 1989 when other *matai* and families were also suspended from the village. Thereafter, *matai* in the main council resolved to change the traditional composition of the village council. Traditionally, Leulumoega village council comprises nine *tulafale* (thus Leulumoega's socio-political and ceremonial greeting, 'house of nine')[7] and 'Alipia (greeted the *matua* – leader – of the house of nine following his designation by Fonotī's half-sister, Samalāulu, during the national war of succession in the 1640s). Although Leulumoega had origi-nally been established as a village of *tulafale*, it had over the years incorpo-rated *ali'i* and the *aualuma*, a female sub-organization of the village whose origin is traced to So'oa'emalelagi, an historically renowned ancestress of the *ali'i*, Tuioti and Taualofae. In the 1989 dispute, Liufau Pisia and Logo Vaeoso, the village's female sub-organization, Tuioti and Taualofae and the other two holders of the Tupuola title, were suspended from formal village participation by 'Alipia Siaosi and the other *matai* of Leulumoega. In all, 68 families (63 which have *matai* and five which had no *matai*) left following the 1989 dispute. All these families went over to Lepou Rōpati and Sāmoa Pita (who were originally suspended in 1982) and formed a rival village council.

The two rival councils of Leulumoega were not reconciled until late 1995. Such electoral divisions can create severe problems for a village. Most villages build, maintain and own their own school buildings and lands on which the schools are built, although the teachers are supplied and paid for by the government. In some cases, *matai* in rival councils expel from school the children of their counterparts, claiming that they alone comprise the legitimate council, and therefore control all school-related activities.

Other instances where the exercise of individual freedom of choice has come into conflict with traditional values include a case in Sāfa'atoa village. There, an HRPP supporter was suspended by his village because he defied village instructions to vote for the candidate that his village supported.

Sāmoa's strong family-oriented culture has been adversely affected by inter-party competition. Divisions have affected extended families of closely related people such the Va'ai[8] and Pētaia[9] families, as well as tra-ditional families, such as 'Āiga Sa Fenunu'ivao. An instance was in Falefā village. A man who was a strong supporter of Tupua Tamasese 'Efi was opposed by his own son, who supported a lower-ranking titleholder. The father was a holder of a high-ranking *tulafale* title of 'Āiga Sa Fenunu'ivao whose *tama-a-'āiga* was Tupua. The father assaulted his son, and both were wounded. In a neighbouring village, Lufilufi, another high-ranking *tulafale* encountered the same problems. He and his village campaigned strongly for Tupua because, among other things, Tupua also holds the Tui Ātua title that Lufilufi traditionally supports and protects. However, his niece campaigned for Tupua's rival, and was later suspended from the village.

Competition and political participation

O le ala i le pule o le tautua (The way to authority is service) is the traditional ideology that governs the relationship between those in positions of authority and those who are likely to hold the same positions in the future. Family members elect their *matai*. Thereafter, the *matai* expects from family members the respect and obedience befitting of his new position, a state of affairs that continues until the titleholder passes away and is replaced by another family member. In modern Sāmoa, however, there are many roads to service – such as the provision of money, and, in a monetized economy, most people are able to contribute to their families and thereby claim recognition of their service with a title.

Universal suffrage was generally seen as the answer to the proliferation of titles. It was reasoned that, if all adults could vote, families and villages would not have so strong an incentive to divide their titles, and create new ones. In 1968, parliament rejected the right of all people over 21 to vote, as it was seen as an erosion of *fa'asāmoa*, the rights of *matai*; but, by 1990, universal suffrage had been accepted by a majority of the people. Tofilau 'Eti, at the helm of the HRPP government, in 1990, initiated this development, asserting that universal suffrage addressed the modern democratic and human rights of the people. He explained that he had not supported earlier parliamentary motions to this end, because:

> … motions of this sort had been put to the House before and were heavily defeated, because the majority of the members were *matai*. I suggested that [Matatūmua] withdrew her motion until after the general election in 1985, pledging that if my party, the HRPP, was returned to power, I would introduce a general referendum on universal suffrage so that the people might express their view. The then leader of

the opposition, Tupua Tamasese 'Efi, also pledged that should his party be returned to power, he would introduce a plebiscite, which he did not do when we were ousted from power shortly thereafter. I won that election, obtaining 31 seats, but after only three months, a motion of no-confidence, engineered by some members of my own HRPP party, was moved against me. Some of them were not appointed to Cabinet by myself, so they turned around and formed a faction and that faction moved the motion, which ousted us from power (*The Courier*, 128, July-August 1991, pp. 37-8).

Having passed the legislation that provided for the holding of a plebiscite, the HRPP government set 12 November 1990 as the day on which the referendum would be held. Voter turn-out was relatively low, but responding to the question of whether or not those over the age of 21 should be given the right to vote, while restricting the right to stand as members of parliament to *matai* only, 20,149 voted 'yes', 18,141 voted 'no', and 1,844 votes were classified informal (and were rejected).[10] Thus, the 'yes' vote won, but with only 50.2 per cent, a winning margin of 0.4 per cent.

Whatever the explanation for the low turnout in the plebiscite, one thing seems clear: There was no overwhelming support for the introduction of universal suffrage.

A few issues relating to universal suffrage are worth noting. Some of the HRPP MPs who left the party and joined the coalition (which – as Tofilau mentioned – engineered the no-confidence motion to remove him from power, and when in power did not table any legislation for the introduction of universal suffrage) were among the critics of universal suffrage. One of them, Le Tagaloa Pita, was one of the eight *matai* who filed a lawsuit in the Supreme Court against it. When judge Sir Maurice Casey dismissed the lawsuit, Le Tagaloa and his supporters filed an appeal against the decision. The appeal was dismissed by the Sāmoa Court of Appeal on 18 December 1995. Tupua Tamasese 'Efi, the leader of the opposition and deputy prime minister in the coalition government, possibly reneged on his pledge that, 'should his party be returned to power, he would introduce a plebiscite' to ascertain the public's views on universal suffrage, because he lacked the support of his colleagues.

Doubts about the possibility of introducing universal suffrage cut through all political groups. The HRPP cabinet, when debating the issue before tabling the legislation, was deeply divided on the issue. The issue was so sensitive that one cabinet minister, an ardent traditionalist and devoted

HRPP supporter, had to have a private discussion with the prime minister in order to explain his behaviour, following his remarks at a public function which implied distaste for universal suffrage. When Le Tagaloa tabled a petition in parliament that included the rejection of universal suffrage, the same minister praised Le Tagaloa and his organization for their efforts in trying to preserve Sāmoan custom and tradition. However, the legislation to enact universal suffrage came up for debate in cabinet too close to the next general election for the incumbent ministers' comfort – it was the prime minister's prerogative to appoint cabinet ministers – and so, despite the numerous sensitive cultural issues associated with universal suffrage, the prime minister eventually had his way.

At the caucus level, the need to maintain party solidarity in order to remain in power outweighed any cultural risks associated with the introduction of universal suffrage. Moreover, when the HRPP MPs were elected, they had signed a legal document in which they pledged loyalty to the party. One HRPP MP decided not to stand in the 1991 general election because it was clear to him that his constituency did not support universal suffrage. Thus, it was due to the existence of political parties rather than to genuine support for universal suffrage *per se,* that the plebiscite registered a slim positive majority. The HRPP's victory in the 1991 general election was probably an indication of the appreciation of untitled members of the public for Tofilau's efforts in giving them a political voice.

Despite significant public disapproval of universal suffrage it greatly increased the level of public participation in political activities, increasing the proportion of the national population who cast votes in general elections, from 8.0 per cent in 1988 to 37.3 per cent in 1991 in all electorates, and from 7.6 per cent to 35.6 per cent in the Sāmoan constituencies. The number of voters increased from 57,904 in 1991 to 72,511 in 1996, an increase of 14,607 (25 per cent) of voters.

Democracy reverses traditional practices of political participation. For example, at the village government level, the only means of influencing policies is through the established structures. The saying *Ua tōfia e le Atua Sāmoa ina ia pūlea e matai* (God has designated Sāmoa to be governed by the *matai*) justifies the unchallenged authority of *matai* in village governments and other supra-village institutions. Generally, socio-political affairs in the indigenous structures are so tightly controlled by their respective governing bodies that public protest against the central government is rare, and when it occurs, it is conducted through *matai*.

Before the introduction of universal suffrage, a relatively low proportion of voters were wage and salary earners. Since independence, the only two major protests against government policies, in 1965 and 1981, were staged by wage and salary earners, and the main issue in both protests was to do with pay rises to accommodate the rising cost of living. Neither was a national protest because the existing indigenous socio-political structures were not directly involved. However, the protest movement against the introduction of a Value Added Goods and Services Tax (VAGST) in 1994 was significantly different and is discussed in the next chapter.

Public policy and accountability

The period from 'quiet opposition' (1962–69) to 'recognized factions' (1970–81) can be characterized by two general approaches to economic policy. The first was roughly represented by the Matā'afa prime ministership (1962–69, 1973–75), the general feature of whose economic policies was cautious conservatism. Though development was one of the most important items on the government's political agenda, it was not allowed to become the sole objective to the detriment of the nation's general economic situation; there was a constant effort to balance expenditure against revenue. The second approach, witnessed during the prime ministerships of Tamasese (1970–72, 1975) and Tupuola 'Efi (1976–78, 1979–81), generally put more emphasis on development than on avoiding a national deficit. These differences in orientation generally were 'hidden' within the confines of parliament.

The creation of the HRPP established a new precedent in the country's political history. The general election in 1982 was the first in which the names and photographs of candidates for a party – in this case the HRPP – were publicized in a collective party-statement. Then, in the 1985 general election, the HRPP included in the party statement the policies it hoped to implement if elected to power. These practices have now become a matter of course in all general elections and by-elections. Despite this, the overwhelming trend in selecting political leaders has been to do so on the basis of family and village affiliations, personal allegiances, and other cultural factors. This raises the issue of how parties discipline their members, and establish and retain a party identity and vote in the electorate. Though concerned with improving the level of participation in the formulation of party policies, those concerned also attempted to solve the problem of how to make the MPs more accountable, not only to the party but also to the voters in their respective constituencies.

To solve the problem of 'the unreliable link' between the central government (or the political party in power, or any political party for that matter) and the voters, the HRPP, as mentioned earlier, submits for party executive committee approval the names of all the *matai* who want to contest as HRPP candidates, and requires its candidates to sign a legal document pledging loyalty to the party if elected. However, the acceptance of factions within the party has proven to be potentially destructive if it is not carefully managed by party leaders; and preventing party-endorsed parliamentarians from switching parties has been a challenge. The Electoral Amendment Act 1995 was one attempted solution. It requires candidates to declare their political parties on ballot papers, prevents candidates from contesting seats as independents if they contested seats as members of a political party before the current election, and allows only candidates who polled at least 50 per cent of the total number of votes polled by the person elected or returned at the election' to file an election petition. The Electoral Amendment Act 2000 went further by legally recognizing for the first time the existence of political parties. It provides for the registration of political parties, but these must be registered before the day on which the writs for an election or by-election are issued. It also gives the chief electoral officer the power to cancel a political party on its own request or when the chief electoral officer becomes aware that the number of current members of the party has fallen below 100. Following the recommendations of the 2001 commission of inquiry into the *Electoral Act 1963*, the Electoral Amendment Act 2005 prevents the movement of elected MPs between parties or them becoming independent members after taking the oath of allegiance. However, an independent member may join a political party, and an elected member of a party that is too small to be recognized as a party in parliament may also join another party, provided all such changes take place before the oath of allegiance is taken. Any other such movements thereafter result in the seats of those MPs being declared vacant. The 2006 commission of inquiry reaffirmed the Electoral Amendment Act 2005.

The 'Ugapō model' suggests another way of dealing with the problem of switching parties, and may at the same time remove indefinitely most, if not all, of the election candidates' nightmare, of spending excessively to gain the sympathy of the voters. The Ugapō model refers to the document entitled 'Proposed restructure and reorganization of the Human Rights Protection Party'; it was drafted by Ugapō Pusi Ulale. Ugapō was the HRPP secretary until his appointment to his new job in the prime minister's department in late 1992. In early 1991, Ugapō submitted his 'Reorganization' draft to the prime minister to make known his views on how the party's organization might be improved. As he put it:

> HRPP does seem to be a Political Party only by name, because in reality it is not functioning at all as a party, but rather, like scattered iron filings all rushing and clinging to a magnet in any unorganised way whatsoever. … there is simply no co-ordination whatsoever'! …
>
> The Party's policies, manifestos and development programmes are instigated, promoted and given approval within the Caucus. Problems even of unrelated nature are taken to and resolved in Caucus. Issues of national importance that should carry party-consensus, were known to have been decided upon and set to motion within the narrow confines of the Caucus body; hence the inevitable discontentment and confusion among even Caucus members. Then what of the party member and voter! What of a Constituency which has no representative in the Caucus? How are our party members in such a case communicated with? How are ideas or complaints – born at the village level, channeled and conveyed to the Party's top echelons? (Ulale 1991:1)

In suggesting ways to improve the party's organization, Ugapō hoped to 'have participation improved at all levels of membership'. Most importantly, the party MPs would be 'bound to the collective decisions not only of the PPC (parliamentary party caucus), but also of the PEC (party executive council)'. Ugapō's uppermost concern has been the tendency of MPs to remain detached from both the party and their respective constituencies following their election victories. The Ugapō model attempts to provide a two-way link between the party's governing body and the voters in the constituencies, and to provide a stronger link between the extra-parliamentary and the parliamentary sections of the party.

Notes

1   See Chapters 1 and 2 and Appendix 3.
2   Thus the socio-political and ceremonial greeting of Tofilau, *O le to'ot'ooāli'i* (The orator-chief, or the chief [*ali'i*] who can also deliver speeches as an orator [*tulafale*]).

3   The Fuimaono title was first established in the 1720s. See also Appendix 3.

4   Tuila'epa Sa'ilele has been an MP since winning a by-election in 1981; Pule
     Lameko has been an MP in the parliamentary terms 1979–81, 1982–84,
     1985–87, 1988–90 and 1991–95, and 2001-06; To'i has been an MP in the
     parliamentary terms 1979–81, 1982–84, 1985–87, 1988–90 and 1991–95; and
     Polataivao Fosi has been an MP in the parliamentary terms 1964–67, 1970–72,
     1973–75, 1976–78, 1982–84, 1985–87, 1988–90 and 1991–95.

5   In contrast to the HRPP's method of selecting its leaders, the Temokalasi Sāmoa
     Fa'amatai Political Party in its draft constitution stipulates that although the
     leader of the parliamentary wing of the party is elected by that forum, and is later
     to be also endorsed by party's executive committee comprising the *matai* of both
     the parliamentary and extra-parliamentary wings, he/she can only be dismissed
     by the *unanimous* (my emphasis) agreement of the executive committee (Section
     VII). That is, the leader of the caucus will be very difficult to remove. The party
     deliberately rejects the method of arriving at decisions by a ballot, and thus also
     the majority principle (Section III[2]).

6   Sāmoa is another high-ranking *tulafale* title of Leulumoega village like the
     Tupuola, 'Alipia and Lepou titles.

7   For more information on the composition and the traditional rights, privileg-
     es and responsibilities of the Leulumoega orator group and Leulumoega as a
     village, see Chapter 1 and Appendix 6.

8   When Lesātele Rapi (aged 70) remained loyal to Tupuola 'Efi in the 1979 prime
     ministerial elections against his younger brother, Va'ai Kolone (69), who was
     the opposition faction's prime ministerial candidate, there was a public murmur
     that Lesātele had deprived his own brother of victory (interview with Lesātele's
     daughter, 23 September 1993). The two men's children were deeply divided
     on the issue. In a tribute to Lesātele Rapi in the *Sāvali* (28 December 1979),
     following his death on 14 December 1979, the author wrote:

     He (Lesātele Rapi) must have known that most of us value blood and *'āiga*
     connection above all else; we even place it above individual conscience. To vote
     against one's brother is viewed by most of us, as the worst betrayal any one
     can commit [This particular section of the tribute complemented Lesātele's
     loyalty to Tupuola 'Efi].

     The minister of Education in the 1991-96 HRPP government said that she
     was very disappointed when her father's first cousin supported Tupuola's
     prime ministerial candidacy in 1979, when he should have supported the
     opposition faction of her mother (the wife of the former prime minister,
     Matā'afa F. M II). When Le Tagaloa Pita's older brother entered parliament
     for the first time in 1988, he supported the HRPP despite the fact that Le
     Tagaloa was cabinet minister in the previous SNDP government. Le Tagaloa
     later in that parliamentary term declared himself an independent, and has
     since retained that status. His older brother still held his seat but he was not
     appointed to cabinet in the 1991-95 HRPP government.

9   Members of the Pētaia family include the late prime minister Tofilau E. Alesana (MP in 1958–1960, 1967–69, 1970–72, 1976–78, 1979–81, 1982–84, 1985–87, 1988–90, 1991–95, 1996–98), Matā'afa F. M. II's wife Lā'ulu Fetauimalemau (MP in 1975, 1979–81), Matatūmua Maimoaga (Lā'ulu Fetauimalemau's sister – MP in 1982–84, 1991–95), Nomumalo Sōfara (whose wife 'Eni is a sister of Lā'ulu and Matatūmua – MP in 1979–81, 1982–84, 1991–93), Fiamē Nāomi (Lā'ulu's daughter – MP in 1985–87, 1988–90, 1991–95). Lately, some non-parliamentarian members of Sa Pētaia have complained that as prime minister, Tofilau 'Eti seems to have neglected the parliamentarians of his Pētaia family, especially following his elevation to the prime ministership. Evidence of this, for example, is that Nonumalo L. Sōfara (whose wife 'Eni is a member of the Pētaia family and a founding HRPP member) left the HRPP in 1993 and subsequently formed the Sāmoa Democratic Party. Also, following the 1991 prime ministerial elections, Matatūmua Maimoaga ('Eni's younger sister) has been a strong critic of the Tofilau 'Eti and some of his policies in parliament, despite the fact that she is an HRPP MP. This can also be interpreted as a deliberate attempt by Matatūmua to divert public attention from the fact that most of the Sa Pētaia MPs have supported the HRPP, one of whose leader since late 1982 is another Sa Pētaia. Either interpretation nevertheless implies the importance of families in Sāmoan society.

10   Official results of the plebiscite from the office of the clerk of the legislative assembly.

8 | The impact of 'constitutionalized' rights[1]

THE INCORPORATION INTO Sāmoa's constitution of provisions to safeguard civil and political rights has helped these rights gain the upper hand over 'customary laws' associated with indigenous institutions. This impact is examined in this chapter by way of case studies.

Civil and political liberties, and customs and traditions

Not surprisingly, the Sāmoan constitution has not recognized village governments *per se*. Nor has it recognised *Tūmua* and *Pule*, which collectively governed Sāmoa before European contact. Their exclusion from the constitution undermines their position in the present democratic framework. Furthermore, the *Village Fono Act 1990* failed to give village governments all the powers they used to have in relation to customs and traditions, because their recognition would have contradicted a number of individual rights provisions in the constitution.

Significantly, the 1990 plebiscite dealt another (and probably final) blow to *Tūmua* and *Pule's* traditional authority and rights, in that 56% of those voting voted *against* a second house in the parliament; a house that would have been representative of the 11 traditional political districts associated with *Tūmua* and *Pule*.[2]

Village councils and constituencies

As discussed elsewhere in this book, village councils sometimes dictate to the rest of the village the choice of parliamentary candidates, apply pressure on certain candidates to withdraw their candidacy, and so forth. This section revisits some of those issues using two case studies in the

2006–11 parliamentary term – Fa'asalele'aga No. 4 and Faleata East constituencies – in the context of civil and political liberties.

Fa'asalele'aga No. 4 constituency

The 2006 general election result of Fa'asalele'aga No. 4 constituency was keenly awaited by the public: The incumbent MP, Mulitalo Siāfausa Vui, was a high-profile member and the incumbent minister of health of the ruling HRPP government, and his main rival, Su'a Rimoni Ah Chong, was not only leader of the newly established Sāmoa Party but had also taken a firm and highly publicized stand against the late prime minister, Tofilau Eti Alesana, and his HRPP government in the 1991–96 parliament. When Su'a was controller and chief auditor, his report to parliament pointed out corruption in high places in the HRPP government. Unhappy with Su'a's report, the late prime minister put pressure on Su'a to amend some of the points he had made in the report; Su'a refused and resigned. A direct result of this controversy saw the constitutional position of controller and chief auditor, originally for a life term, re-advertised as a contracted position for a term of three years. For his firm stand on what he believed was right, Su'a was awarded a Transparency International medal.

When the general election result was finalized, Mulitalo had polled 689 votes to Su'a's 436, thus guaranteeing Mulitalo another parliamentary term. Convinced that certain provisions of the electoral act had been breached during Mulitalo's campaign, Su'a filed an election petition against Mulitalo. Lano, Su'a's and Mulitalo's village in the constituency, immediately put pressure on Su'a to withdraw his petition against Mulitalo. When Su'a did not, he was banned from the village (Ah Mu and Semu 2006:1–2). In the course of the petition hearing, the bench conducted an impromptu inquiry into Lano's involvement in Su'a's ban. The leading *matai* of Lano was told by one of the supreme court judges – in no uncertain terms – to lift the ban on Su'a and have him re-instated in the village by a date set by the court (Ah Mu 2006a:1–2). Lano detested the court's intrusion into their village affairs. After discussions with the chief justice, a Sāmoan, the supreme court judge amended his earlier statement and advised Lano's *matai* instead to file a petition with the Land and Titles Court relating to their ban on Su'a (Ah Mu 2006b:1–2). In the hearing, all counts of breach of the electoral act by both men were dismissed except one against Mulitalo. In the end, the court found Mulitalo guilty of that last count and declared void his seat. On the day after the court's decision was handed down, the traditional residence of the Su'a title at Lano, Lotolano, was burned to the ground in mysterious circumstances (Ah Mu and Semu 2006b:1–2).

During the hearing, Mulitalo learned that charges could be filed in the criminal court for some of the allegations against Su'a – and after his seat had been declared void, Mulitalo filed these charges. The court found Su'a guilty of one charge of bribery and was fined ST300. Immediately thereafter, Su'a announced that he would return the Transparency International medal (Sio 2006:1–2). The court decision meant that, like Mulitalo, Su'a could not contest the seat in the by-election resulting from the disqualification of Mulitalo's election victory. The by-election elected another HRPP candidate. Lano's ban on Su'a was lifted on 31 October 2006, the day before the Land and Title Court's deadline for Lano to do so (Ah Mu 2006c:1–2). The new MP, Vui Tupe, also from Lano, was eventually able to bring together the two Lano village factions to reconcile their differences and continue with normal village life.

Faleata East Constituency

Although Faleata East constituency comprises the three villages of Vailoa, Lepea and Vaimoso, the contest for the parliamentary seat is usually between the last two, the bigger villages in the constituency. Faumuinā Anapapa of Lepea was elected in 1985 by 40 votes to Manuleleua Fouvale of Vaimoso's 14. Faumuinā won again in 1985 by 29 votes to Matai'a Visesio Europa of Vaimoso's 23. In 1991, Matai'a was elected by 1,010 votes to Faumuinā's 463.[3] He was elected again in 1996 by 1,443 votes to Faumuinā's 1,010. When Matai'a was appointed to the council of deputies in 1997, Faumuinā was elected unopposed to complete Matai'a's parliamentary term. He was re-elected unopposed in the 2001 general election. When Faumuinā was, in turn, appointed to the council of deputies to succeed Mata'ia, who passed away in office in 2002, another Lepea *matai*, Lepou Petelo II, succeeded Faumuinā to the constituency's parliamentary seat. No by-election was held. When Lepou succeeded Faumuinā, an agreement was reached between Vaimoso and Lepea that it would be Vaimoso's turn to nominate the constituency's parliamentary candidate in the next general election in 2006.

However, at the close of nominations for parliamentary candidates for the 2006 election, Lepea was shocked to discover that Lepou had registered his name as one of the candidates for the constituency's seat. The only other candidate was Vaimoso's nomination, Manuleleua Lalagofa'atasi Manuleleua, who would have been elected unopposed had Lepou not registered his candidacy. Furious that Lepou had defied the village council ruling, Lepea expelled him from the village. After the ban on Lepou had become public knowledge, Faumuinā received a letter from the Land and Titles Court to lift the village ban on Lepou as it violated the constitution (Ah Mu and Semu 2006c:2). The following day, 22 March 2006, Lepea village applied to the Land and Titles Court to have Lepou removed from the village because he had defied the village's agreement with Vaimoso and Vailoa villages. The court ruled that Lepou's dismissal by his village was illegal and excessive (Ah Mu 2006d:2). Reconciliation between Lepou and his village later took place at Lepea, and Lepou was allowed to return to his family. Manuleleua was elected as the constituency's member of parliament by 331 votes to Lepou's 120 (*Observer*, 16 April 2006). The result of the election seemed to indicate that the majority of voters respected the agreement among the constituency villages that it was Vaimoso's turn to nominate the constituency candidate for the 2006–11 parliament.

When Manuleleua passed away on 15 February 2007, aged 82 years, Vaimoso village met to select one of its members to succeed him. They eventually decided on 82 year-old Pātau'ave Etuale, a former member of parliament and the oldest *matai* of the village. The decision to nominate him was based primarily on his age and, secondly, on his service to the village. After the people of Vaimoso had made their choice, Lepea and Vailoa villages were notified (Fa'afia 2007a:1–3). Aveau Niko Palamo, CEO of the‾ Sāmoa Association of Sports and National Olympic Committee (SASNOC), took issue with the decision, arguing that not only was he absent from that meeting but it was also supposed to be his family's turn to nominate a parliamentary candidate from Vaimoso village. Worse still, his Manuleleua family (to which the deceased MP belonged) had not been consulted. Aveau believed that another *matai* from the Manuleleua family should have been nominated to replace their deceased member (Ripine 2007a:1–3). Aveau elected to stand as a candidate in order to 'do the right thing' – make those points to his village of Vaimoso. Furthermore, he contended, he had the right to contest the seat regardless of the village council's decision (Ripine 2007b:2). Despite threats to have him banned from his village if he did not withdraw his candidacy and despite pressure from the Manuleleua family, Aveau held his ground. In the by-election he polled 470 votes to Pātau'ave's 615 (Fa'afia 2007b:1–2).

The Faleata East by-election and the war of words between the high-ranking *matai* of Vaimoso and Aveau associated with it could also be seen as a contest between tradition and modernity. The 82 year-old Pātau'ave and his supporters stood for tradition and the 49 year-old Aveau for modernity.

Traditionally, major village decisions are made by high-ranking/senior *matai*. The agreement among the three villages of the constituency was one of those decisions. The decision that Pātau'ave succeed Manuleleua was also greatly influenced by the senior *matai* of Vaimoso, and was strongly defended by Une, a high-ranking *matai* of Vaimoso, and by Vaimoso's village mayor and Lepea's village mayor.

The village tactic to have Aveau withdraw his candidacy was twofold – first, there was the implicit intention of banning Aveau from Vaimoso, as Lepea had banned Lepou; and, second, there was the intention that the leading *matai* of the Manuleleua family would convince Aveau to withdraw. In the war of words between Vaimoso's senior *matai* and Aveau, Vaimoso kept referring to Aveau as a 'kid', implying that, although Aveau was a *matai* of the Manuleleua family, his title was a low-ranking one not only in his family but also in the village.

Pātau'ave's first comments after winning the by-election indicated that he wanted the constituency to develop agriculture and return the people to the practices of the past: his vision for the future of the constituency was a return to the past. In contrast, Aveau in his campaign had talked up the importance of modern education for the future of the constituency. He also stood for 'rights'; the right of his family to be consulted and his own individual right to contest the seat regardless of his title rank and village opinion. Aveau's candidacy was also a stand against village authority and the traditional means by which their decision was reached. Although Pātau'ave won, the fact that the race was relatively close suggested that Aveau had fairly good support. But, most importantly from a traditional perspective was the fact that high-ranking *matai* of Vaimoso village and the constituency had the candidate of their choice.

The cases of Lano of Fa'asalele'aga No. 4 constituency and of Lepea and Vaimoso villages of Faleata East constituency show the persisting influence of village councils in deciding candidates for parliamentary elections. Lano put pressure on Su'a to withdraw his election petition against election-night winner, Mulitalo Siāfausa, and, when Su'a went ahead with his petition, he was banned from the village. Furthermore, when Mulitalo eventually lost his seat, the Lano residence of Su'a was burned to the ground. Lepea wanted Lepou not to contest their parliamentary seat and when he did, he was banned from the village. Vaimoso applied similar pressure on Aveau Niko Palamo. Fortunately for Aveau, the Land and Titles Court decision ordering Lepea to lift its ban on Lepou and have him reinstated in the village was still fresh in the minds of the people of Vaimoso village, so Aveau was spared the punishment dished out to Su'a and Lepou by their respective villages.

Some observations can be made from these elections. First, despite village councils continuing to influence the choice of candidates for their respective constituencies, the law, as administered by the Land and Titles Court, has the final say. Therefore, as long as similar cases are brought before the court, village councils will be on the losing end. Second, despite Lepou's and Aveau's insistence on their right to contest the seats of their respective constituencies, the winning candidates in both cases have been those preferred by the village councils. The case of Fa'asālele'aga was different in that the candidacies for by-elections of both Su'a and Mulitalo were disqualified by the court.

In general, the provisions in the constitution to safeguard civil and political rights have so far been a success. The legal victory of the *Tūmua* and *Pule* protest movement against the HRPP government (discussed below) is a classic example. Moreover, the HRPP government did not interfere with or put pressure on organizers of the RHD protest march to prevent the march from going ahead as planned (discussed below).

The practice whereby some candidates and their campaign committees withheld voters' identification cards (IDs) until election day to induce them to vote for certain candidates was common in 1991 (see, So'o 1993) and in all general elections until after the 2001 election, even though the Electoral Amendment Act 1995 forbids this practice (Art. 30). Following recommendations of the 2001 Commission of Inquiry in to the *Electoral Act 1963* as amended, IDs were replaced in the 2006 general election by a new electoral registration system that used photographs and fingerprints to identify registered voters. Although the new system was generally a success, it was discovered that some voters voted twice.

Another Commission of Inquiry into the Electoral Act was established after the 2006 election. It endorsed the new system and added stiffer penalties for double voting. For example, it recommended that the penalty for double voting be increased to a term of imprisonment of up to two years and/or a monetary fine of ST5,000 or 50 penalty units. In addition, it recommended that an individual convicted of double voting, or any candidate aiding and abetting double voting be automatically disqualified from standing as a candidate for election for 10 years from the date of conviction (Report 2006:36).

The issue of village councils deciding which candidate village members should vote for is still a problem. For example, before the general elections in 1996 and 2001, Sāvaia village ruled that all village members were to vote for certain candidates for its constituency's seat. Lano and Lepea had the same problem in the 2006 general election, and Vaimoso village in the 2007 by-election, though to a lesser extent. The government has yet to come up with a solution to this problem, even though, by right, any village practising this strategy has breached the undue influence provision (Art. 98 of the *Electoral Act 1963*).

Perhaps all that is needed is to enforce this legislation, as the Land and Titles Court did in the cases of Lano and Lepea. But, as seen in the cases of Lano and Lepea villages, village councils still demonstrate strong resistance to state interference in their traditional authorities. As the Land and Titles Court becomes increasingly involved in defining the limits of village councils' authority come parliamentary elections (and in other issues generally associated with civil liberty and individual rights and freedom), hopefully, village councils will eventually learn to refrain from interfering with candidates and voters constitutional rights. To date, the Land and Titles Court has consistently ruled against village councils. Only if this continues and only if, in the process, village councils are made aware of the limitation of their traditional authorities, will the constitutional ideal of respecting civil and political rights of citizens be fully realized.

Freedom of expression

Case studies of two events that took place in the early 1990s – the conflict between the vice chancellor of the National University of Sāmoa and a local newspaper, and the expulsion of an MP from parliament – gauge the extent to which freedom of expression has been practiced in Sāmoa and the kinds of responses elicited when it is exercised.

The Vice-Chancellor vs Sāmoa Observer

The vice chancellor (VC) of the National University of Sāmoa sued the local newspaper, *Sāmoa Observer,* for ST250,000 damages in respect of an article that appeared in the newspaper on 22 September 1989. The hearing took place between 27 August and 5 September 1991. Chief Justice Ryan found that the VC had indeed been defamed in relation to his administrative and management abilities and his honesty and integrity. The chief justice found that:

> ... the defence of justification has been made out in the first instance as to the Plaintiff's administrative and management abilities but that it has not been made out insofar as his honesty and integrity are concerned. In respect of that second defamation I fix damages in the sum of S$20,000 and costs...The amount claimed by the Plaintiff was in my view grossly excessive and would have been so even if the defence of justification on the first ground had not been made out.[4]

Chief Justice Ryan explained that not only had the article defamed the plaintiff but so also had the publication of six subsequent articles.[5] In explaining his decision, Chief Justice Ryan said that the:

> Plaintiff's counsel suggests that when looked at overall the only interpretation that can be placed on such a series of publications is the Defendants are biased and prejudiced against the Plaintiff and that at all times they have endeavored to place before the public a one-sided and totally prejudiced view of the plaintiff's involvement with the University as its principal administrator.
>
> ....The Plaintiff's view is that when the whole article is looked at and in particular when the foregoing paragraphs are considered, the only interpretation which can be placed on the Article is that he (VC) is a dishonest man and a thief – that he has "dipped into" University funds, that he has cheated on expenses, that he has attempted to manipulate university finances to his own ends, that he has been involved in questionable activities.
>
> The Defendant Mālifa in his evidence conceded that he did not approach the Plaintiff to discuss with him the allegations which some of the students had made to him.
>
> It hardly needs to be re-stated but that the media, and in particular the print media, whose images induce beyond the spoken word, must

exercise its power in a balanced and impartial manner. Here there was no reasonable effort made by the Defendant to provide the Plaintiff with an opportunity to answer the allegations made. There was <u>no attempt at impartiality or fairness</u> and the Plaintiff was portrayed in a manner which encouraged denigration by the many readers of the paper.

Mr Mālifa in his evidence said he "tried to get in touch with someone" – hardly a strenuous effort for the champion of the freedom of the Press, which he then admitted to being.

.....I must say that I was in no doubt when I read the article but that the Plaintiff was involved in some financial skullduggery, that he was misappropriating University funds and that he was a dishonest person. He has <u>satisfied me in the witness box that he was defamed.</u>

.....I take from the evidence as a whole on this topic that the allegation that: the administration dipped into the Canadian grant of $40,000 <u>was a blatant lie on the part of the Defendants</u> ....The witness denied telling the Defendant Mālifa that this had occurred and in my view the Defendants falsely and maliciously fabricated this allegation.[6]

Expulsion from parliament of Leota Itū'au

In parliament on 1 March 1990, Leota Itu'au Ale, a former speaker of parliament (1976–79), accused the incumbent prime minister of 'unlawfully taking a refrigerator from the government house at Malae-o-matagofie at Matāutu', among other items (*Observer*, 9 March 1990). The speaker ordered Leota to substantiate his allegations against the prime minister. Five days later, when Leota had failed to come up with any evidence to support his allegations, parliament passed another resolution giving him an extra 24 hours to come up with evidence. At this point, Leota provided as evidence letters from the financial secretary (the head of the treasury department) and the manager of the Development Bank of Sāmoa. The letter from the financial secretary to Leota's lawyers, who had inquired into advances made to the prime minister by the government, stated that 'the Public Monies Act does not authorize any such disclosure'. The letter from the manager of the Development Bank noted that 'banking principles do not allow [him] to provide any information on a client without the written consent of the client'.

At this point, Leota arose and began reading from a series of papers, alleging improprieties in the management of government property and regulations. The speaker judged that he could not accept the papers submitted by Leota as they did not address the 'issue at hand, which was to substantiate the allegation that the prime minister had unlawfully taken a refrigerator, spoons and other property from the government residence at Pilot Point' (*ibid.*). Immediately thereafter, the MP whose daughter, Leota claimed, had told him that the prime minister had removed the refrigerator, moved that Leota be suspended from parliament for 12 months without pay and without the privileges normally accorded to MPs. The speaker ruled that Leota could not be suspended for 12 months because there were only 10 months left before the end of the current parliamentary term. The original motion was then amended and passed that Leota be suspended for the rest of the current parliament. Before the motion was passed, the prime minister denied the original allegations against him as well as those that were made when Leota read out his list of alleged improprieties.

Following his suspension from parliament, Leota said that 'if we become the government we will call a commission of inquiry to investigate the government's alleged mismanagement of public money' (*Observer*, 14 March 1990). Leota thought that the assembly's privileges committee would look into his allegations but 'it is obvious that this would not be so'. Moreover, Leota claimed, there was also an unfounded allegation made in parliament by the MP who had moved the motion to have him suspended, which resulted in the Nauru government withdrawing all its investments from Sāmoa. That allegation cost the country 'lots of money' but there was 'no attempt to seek substantiation', Leota said. Commenting on Leota's suspension, the leader of the opposition said that it was 'a sad day for democracy [in this country] and a sad day for the truth' (*Observer*, 9 March 1990). The leader of the opposition was particularly unhappy that a number of similar allegations had been made in parliament by government MPs. Referring to the minister who had made allegations against the Nauru government, the leader of the opposition said 'We had asked the minister to provide the substantiation but this was never done.... When they want to silence opposition all they do is band together and there's nothing anybody can do about it' (quoted in *Observer* [*ibid.*]).

Freedom of the press

The two cases cited above are important in three respects. First, they set precedents. Secondly, indirectly if not directly, they probably influenced the passing in early 1993 of the *Newspapers and Printers Act 1992/1993*, and the *Defamation Act 1992/1993*. Thirdly, they occurred in the context of an operative political party system. Clause 10 of the Newspapers and Printers Act allows a plaintiff to discover the:

> name of the printer or publisher of any newspaper or of any matter relating to the printing and publishing thereof, including any correspondences, written materials or other sources of information whatsoever, in order to enable him more effectual to bring or continue an action for damages....

In other words, Clause 10 requires journalists and editors to reveal their sources of information. A breach of this clause can result in a three-month jail term and a fine of up to ST5,000 (Clause 18).

The journalists' main concern about the Defamation Act revolves around Clauses 6, 7 and 8 (*Observer*, 17 February 1993). Clause 6 makes it an offence to publish defamatory statements made in court about someone who was not a party to the court proceedings. Clause 7 deals with matter printed about a member of a group when the member is unidentified. Any member of that group who feels 'aggrieved' by the report and has 'reasonable grounds' for believing others 'may suppose that the words are intended to apply to him' can demand a written 'disclaimer' saying the published words did not refer to him. Clause 8 requires 'a person who has published words alleged to be defamatory of another person' to 'make an offer of amends under this section if he claims that the words were published by him innocently in relation to the other person' (8[1]). 'If the offer is not accepted by the party aggrieved', then the publisher has to defend his innocence in court (8[1.b]).

Understandably, the passing of the two laws drew criticism from both the media and some sections of the public. The Pacific Islands News Association (PINA) and PNG Journalists Association called on the Sāmoan government to repeal the Newspapers and Printers Law, arguing that 'Protection of sources by journalists and editors is a fundamental aspect of the freedom of the media and our profession to inform the public' (cited in *Observer*, 17 February 1993). The publisher of the *Observer* argued that,

'Any attempt to tamper with freedom of expression....is a serious threat to democracy. Forcing newspapers to disclose their sources is another way of silencing critics of the government' (Aiāvao 1993:58). Fata Fa'alogo Pito, life member of PINA and former publisher of the *Sāmoa Times*, said:

> .....it comes as no surprise that a government with skeletons in its cupboards would wish to lock the doors, bolt the windows and gag the servants....a statement is libelous or slanderous because of its contents not because of its source. How soon will it be before the police is given the authority to bug telephones and intercept mail? How long will it be before lawyers and doctors lose the protection of the confidentiality of their information? (cited in Aiāvao 1993:58).

Le Tagaloa Pita – a former MP, publisher of the local newspaper *The South Sea*, and whose wife had been one of the witnesses for the defendants in the *VC vs Observer* case – said that in view of the successful defamation lawsuit by the VC against the *Observer*, it was absolutely clear that 'the rights of those who felt wronged were already protected' (cited in Ah Mu 1993:28). Misa Telefoni, lawyer, former attorney general and currently deputy prime minister, defended clause 10 in the Newspapers and Printers Act saying that individual rights were not removed, and that the Act was aimed at people who use aliases and write misleading information (cited in Aiāvao 1993:58). In defense of the same law, then prime minister Tofilau 'Eti Alesana said:

> I believe that by introducing this Act, the standards of the press in Western Sāmoa will be enhanced, and that the public and the international community can look forward to a higher standard of reporting in terms of accuracy, relevancy and fairness (*Sāvali*, 18 February 1993).

He asked: 'Where is the right we protect and not protect? Let the hammer fall on the nail....let not just the publisher carry the full burden, but also the source' (quoted in Aiāvao 1993:58). Commenting on Pacific Islands leaders in general, Jagmohan wrote:

> Perhaps a reason for the sensitivity of our leaders is steeped in cultural traditions of the islands. Traditional leaders of the Pacific – be they the chiefs, nobles or *matai* – have been accustomed to unquestioning loyalty and respect from subjects. Their positions and actions are un-disputed.
>
> .....But as the Pacific media grows away from being largely government-owned or government-controlled entities and assumes its new

responsibility as the watchdog of the nation, the governments are perhaps retaliating in an attempt to check the trend.

But the clock cannot be turned back. The public have begun to expect the media's new role – of being the voice of the people in demanding greater accountability from the governments (1993:4).

In explaining the reasons behind the enactment of the Newspapers and Printers Act, he went on to say:

Western Sāmoa is a developing nation in terms of Western civilization. In this development, it has become inevitable that new ideologies, influences, rights and responsibilities have needed to be assimilated into its society. It is true to say that Sāmoa must retain its own culture and identity. That is why, a responsible Western Sāmoan government must not hasten to import Western ideas and beliefs automatically no matter how attractive they may be (quoted in *Savali*, 18 February 1993).

The debate over freedom of the media and freedom of expression was well summed up by Ioritana Leāuga in a tactful article in the *Sāmoa Observer* (17 February 1993):

Personally I would feel at ease as a free Sāmoan if this piece of legislation (Newspapers and Printers Act, clause 10) is retracted. It's like a gun. In the right hand it's safe. In the wrong hand it's lethal.

I have no serious problems with it in Tofilau's hands [but] will the hands after him be guaranteed? No siree, better recall it before it haunts their creators to their dying day.

...If retracted, everyone from government to opposition, to newspapermen to the public must exercise this freedom responsibly.

When things get choppy, let's accept it as democracy reacting to safeguard the citizens from the power of the state.

Leāuga's words of caution went unnoticed and the two pieces of legislation are still in force. Looking back, however, perhaps the late prime minister's defence of the legislation – that it would result in higher standards of reporting in terms of accuracy, relevancy and fairness – made sense. Following the enactment of the two pieces of legislation, it has become common practice for newspaper readers and the general public to write to editors and publishers of newspapers to have published articles or details contained therein amended or corrected. Likewise, editors and publishers, if they believe that the complaints and requests are valid, respond appropriately with an apology to the aggrieved. Moreover, the authors of all articles published in newspapers are identified by name. It seems, therefore, that the two pieces of legislation have improved the standard of media reporting and resulted in greater accuracy, relevance and fairness. Both the media and the public have taken on board these changes as normal parts of daily life.

Freedom to form and join organizations

As already mentioned, the freedom to form and join organizations is well protected under the constitution's provisions on fundamental rights (Art. 13[b-c]). Two examples of how two particular organizations have been dealt with by the 1991–95 and current (2006–11) HRPP governments indicate how effective the justice system has been in safeguarding this provision of the constitution – how organizations in Sāmoa are operating in a constitutionally established democratic state. The two organizations are *Tūmua ma Pule* (*Tūmua* and *Pule*)[7] and the Right Hand Drive (RHD) movement. *Tūmua ma Pule* is a nationally encompassing concept, discussed in chapters 1–3, while the RHD movement was an ad-hoc organization created to protest against the government's proposal to change Sāmoa's road rules so that driving would be on the left side of the road rather than the right.

The Tūmua *and* Pule *protest movement*

The origin of the *Tūmua* and *Pule* protest movement can be traced to the introduction of the 10 per cent VAGST on 1 January 1994. A misunderstanding between the government and the Price Board, which sets the price or price range for selected goods and services, resulted in the enforcement of a new price order on the day the VAGST became effective; the combined effects of these developments was a 40 per cent increase in the cost of living (*Observer*:11 February 1994). Public reaction gave birth to the *Tūmua* and *Pule* demonstration, or more correctly, the re-activation of that traditional sociopolitical structure. Initiated by the *Tūmua* political centres on Upolu island, the organizers of the demonstration met with and obtained the support of the six *Pule* political centres on Savai'i as well as that of the traditional political district of 'Āiga-i-le-Tai. As one spokesman of the movement pointed out, the six *Pule* 'didn't have any sense of hesitation'; they had 'been waiting for *Tūmua* to make the move' (*ibid.*). In an article explaining the developments that led to the formation of the *Tūmua* and *Pule* demonstration, the *Observer* referred to *Tūmua* and *Pule* as the 'traditional arbitrators over national crises' (*ibid.*). Another article in the same edition called upon *Tūmua* and *Pule* to save the country from the current crisis.

On 24 February 1994, *Tūmua* and *Pule* stated that the two objectives of its planned demonstration were the abolition of the VAGST and the changing of the government (*Observer*, 1 March 1994). On national television on 27 February 1994, the prime minister responded to the second objective by stipulating the various constitutional ways in which a government could be changed.[8] He was driving home the point that *Tūmua* and *Pule* could not force an immediate change of government by their planned protest march (*Observer*, 1 March 1994). A *Sāmoa Observer* editorial (23 January 1994) had alluded to the possibility that the head of state:

will most likely "declare a state of emergency exists if the protest march against the high cost of living goes ahead on 2 March as planned. He is empowered under the Constitution to do this. But only if he is satisfied "acting in his discretion after consultation with Cabinet" that the "economic life of Western Sāmoa" is threatened by an "internal disturbance".

The protest march went ahead as planned on 2 March 1994; close to 20,000 participated. About half of them were *matai* (*Observer*, 3 March 1994). The demonstrators marched for about five miles (eight kilometres) from Vaimoso[9] to the main government building in the centre of Apia to deliver their petition to the prime minister and his cabinet. *Tūmua* and *Pule* designated the leader of the opposition, Tui Ātua Tupua Tamasese 'Efi, to be their spokesman and officially deliver their petition to the government. Prime minister Tofilau replied that the head of state had agreed to an Executive Council meeting on 4 March to discuss the matter. Furthermore, the government was planning a further reduction in prices of items on the price order (*Observer*, 3 March 1994). Insisting that the VAGST be abolished, *Tūmua* and *Pule* refused to disband until that objective was realized, and commenced a two-week vigil in front of the government building. Responding to the prime minister's reply to their petition, Tupua said, 'If you cannot see what is happening, then you must be blind. And if you cannot hear the people's moaning, then you must be deaf' (*ibid.*).

In an announcement on national radio 2AP, the prime minister said that, following a decision of the executive meeting on 4 March, the VAGST would remain unchanged but duties on all basic commodities would be reduced. The details would be officially announced in parliament when it met on 15 March (*Observer*, 6 March 1994). With the government prepared to compromise, satisfaction of the demonstrators' demands seemed imminent. *Tūmua* and *Pule* leadership sent a second delegation to the head of state, asking him to hold a referendum to ascertain the public's views on how the cost of living was affecting them (*ibid.* 9 March 1994). When parliament convened on 15 March 1994, the minister of finance identified the 32 basic commodities on which tax would be reduced. The tax reductions ranged from total abolition to a 50 per cent reduction (*ibid.* 16 March 1994). With this announcement, the demonstrators decided to disband. However, *Tūmua* and *Pule* leadership agreed to keep up the pressure to have the VAGST abolished on all goods.

Another *Tūmua* and *Pule* delegation was sent to the head of state in August that year, asking him to abolish the VAGST and to acknowledge the chief auditor's report – in which, among other things, the chief auditor 'gave detailed instances of wide-scale corruption and implicated a number of ministers and government officials' (*ibid.* 13 January 1995).[10] The head of state asked the delegation to give him a written petition and an indication of the number of people who supported it (*ibid.* 13 September 1994). A signed petition was presented on 11 March 1995 by a *Tūmua* and *Pule* delegation, immediately following another public march in which about 30,000 people participated. A total of 133,354 people were claimed to have signed the petition. Of these, 122,954 were Sāmoans residing in Sāmoa while the other 10,400 Sāmoans were residing in Wellington, New Zealand. People in the latter group 'were concerned that the remittances they were sending over for their families' upkeep here were being subject to the 10% tax when the funds had already been taxed in New Zealand' (*ibid.* 10 March 1995). That same day, a special fourteen-member committee was appointed by the government to, amongst other things, investigate the validity of the signatures on the petition (*ibid.* 12 May, 6 June 1995). Its report, presented to the government in mid-August 1995, invalidated the

Tūmua and *Pule* petition, claiming that it was illegal because any petition was supposed to be presented to parliament. Furthermore, of the 12 *matai* who signed the petition, one had not officially registered his title with the Land and Titles Court; of the alleged signatures in the petition, 122,179 had not personally signed their names[11]; and, the issues of the VAGST and the chief auditor's report had all been debated and passed in parliament (*Sāvali*, 15 September 1995; *Observer*, 27 September 1995).

Tūmua and *Pule* had a victory on one front, however. In its 24 June 1994 edition, the *Observer* had noted that the police department was probing whether there were seditious intentions behind the *Tūmua* and *Pule* national protest of 2 March 1994. The government pressed ahead with sedition charges against the president of *Tūmua* and *Pule*, Fa'amatuāinu Tala Mailei, and one of its executive members, To'alepai T Si'ueva, despite persistent pressure from the local and international media and Amnesty International to have the charges dropped (*Observer*, 15 March, 28 June 1995). Fa'amatuāinu was charged under the Criminal Act with two charges of speaking seditious words and two charges of publishing seditious libel. To'alepai was charged with two counts of speaking seditious words and one of publishing seditious libel. The charges originated from events leading up to the protest march of 2 March 1994. In court, magistrate Lussick dismissed all seven charges 'when the prosecution failed to produce any evidence' (*ibid.* 30 June 1995). The magistrate's decision contrasted with the police commissioner's earlier remarks, that 'the charges were valid and would not be withdrawn by the police' (*ibid.* 31 March 1995). Following this court decision, the two men planned to sue the government for ST1,000,000 'for the unconstitutional way in which we were both charged for sedition' (*ibid.* 4 August 1995).

Reflecting upon the sedition case, Tupua, leader of the opposition SNDP, in an article in the *Observer* (30 June 1995) said:

> It was an attempt to portray the *Tūmua* and *Pule* movement as a real threat to law and order.

> The objective was to discourage the local council of churches and those who are supporting or sympathetic from a more public demonstration of support for the *Tūmua* and *Pule* movement.

> Additionally it was intended to distract attention from the acute economic problems and corruption raised in the Auditor's report.

The tight government control on TV and radio, combined with the fact that the constituency is relatively uninformed, ensure impact and effectiveness of the message, ie. that the *Tūmua* and *Pule* movement is a threat to law and order.

From a democratic perspective, there were important political gains arising from the *Tūmua* and *Pule* demonstrations and the sedition charges that resulted from them. One of them was noted in the *Sāmoa Observer* editorial of 28 June 1995, the day the sedition charges were heard in court:

> ... this hearing will set a standard by which future court cases of this kind will be judged against.

> It will serve as a powerful indicator to the nation of the amount of freedom we can really expect to have in the future.

In other words, the sedition charges were the ultimate test of the individual rights provisions in the constitution. The *Tūmua* and *Pule* legal victory was particularly significant given that one political party had such a large majority in parliament that its power and political influence appeared to be unlimited. Yet, against such power, and under a political system that co-exists with an indigenous socio-political system emphasizing traditional loyalty, the justice system is now the last resort for examining and, if necessary, curbing that power.[12]

The publicity generated by these developments was another milestone in educating the voting public and creating an awareness among them of the political importance of government policies. While earlier demonstrations (in February 1965 and mid-1981) were started by wage/salary earners – then only a small section of the population, *Tūmua* and *Pule* was a 'national' protest movement, as everyone was affected by the VAGST. However, given that the HRPP was returned to power in the 1996 general election (and the 2001 and 2006 elections) it would seem that the voting public was not able to rise above issues of title, family, village, personality and other traditional affiliations to select their political leaders on the basis of policies directly or indirectly affecting daily lives.[13] Adherence to traditional values does not necessarily guarantee one's livelihood under the modern state and its infrastructure. On the other hand, the fact that HRPP was returned to power in the 1996 general election probably meant that the *Tūmua* and *Pule* protest march did not have the support of the majority of the public.

Right hand drive protest

Cars in Sāmoa drive on the right hand side of the road, which means that car steering wheels are fixed on the left side of cars. The first public statement indicating a change to that system was made in the 2006 campaign platform of the *Sāmoa La'ala'a* political party. The party promised that, if elected to government, it would change the code to enforce driving on the left hand side of the road. The HRPP picked up the idea and, after September 2007, the prime minister repeatedly pronounced that the switch would come into effect on 1 July 2008. Moreover, the prime minister used the highly publicized 28th birthday celebration of the HRPP on 14 December 2007 to announce changes to the government's proposal – these would bring forward the date for the commencement of imports of right hand drive (RHD) vehicles to February 2008 and delay to 1 July 2009 the switch to driving on the left hand side of the road (Ah Mu 2006a:2).

In his speech, the prime minister argued that the main reasons behind the proposal were that:

1. It would allow the importation of cars from New Zealand and Australia, countries to which 99 per cent of Sāmoans travelled
2. It would encourage Sāmoan families in New Zealand and Australia to send cars to Sāmoa, so that local Sāmoan families could enjoy a similar standard of living to that currently enjoyed by lawyers and business people [who, ironically, have been the most vocal, although minority, opposition to RHD]
3. It would be a great help in times of tsunami as a lot more families would have cars and, therefore, be able to escape the tsunami-prone shorelines quickly
4. It would benefit tourists from New Zealand and Australia – because they drive on the left side of the road in their home countries – and stimulate rental car businesses
5. It would benefit the substantial majority of the public because of the expected drop in prices of secondhand cars as more were sent from New Zealand and Australia
6. It would allow for savings in fuel bills as secondhand cars from New Zealand and New Zealand would be less fuel-consuming than cars imported from USA.

To further support his argument, the prime minister pointed out that, in the whole of 2004, there were only 6 traffic accidents involving RHD vehicles in Sāmoa compared with 231 involving LHD vehicles. Furthermore, in eight countries which switched driving sides in the last century, there was noticeable drop in traffic accidents in the first year of introduction of the switch (Kelekolio 2007:1–2).

Following the prime minister's first mention of his government's intention to switch from LHD to RHD, the media was bombarded with objections from the public, and a voluntary organizing committee – People Against Switching Sides (PASS) – was formed to coordinate a public protest movement. PASS decided to organize a public petition to be relayed to parliament in a protest march planned for 17 December 2007.

At 8:30am on 17 December, about 12,000 protesters marched from in front of the government building in Apia to parliament, where PASS coordinator and high profile lawyer Tole'afoa Solomona To'ailoa handed over to the speaker of parliament a public petition containing 33,000 signatures; more were being gathered to be submitted later. As stated in the petition, the main arguments against the shift to RHD were that:

1. There was very little, if any, consultation between the government and stakeholders to determine the implications of such a huge change on all sectors of the community

2. There would be a great safety risk to all road users and pedestrians when the 17,000 existing LHD vehicles started driving on the other side of the road

3. The private sectors estimated that the switch would cost the economy at least ST790 million – the government had yet to release any figures on the cost to the country's economy

4. The business community would suffer greatly given that car-related businesses would close and people would lose their jobs

5. The downturn in business resulting from the shift would mean a loss in VAGST and income tax revenue for the government

6. Existing LHD vehicle owners would lose 50–75 per cent of the value of their vehicles

7. Investor confidence would suffer as the government's decision had been made without any consultation and without proper studies on how the switch would impact on the public

8. The switch would make Sāmoa less attractive to tourists and, consequently, the tourism industry – touted by government as the priority sector – would suffer

9. The institute of professional engineers of Sāmoa had identified the following costs if the policy were to be implemented: ST340 million to convert 17,000 existing cars to RHD; ST175 million to modify, redesign and reconstruct intersections, corners, round-abouts, bus stops, and so forth; ST4.6 million to redesign appropriate infrastructure; ST549 million to complete all the necessary changes in order to meet road design codes; and ST10 million to alter road signage, all lane markings, drainage signs, bill boards and so forth

10. The costs of the change would outweigh any benefits it would bring

11. The 'aesthetic' implications would be of grave concern as LHD vehicles would remain the majority on the roads for many years to come (cited in Ah Mu 2007a).

Present to receive the petition were the prime minister, deputy prime minister, ministers of cabinet and other parliamentarians. The speaker told the protestors that there are parliamentary procedures to follow: The petition would be tabled and a public petitions committee would sit to discuss the petition and make recommendations to parliament. He also told protesters that no legislation has been tabled in parliament to enact a switch in the driving code from the left side of the road to the right. Later in the afternoon, after the protesters had retired and parliament resumed, an independent MP tabled the petition in parliament and it was referred by the speaker to the parliament's public petitions committee for deliberation and recommendation.

Well before the protest march, the media had widely publicized the fact that the HRPP caucus had already discussed the switch issue and had agreed unanimously (with the exception of two members who were absent) to adopt the change. Given the HRPP's overwhelming majority of 37 seats in parliament, it is unlikely that the public petition will change anything, unless the HRPP, in particular the prime minister, has an unexpected change of heart.

The RHD protest march makes an interesting comparison with the *Tūmua ma Pule* protest marches.

The latter involved politicians, and the leaders were chosen from among *Tūmua* and *Pule* traditional orator groups. The leaders of the former were not of the *Tūmua* and *Pule* traditional leadership *per se*, even though

To'ailoa was a *matai*. Furthermore, To'ailoa made explicit appeals to politicians not to be involved in the march in case it might be construed by the government and the public as means of the opposition MPs scoring political points and so weaken the credibility of the protestors' genuine concern with the government's RHD policy. In his speech to hand over the petition, To'ailoa told politicians present that the protestors were not against the prime minister or cabinet or the HRPP, nor was it their intention to overthrow the government; their aim was merely to show their heart-felt concern about the negative impact on people of the RHD policy if it were implemented.

Also, the RHD protest did not have the extreme political sensitivity associated with it that was so acutely felt at several points during the *Tūmua* and *Pule* protest marches. On the other hand, the *Tūmua* and *Pule* protest succeeded in reducing VAGST on some items and eliminating others completely. Time will tell whether the RHD protest will succeed in achieving its main objective.

As the prime minister mentioned in his speech at the HRPP's birthday celebration, the RHD protest march on 17 December 2007 was important in that it signalled to the rest of the world that democracy was alive and well in Sāmoa – although that statement was accompanied by a rather sarcastic remark to the effect that the march would also be important physical exercise for the marchers.

Notes

1   An earlier version of this chapter appeared in So'o (2000) and in Firth (2006).
2   Official figures I obtained from the Legislative Assembly office. Of the 39,941 who voted on this question, 14,383 voted Yes, and 22,299 voted No. 3,329 votes were classified as Informal, or were rejected. They included ballots that were not properly marked.
3   Universal suffrage was introduced in the 1991 general election, thus the great increase in voter population. Before that, only *matai* had the vote.
4   Judgement of Chief Justice Ryan in *Tau'ili'ili Uili (Plaintiff) vs Porotesano Mālifa and Ieti Lima (Defendants), 4 October 1991*. The dates of the hearing were August 27 and 29–30, and September 2–5, 1991.
5   These articles were published in the *Observer* on 27 September 1989, 4 October 1989, 15 December 1989, 25 January 1990 and 13 June 1990.
6   Judgement of Chief Justice Ryan in *VC vs Observer*, 4 October 1991. The underlined phrases are as presented in the written judgement.
7   In the latter stages of the demonstrations, the movement called itself *Tūmua ma*

Pule ma 'Ā'iga (*Tūmua* and *Pule* and '*Aiga* [TPA]). This was the name the WSLP later adopted.

8   These included a vote during the general elections, a vote of no-confidence against the government in parliament, the resignation of the prime minister or his absence from the country without having first consulted the head of state (*Observer*, 1 March 1994).

9   A village on the western outskirts of the national capital Apia.

10   A government-appointed commission of inquiry, which was set up 'to look into allegations in the report to allow those implicated the chance to defend themselves', 'downplayed the report and exonerated most of those implicated in it' (*Observer*, 15 July 1994, 13 January 1995). Substantial sections of the chief auditor's report had been published in the *Observer* (15, 22 July 1994).

11   The president of *Tūmua* and *Pule*, Fa'amatuāinu, said that 'even babies and children who can not read or write were included in the petition as their parents can sign for them as they are the ones taking care of them and feed them' (*Sāmoan Bulletin*, 22 September 1995).

12   The author would argue that the events that led eventually to the *VC vs Observer* defamation case mentioned above had been indirectly, if not directly, affected by political developments of the time. The defaming articles against the VC had been a reaction (by those who were directly and indirectly affected by the manner in which the VC had administered the National University of Sāmoa) to the VC, who had been unnecessarily victimized in a political tussle between the outgoing coalition government and the incoming HRPP government. The new professor of Sāmoan language and culture (whose job was terminated by the VC in late 1989, but later reinstated following a court injunction) and the minister of education (who was also the chancellor of the university and the chairman of its council, and under whose chairmanship the appointment was made in 1988) were two of the 12 HRPP MPs who defected and formed the coalition government 1985. The coalition lost the general elections in 1988. The VC's original appointment was made in 1984, at the time the coalition government's outgoing minister of education was holding the same portfolio in the HRPP government. He was therefore directly responsible for the VC's original appointment.

13   The official results of the 1996 general election were HRPP 24 seats, SNDP 11 seats, SLP 1, and Independents 13. The results indicated a number of points. First, the leader of the SLP, To'alepai Toesulusulu Si'ueva – who defeated the speaker – registered his party as the Sāmoa Labour Party, not as *Tūmua* and *Pule* and '*Āiga* political party as discussed in the section on political parties. Second, candidates in other parties registered themselves as independents. Third, the two main parties in 1996 were still the HRPP and SNDP. Fourth, HRPP still has substantive support among the public. Fifth, it is reasonable to conclude that voters value other considerations in the selection of their MPs above their traditional affiliation to *Tūmua* and *Pule*. Or perhaps *Tūmua* and *Pule* are powerless when it comes to election of leaders under the current political set-up because their traditional influence has already been substantially, and adversely, affected

by the concept of parliamentary constituencies. In the 1996 prime ministerial election, Tofilau polled 34 votes to Tupua's 14. Parliament, following the 1990 constitutional amendment which increased by two the number of parliamentary seats, now has 49 seats. Clearly, most of the independents ended up supporting the HRPP.

9 | The current status

THE IMPACT OF CUSTOMS and traditions on democracy, and vice versa, in the period following Sāmoa's independence has been both negative and positive. This two-way impact has been examined in relation to cultural themes that were passionately discussed in the 1960 constitutional convention – themes including village government, district representation, *fono* (parliament) and suffrage, political parties and the head of state. To gauge the extent of democracy in Samoa, to date, these cultural themes have been analyzed against the democratic yardsticks of competition, participation and civil and political rights.

Village governments

Village governments (or councils) have almost unlimited power in their sphere. Backed up by the threat of punishment, this power has been used by several villages to decide which parliamentary candidates villagers (first matai and more recently all adults) were to support. A village's decision to support one candidate prevents other eligible village people from standing and prevents voters from casting their ballots in favour of other candidates they may individually prefer. Village decisions on which candidate to support have been partly influenced by the traditional value of maintaining *matai* rank within villages and constituencies. The same traditional attitude influenced the 1954 and 1960 decisions that only *matai* be given the rights to vote and to stand in parliamentary elections. Customary procedures used by councils of *matai* in arriving at collective decisions give certain *matai* greater influence in village affairs. This means that, in a substantial majority of cases where candidates are either elected unopposed or elected through bloc-voting, the elected candidates have been determined by only a few *matai*, if not by a single *matai*.

The gradual disappearance of the practice of unopposed election, the operation of the party system and the introduction of universal suffrage have seriously affected village governments' traditional grip on power. Generally, village governments can no longer guarantee the election to parliament of their high-ranking titleholders, or of any candidate they (as a collective authority) prefer. Instead, any matai, regardless of rank, who is capable of influencing voters can win at election time.

In some cases, where village councils have meted out punishments, the victims have filed complaints with the Land and Titles Court – the decisions of which have almost always come down in favour of the complainants. Conversely, village councils that have lodged complaints with the Land and Titles Court against the undermining of their authorities by villagers have not been successful. In either scenario the authority of village councils have been both deterred and marginalized.

Fono (parliament)

Parliament has become an entrenched and respected institution of democracy, despite doubts sometimes cast over its legitimacy and ability to deal with sensitive national issues that had traditionally been the sphere of *Tūmua* and *Pule*. Doubts raised in the 1960 constitutional convention about the legitimacy of appointing future heads of state without the blessing of *Tūmua* and *Pule* were dispelled in 2007, when the new head of state, Tui Ātua Tupua Tamasese 'Efi, was unanimously appointed by parliament for a five-year term. It followed the passing away of the remaining joint head of state, the late Mālietoa Tanumāfili II. Since independence, *Tūmua* and *Pule* have not agitated for a specific place in the state structure. *Tūmua* and *Pule* is right on at least one count, however; as they argued in the 1960 constitutional convention, if they were not part of the state and not involved in the appointment of future heads of state, their traditional influence and respect would be marginalized.

Although the constitution does not explicitly stipulate that only *tama-a-'āiga* can be appointed head of state – instead stipulating that anyone eligible to contest parliamentary elections can hold that office – it is unlikely in the near future that a non-*tama-a-'āiga* titleholder will be appointed to that position. While this remains an acceptable preference, democratic competition for that office will be restricted. Nonetheless, given current Sāmoan feeling, this is a realistic and practical compromise in this metaphorical marriage between custom and tradition, and democracy.

The office of council of deputies was specifically created to accommodate the other three *tama-a-'āiga*, should one of the four *tama-a-'āiga* be appointed head of state. Since 1993, three non-*tama-a-'āiga* titleholders have been appointed to the council of deputies – begging the question of whether or not this office has rendered itself redundant. However, whilst the appointment of non-*tama-a-'āiga* to the council of deputies may still be culturally sensitive, it is in line with the democratic ideal of un-restricted competition for all offices of state. In contrast, candidacy for parliamentary elections in territorial constituencies remains restricted to *matai*, and it is unlikely that this will change for a long time to come. Sāmoans are comfortable and happy with this compromise between custom and tradition, and democracy.

Political participation, in terms of being electors in general elections, gradually increased in the 30 years after independence with the proliferation of *matai* titles (*matai pālota*) – a move intended primarily to improve candidates' chances of winning parliamentary seats. A much-increased level of political participation followed the 1991 introduction of universal suffrage, by which every citizen aged 21 years and over was given the right to vote. While universal suffrage has been hailed by the outside world and some Sāmoans as a sign of a maturing democracy, it has been seen by conservatives as contributing to the breakdown of village order and the general erosion of traditional values.

The widening of the franchise following the adoption of universal suffrage, the operation of the political party system, and the discouragement and prevention by law of village councils influencing the choice of parliamentary candidates have contributed to the election to parliament of all categories of *matai* regardless of title rank and status in their respective villages and constituencies, and thereby increased the competition for parliamentary seats.

However, parliamentary candidates' campaign strategies and methods of election have been (and still are) a challenge in terms of modern democracy. It is still far away from a time when voters vote on the basis of party policies and issues only. Furthermore, given the persistence of the traditional mentality of cultural reciprocity, campaigns still require candidates to go through village councils – whose support is 'reciprocated' by the giving of gifts by the candidates – despite electoral provisions against bribery and treating. Conversely, most of the enfranchised 21 year-olds and over, have taken advantage of their voting rights to befriend candidates and sometimes demand gifts and other material rewards in return for their votes.

Impersonation at general elections has also been a challenge. To minimize the chance of voters casting votes for the deceased, whose names could be still on the electoral roll, or for voters who may be overseas at the time of the election, ballot identification cards (IDs) were introduced for the 2001 general election. However, when several candidates attempted to retain loyalty by holding on to the ID cards of their prospective voters, only returning them on polling day, a new system of voter identification was introduced. Implemented for the 2006 general election, it involved photographs of voters along with other details, including their finger prints, being included in the electoral rolls. But the new system has not prevented double voting, and the office of the electoral commission is already looking at ways of strengthening this new system. The commission of inquiry into the electoral system that was established after the 2006 general election recommended heavier penalties against breach of that provision of the electoral act. The establishment of the office of the electoral commission to handle all issues associated with elections, following a recommendation of the Commission of Inquiry into the Electoral Act 1963 and its amendments, that was set up after the 2001 general election, has greatly improved all aspects of the electoral process.

The freedom of members of parliament to contest all parliamentary positions was restricted in the first 14 years following independence because of members' traditional deference to a *tama-a-'āiga* as prime minister. However, once *tama-a-'āiga* Matā'afa Fiamē Mulinu'ū II and Tupua Tamasese Lealofi IV were no longer in parliament, seeds were planted for the emergence of the political party system.

Political parties

The fact that it took 17 years after independence for the first political party to be established was due partly to the conservative nature of Sāmoan society at the time – as reflected in parliament's deference to *tama-a-'āiga* as prime ministers – and partly due to the public perception of political parties as potentially divisive agents of society. Nonetheless, now that political parties have become legal and legitimate institutions of state, with visibly functional roles in the affairs of parliament, they are here to stay.

Political parties have contributed positively to effective governing for the development of the country. For example, the first parliament after independence managed to pass only 59 per cent of bills it tabled in parliament and for which divisions were called, whereas, following the establishment of political parties, governments have passed every bill tabled in parliament.

On the other hand, speaking in one voice has also enabled the HRPP to pass controversial pieces of legislations – such as those to enact universal suffrage, introduce parliamentary under-secretaries, associate ministers and special posts, and put under a three-year contract the supposedly lifetime post of controller and chief auditor. A disadvantage of the party system is that, when the party in government obtains too much power and has been in power for a long time, parliamentary opposition is rendered meaningless. The continuing electoral success of the HRPP since the 1980s, and its ability to obtain huge majorities has made it extremely difficult for parliament to challenge, let alone check, its power. This is a major challenge in Sāmoa's party system, and its governing system generally.

Although the relatively smooth transition from consensus politics to political parties can be hailed a democratic success, it has not been without cultural casualties. Sāmoa being a family-oriented society, political parties have divided members of close and extended families, villages, districts as well as members of traditional lineages and allegiances. While the party system has provided political opportunities to contest parliamentary seats and party leadership positions, political parties have also marginalized cultural considerations of rank and traditional recognition. But not all is bleak; holders of some ranking titles have successfully perpetuated their traditional status and rank through political parties and through being members of parliament.

Three points can be made about the divisiveness associated with the establishment of political parties and the operation of the party system. First, villages and families (nuclear, extended and traditional), divided because of political party affiliations and other influences, have, over time, reconciled their differences and restored amicable relations. Secondly, such divisiveness has been a feature of Sāmoan society in the past, such as during the Mau movement (1920s–1930s) and during the prolonged political struggles throughout the nineteenth century. In the pre-colonial and early colonial period up to 1900, political competition led to warfare – although, as with divisions brought about by party affiliations, amicable relations among the people involved were later restored. Thirdly, the idea of political parties as a divisive factor in society was a common concern in democratic nations until political parties gained legitimacy. What was required was management of the divisiveness associated with political parties in order to attain positive democratic ends – such as participation in debates and the putting forward of different points of view – and to disseminate new knowledge and values upon which final decisions could be based. Just as Sāmoans have been able to reconcile their differences in the past, they have also been able to following the adoption of the party system. This is a positive step towards accepting political parties as legitimate democratic institutions, the establishment of which is an inevitable part of the development of representative democracy.

In the mixing process, despite tradition and democracy trying to accommodate each other, custom and tradition have been relegated to the periphery – although some aspects of custom and tradition still stand in the way of a fully-fledged and an unhindered democracy flourishing in Sāmoa. However, custom and tradition have not been extinguished. Not at all. They are there and will continue to be practiced as a way of life in the foreseeable future.

Undoubtedly, the relegation to second fiddle of custom and tradition has been a tough experience, but Samoans are slowly realizing that it is the new reality, that democracy and custom and tradition do not always operate in the same sphere, and that there has to be a give and take if the two systems are to continue to co-exist until such time as the two have totally merged into one – a merger that is still quite some time away.

The campaign strategies used by politicians to obtain public support in their electorates, and among MPs in order to win government and parliamentary positions, have provided strong evidence of the mixing of tradition and democracy. Democratic institutions have been used to maintain and/or advance the traditional status, rank, prestige, influence and recognition of *matai* titles held by certain politicians, such as leaders of political parties. Conversely, as leaders of political parties, these *matai* have used the traditional influence, rank, recognition, etc. associated with the titles they hold in order to obtain public support. In this sense, both democratic and traditional indigenous institutions have been used indiscriminately by politicians to attain their goals, be they in 'traditional' or introduced, constitutional spheres.

Public concern about the divisiveness of democratic institutions such as political parties, universal suffrage, elections and the general confrontational nature of the Westminster parliamentary system has not necessarily been shared by politicians. The attainment by politicians of their political goals has been paramount and one sphere has ultimately reinforced the other.

Although the mixing of traditional and democratic procedures, practices and values by politicians and their supporters, for political purposes, is generally perceived by the public as degrading, it nevertheless reflects the present status of politics in Sāmoa, and suggests what to expect in the near future. Viewed in historical perspective, Sāmoa has progressed from the establishment and development of its indigenous institutions before European contact, through the adaptation of those institutions to introduced European political ideas throughout the nineteenth and early twentieth centuries, to further adaptation in terms of a legal democratic framework in 1960 and 1962, with the enactment of the independence constitution. Despite the heavy emphasis on tradition in all historical phases, Sāmoans have been able to adapt to changes associated with each phase. The mixing of tradition and democracy is another phase in the process of continuous social and political change, as old political practices and values which no longer fit current circumstances are discarded for new ones that are more relevant and appropriate.

Thus, a famous Sāmoan saying: *O le fuata ma lona lou* (There is a new picking stick for every breadfruit season).

Appendix 1

Chronological calculations

GENERALLY, THIS BOOK uses a two-part technique to calculate approximately when past events occurred. The first part involves calculating the number of years per generation. The second, explained later, involves constructing a genealogy, or sets of genealogies.

The number of years per generation is calculated on the basis of the number of generations and titleholders from known people in the past until their descendants who are alive today (2008). The dates (year) at which these known people in the past died are then subtracted from the present year (2008) to give an estimate of the number of years between then and now. The number of generations or holders of particular titles is then used to divide the number of years between the known people of the past and their presently surviving descendants. This gives a rough estimate of the number of years in one generation. Several such results are then averaged out to give the number of years per generation that is used in this book.

This number is then used to calculate the estimated time period at which events occurred in the history of Sāmoa, and when certain personalities lived. This second part of the process requires having sets of genealogies (called Gx). For example, if in genealogy Y, person Z lived five generations ago, then the number five is multiplied by the number of years per generation (x) to give the estimated time in the past at which person Z lived. In this example, person Z lived in year 2008 − 5x. The more common method of estimating the time at which events happened in the past or when people lived is to state the number of generations. That method could have been used here. However, because periods are often referred to, dates rather than a number of generations are used. It is emphasized that the dates used in this study are estimates.

Three procedures have been used to construct Gx. The first involves making use of available sets of genealogies. Some such genealogies include the generally accepted sets of genealogies of a number of Sāmoan families. Among these families are those associated with the nationally recognized titles, such as Mālietoa, Tui Ā'ana, Tui Ātua, Tonumaipea, Tagaloa, Lilomaiava, 'Āiga Sa Tunumafono, 'Āiga Tau Ā'ana, 'Āiga Sa Tuala, 'Āiga Sa Amituana'i, 'Āiga Sa Pesetā, 'Āiga Taulagi and 'Āiga Sa Levālasi. The second procedure makes use of oral traditions. Some oral traditions associate names of certain personalities with certain events that took place in the past. This information allows for adjustments to be made to some of these 'generally accepted sets of genealogies', by matching some of the personalities in them to certain past events that are either explicitly stated, or alluded to, in oral traditions. The third procedure involves placing alongside Gx the generally accepted genealogies of the holders of the Tui Tonga, Tui Ha'atakalaua and Tui Kanokupolu titles of Tonga; this further comparison gives a more reliable estimate of the time periods in Sāmoa's history.

Oral traditions used in this study have been obtained from various sources. A number of oral traditions used are those recorded by various Sāmoans and non-Sāmoan commentators on Sāmoan affairs (see references). Other oral traditions were obtained from the records of the Land and Titles Court of Sāmoa during fieldwork from June to December 1993. Other oral traditions were obtained through formal interviews and informal conversations with Sāmoans, mainly *matai*, during fieldwork, and during the time I have lived in Sāmoa.

The table on page 207 summarizes how the number of years per generation is calculated. Section A shows those who held the titles, while Section B shows the number of generations from known past individuals to their descendants who are alive today (2008).

A.	From past titleholders	To present titleholders	No. of holders	Years/generation
1.	Mālietoa Vaiinupō (d. 1841)	Mālietoa Tanumāfili II	6	2007–1841 = 166; 166/6 = 28
2.	Tamasese Titimaea (d. 1891)	Tamasese 'Efi	3	2008–1891 = 117; 117/3 = 39
3.	Tuimaleali'ifano Sualauvi (d. 1870)	Tuimaleali'ifano Va'alēto'a	4	2008–1870 = 138; 138/4 = 34
4.	Matā'afa Fagamanu (d. 1863)	Matā'afa Pu'elā Pātū (d. 1996)	5	1996–1863 = 133; 133/5 = 27

B.	From past generations	Introduction	No. of generations	Years/generation
1.	Vaiinupō	Present	6	2008–1841 = 167; 167/6 = 28
2.	Tamasese Titimaea	Present	3	2008–1891 = 117; 117/3 = 39
3.	Sualauvi	Present	5	2008–1870 = 138; 138/5 = 28
4.	Fagamanu	Present	5	2008–1863 = 145; 145/5 = 29
5.	Talavou (d. 1880)	Present	5	2008–1880 = 128; 128/5 = 26
Total years per generation for nine sets of generations				278/9 = 31
Average number of years per generation				31*

* The number of years per generation often used in the calculation of past dates is either 25 or 30; however, to be conservative 25 is used.

Appendix 2

Ao (paramount titles) of Savai'i and the settlements that confer them

Ao title	Founders	Time of establishment of settlement[1]	Population[2] (1991 census)
Le Tagaloa[3]	Funefe'ai (1190s)	Sāfune-i-taoa[4]	
		Faletagaloa	439
		Matāvai	209
		Fatuvalu	234
		Vaisala	604
		'Auala	630
		Vai'afai	672
		Sili	1,076
		Population sub-total	3,864
		% of national population	2.4
Tonumaipe'a	Leutogitupa'itea (1390s)	Ālataua-i-Sisifo	
		Neiafu	1,092
		Tufutāfoe	468
		Falelima	532
		Sātupa'itea	1,795
		Population sub-total	3,887
		% of national population	2.4

Ao title	Founders	Time of establishment of set-tlement[1]	Population[2] (1991 census)
Lilomaiava	Tiumalumatua (1620s)	Sagafili[5]	1,579
		Sāfotu	1,423
		Palauli	
		Vailoa	851
		Vaito'omuli	769
		Fā'ala	929
		Population sub-total	5,551
		% of national population	3.4
		Population of villages of above three titles	13,302
		% of national population	8.3

Sources: ALC 11 and LC 3606 (1936, 1971); Kramer 1994; LC 52 (1904), 1969); LC 1515 (1956); Lealai'auloto and Fuataga 1985; 1991 Census Population and Housing, May 1993.

Notes

1   These can be either villages or a number of villages grouped together. The main reason for this is that some of the villages over the years have expanded and formed new settlements that have attained their own status as semi-autonomous villages. On matters to do with the *Ao* title, however, they all claim equal rights to it, as they are all descendants of the people who were involved in its establishment. As new village are formed from the original villages, members comprising them confer new titles. These new titles can include names of people who lived in the past, as remembered in the genealogies of the respective families comprising a village. In some Sāfune villages the title Tagaloa has been bestowed. This title, however, is not the same as the *Ao* title. The difference is that when conferring the *Ao* title, all the four main centres of the Le Tagaloa title are involved. In the former case, only people in that particular village are involved. In other words, the rituals performed in the conferring of the two titles and the people involved, have to be consulted before they are bestowed, distinguishing the status and rank of the two Tagaloa titles. See also footnote 3 below.

2   This gives some idea of the number of people involved in the conferral of these titles. It should be remembered that these figures do not include those in other parts of Sāmoa during the census, and those residing overseas. Neither does

it include *matai* and their descendants living in other parts of the country but whose titles are traced to the founders of these titles. For example, in a Land and Titles Court case on the Tonumaipe'a title held in 1904 (*LC* 52), representatives from three different villages and two different subdistricts on Upolu island were present because of their genealogical connections. All these people, excluding those residing on Savai'i island, were claiming their rights either to be consulted before the title could be bestowed or as descendants of the title who, therefore, had the right to succeed to it.

3   The prefix 'Le' distinguishes the holder of the *Ao* title from others who may also be holding a title bearing the same name. Each of the settlements which confer this *Ao* have over the years conferred the Tagaloa title upon some of their members. These titleholders, however, are not to be confused with the holder of the *Ao* title, the reason being that, in the conferral of the *Ao* title, all the settlements have to consent to it and are involved in its conferral. Holders of the Tagaloa title, however, in contrast to the holder of Le Tagaloa title, are conferred by certain families in a number of villages. As such they can be more appropriately referred to as local titles.

4   The eight *tafa'i* of the Le Tagaloa title and the villages where they live today are:

(i) Sāfuneitaoa	(iii) Vai'afai
1. Tagaloa	5. Sa'e
2. Tūgaga	6. Fataloto
(ii) Vaisala	(iv) Sili
3. Gale	7. Matā'afā
4. Tuiāsau	8. Taliva'a

5   This is a village on the north western end of Upolu island. It was a marriage of the founder of the title to a woman from this village that made this village one of the three villages that confer this title. It was marriages of the descendants of the founder of the title to women from the other two settlements that established them as important centres of the title, which thereafter acquired the traditional rights in the conferral of this *Ao* title. The last two settlements are on Savai'i island.

Appendix 3

'Āiga of *pāpā*: The traditional *'Āiga* of the Tui Ā'ana and
Tui Ātua titles established before European contact, and
the settlements their descendants founded over the years

'Āiga[1]	Founder and time established	Upolu settlements	Savai'i settlements	Population[2] (1991 Census)
Sa Levālasi	Levālasi (1490s)	Apia		549
		Lotofaga		1,784
		Lona		263
		Tanugāmanono		605
			Iva	2,302
			Sub-total Population	5,5033[3]
			% of national population	3.4
Sa Tuala	Tuala Tama-a-le-lagi (1520s)	Lefaga subdistrict		
		-Sāfa'atoa		615
		-Tafagamanu		328
		-Sāvaia		440
		- Gagaifo		563
		- Matāutu		723
		Fasito'outa		1,825
		Nofoāli'i		1,573
		Sātapuala		1,166
		Falese'elā		990
		Faleāsi'u		2,833
			Amoa West	
			- Lano	737
			- Pu'apu'a	557
			- Asaga	230
			Sub-total Population	12,580
			% of national population	7.8

Äiga[1]	Founder and time established	Upolu settle-ments	Savai'i settlements	Population[2] (1991 Census)
Taulagi	Va'afusu'aga (1620s)	Fasito'otai		
		Falese'ela[4]		990
			Faga	1,277
			Sa'asa'ai	622
			Saipipi	613
			Sub-total population	3,502
			% of national population	2.2
Sa Tunumafono	Tunumafono (1620s)	Sā'anapu		1,169
		Sātaoa		1,033
		Lotofagā		655
		Nu'usuatia		389
		Vaie'e		535
		Fusi		546
		Fausaga		387
		Tafitoala		309
		Mulivai		422
			Sub-total population	5,445
			% of national population	3.4
Sa Fenunu'ivao	Tupua Fuiāvailili (1720s)	Falefā		1,390
		Salani		493
			Sub-total Population	1,883
			% of national population	1.2
			Total popu-lation	28,913
			% of national population	17.9

Sources: 1991 Census Population and Housing, May 1993; Kramer 1994; Leala'i'auloto and Fuataga 1985: Anon n.d.

Notes

1 '*Āiga* in this context comprise all those who descended from, or are genealogically connected to the founders of the '*āiga*. Sa Levālasi is a slight variation because its members did not directly descend from Levālasi. Instead they are people who descended from the maternal relatives of Levālasi's husband, Muagututi'a. Later on, however, these people intermarried with the Tonumaipe'a, Tui Ā'ana and Tui Ātua lines, among other important '*āiga*, thereby establishing genealogical connections with that of the family founder. These '*āiga* are among those which are sometimes referred to in the literature on Sāmoa as 'royal families', or '*āigā tupu*.

2 This gives a rough idea of the number of people belonging to these '*āiga*.

3 This is only a rough estimate as many people who descended from this family are scattered throughout other villages, but still identify with and join this family in matters associated with it, such as the conferring of the Tui Ātua title.

4 Falese'elā belongs to both Sa Tuala and Taulagi.

Appendix 4

Other important *'Āiga* that were established before European contact

'Āiga	Founder and time established	Upolu settlements	Savai'i settlements	Population (1991 Census)
Sa Moelēoi	Moelēoi (1490s)		Āsau	1,430
			Neiafu	992
			Falelima	532
			Tufutāfoe	468
			Sātupa'itea	1,795
			Sagone	786
			Vaipu'a	451
			Population	6,454
			% of national population	4.0
Sa Pesetā	Pesetā (1520s)		Matāutu	1,446
			Sāto'alepai	244
			Sāle'aula	1,006
			Sāmauga	1,362
			Population	4,058
			% of national population	2.5
Sa 'Amituana'i	'Amituana'i (1590s)	Solosolo		1,338
		Lalomanu		773
		Apia		4,694
		Vailele		1,077
		Sāle'imoa		2,669
			Vai'afai	672
			Sāfune-i-taoa	
			-Matāvai	209
			-Faletagaloa	439
			-Fatuvalu	234
			Vaisala	630
			'Auala	604

Āiga	Founder and time established	Upolu settlements	Savai'i settlements	Population (1991 Census)
			Faleālupo	1,043
			Sāmata	1,198
			Sili	1,076
			Population	16,926
			% of national population	10.5
Sa Tago	Tago (1620s)	'A'ufaga		581
		Sāmusu		550
		Āmaile		273
			Population	1,404
			% of national population	0.9

Sources: *1991 Census Population and Housing*; Leala'i'auloto and Fuataga 1985; Anon.

Appendix 5

The concept of *tūmua* in traditional politics

AN UNDERSTANDING OF the traditional concepts *matai, tulafale* and *ali'i* is helpful in ascertaining the origin and political significance of the *tūmua* concept. *Matai* is a Sāmoan title or a person who holds a title. It is not certain when the concept *matai* originated (Liuā'ana 1991:30). However, one oral tradition attributes the first Sāmoan *matai* to a son of Tagaloa-a-lagi, who also held that name. Tagaloa-a-lagi (Tagaloa-of-heaven) was one of the gods who was venerated by the Sāmoans at the time of European contact. According to this oral tradition, a war was fought between two groups of Tagaloa-a-lagi supporters (implying also descendants). The two sons of Tagaloa-a-lagi led the two rival groups. The victorious son became the first ever *matai* of Sāmoa. After the war, the two opposition groups reconciled their differences and accepted the victorious son as their *matai* (Ma'ilo 1972:10). Therefore, the *matai* concept implies rivalries between two groups for supremacy, an after-war reconciliation between the rival groups, and perpetuation of the *matai* as a title and as an institution.

It has been suggested that the word *matai* is a contraction of the words mata-i-ai, which have the connotations of being set apart or consecrated (Meleiseā 1987b:7). This conception of *matai* fits well with the oral tradition already mentioned. The son of Tagaloa-a-lagi who won the struggle for supremacy established the concept of *matai* and was therefore the first one to hold a *matai* title. Following a reconciliation between the rival leaders and their respective supporters, the *matai* (or holder of their god's name symbolizing victory) was venerated, and people associated with him were expected to respect him, thus being set apart or consecrated.

There are two categories of *matai*: the *tulafale* and *ali'i*. The concept of *tulafale* is closely related to the *tūmua* concept. The word *tulafale* can have two meanings; it is a contraction of the phrase tūlaga-o-le-fale (literally, 'a place on which a house stands') (Pratt 1862:350; Stair 1895:616); also it can mean *tula-o-le-fale* (the 'top beam of the house') (Liuā'ana 1993:8). These two meanings imply the political significance of *tulafale*. Without the 'foundation' a house cannot stand. Stated differently, without a foundation, there cannot be a house. Likewise, without the 'top beam', a house cannot have a roof. Without a roof, a house (as a place under which people get shelter, protection and comfort) is without a function, and ceases therefore to be called a house. Thus, as 'foundation' and 'top beam' of a house, *tulafale* play(s) a dynamic role in Sāmoan politics' (Liuā'ana 1993:183).

The semantic explanation of *tulafale* fits well with the following oral tradition which alludes to the origin of the first ever *tulafale* in Sāmoa. The story relates that two boys went to 'Atafu (an island in Fiji [Geraghty 1991]) and waged war there, attempting to regain the *fale'ula* (Sāmoan house built of breadfruit wood). While the war was still being waged the boys brought back the *fale'ula* to Sāmoa. Because they carried the house on their backs, they were thus referred to as *tūlaga-o-le-fale* (place on which the house stood), and were therefore the first ever *tulafale* of Sāmoa (Ma'ilo 1972:22). *Fale'ula* in a number of oral traditions symbolizes authority. In having brought the *fale'ula* from 'Atafu island, the boys earned their right to authority.

Tūmua is a contraction of the phrase *tu-muamua* (literally, he/she/those 'who landed first'). It thus implies not only that someone, or some people, landed first, but that others arrived later. The word *tūmua* describes groups of *matai* who are all *tulafale*. Therefore, as a *matai*, a *tulafale* (like the *ali'i*) is someone who is set apart or consecrated, and as a *tulafale*, this category of *matai* symbolizes the foundation and top beam of a house. Given that the *fale'ula* (house) is the symbol of authority, then the *tulafale* plays a very important role in that authority. In fact, without the *tulafale*, that authority is incomplete (*ali'i* being the other part of that authority), and indeed would never have been acquired in the first place.

Note

1. 'Atafu is the Sāmoan term for the island in Fiji called Kadavu (Geraghty 1991).

Appendix 6

The political relationship between Ā'ana district and Leulumoega capital village

AN EXPLANATION OF THE role of Leulumoega vis-a-vis Ā'ana district is necessary because, first, it illustrates the political relationship among *tulafale* comprising a capital village, and, second, it not only compares the customs associated with a district meeting in Ā'ana to those of Tuamāsaga, but also explains the traditions that established the customs. All issues with which Leulumoega is involved, such as the conferring of the Tui Ā'ana title, are discussed collectively by the nine *tulafale* comprising it. However, there is one slight exception, which is related to the political status of one of their number. In the war in the 1640s, 'Alipia sided with the combined forces of Va'afusu'aga and Samalā'ulu, whose side was defeated. In reward for siding with them, Samalā'ulu designated 'Alipia the 'head' of the *faleiva* (Kramer 1994:267), a designation that was later recognised by Fonotī and his supporters when the war was over (Tupua 1995:6). In other words, 'Alipia earned this *tōfiga* (appointment) from Samalae'ulu. The *tōfiga* stipulates the rights and privileges associated with a title, which will be inherited by the descendants of the title, or more precisely, by the successive holders of the title. Privileges, rights, etc. associated with certain titles, because of certain traditions established in the past, are inherited by the descendants of the title. Thus, most titles, villages, subdistricts and even districts have certain privileges and rights associated with them vis-à-vis other titleholders, villages, etc., which had been established from certain past traditions. The holders of the titles associated with these traditions inherit these privileges, rights, etc. *Tōfiga* (appointment, or designation) is the noun derived from the verb *tofi* (to appoint, to designate). 'Alipia's *tōfiga* has been respected to this day, not only throughout Sāmoa but among the *tulafale* of Leulumoega. The political implications of 'Alipia's *tōfiga* are twofold. First, on all occasions in which Leulumoega is involved, it is 'Alipia that the public expect to speak on behalf of Leulumoega. Second, within Leulumoega, it is 'Alipia that takes the leading role, although the consultative process and collective authority inherent in the nature of village governments keeps in check any tyrannical or totalitarian inclinations of 'Alipia.

When a meeting is held at Ma'auga, the meeting place of Ā'ana district in Leulumoega village, the opening speeches are given in a strictly observed order. The first speech is given by Leulumoega, followed by a representative of the two villages Fasito'outa and Fasito'otai. A representative of Lefaga subdistrict gives the final speech. Only after these speeches is the floor opened to the traditionally established speakers in this 'parliament'. Leulumoega gives the first speech because, among other reasons, it is the capital village of Ā'ana. 'Ape and Tutuila, two of the founding *matai* of Fasito'outa and Fasito'otai respectively, were responsible for bringing Salamāsina's father, Tama-a-le-lagi, from Sāfata to Leulumoega in the 1490s to be their *ali'i*. This tradition established the right of Fasito'outa and Fasito'otai villages, also referred to as *uso* (brothers, because of 'Ape and Tutuila's collective role already mentioned), to give the second speech in the meeting. While Salamāsina (1520s) was holding the Tui Ā'ana *pāpā*, she designated two of the founding members of Lefaga subdistrict to be its leading *tulafale*. In recognition of this designation, Lefaga has since been given the third opening speech in the district meeting. The designations of the two *tulafale* have been respected to this day.

Appendix 7

Party affiliation, universal suffrage and traditional support: a case study

THE COMBINED EFFECTS OF party affiliation and universal suffrage have been received by Sāmoans with mixed feelings, though feelings tend more towards the pessimistic end of the spectrum. An example of their 'moderating effect' on customs and traditions is illustrated by the election for the Lefaga and Faleāse'ela constituency in 1991. Although four candidates contested the seat, there were only two contenders with a chance of winning. The winner, Le Māmea Rōpati (the SNDP candidate), and the first runner up, Taulā Ierome (the HRPP candidate), polled 772 and 624 votes respectively.

The constituency comprises six villages. Most significant in this election, however, were the villages of Sāfa'ato'a and Matāutu. Sāfa'ato'a village comprises the main orator group, Tuisāvailu'u, in Lefaga sub-district.[1] Holders of the Le Māmea title reside in Matāutu. An event in the 1670s led to the orators of Sāfa'ato'a asking for the help of the brothers whose original names were Lemalu and Le Māmea. Not only had Lemalu and Le Māmea come to the aid of Lefaga subdistrict (whose spokespeople were the orator group comprising Sāfa'ato'a's village council), but they had also since stayed at Matāutu and become the founders of that village. Thereafter, it has been one of Sāfa'ato'a village's traditional responsibilities to care for Le Māmea, and Lemalu and Matāutu village generally – including upholding their dignity, prestige and socio-political status. In modern terms, this means ensuring that any holder of either title wins the constituency's seat. Thus, in the 1991 election, the substantial majority of Sāfa'ato'a voters voted for Le Māmea Rōpati. The minority of Sāfa'ato'a who voted for Taulā Ierome were those who not only supported the HRPP but had also been greatly influenced by a high-ranking Sāfa'ato'a *matai*. This *matai* got a job at one of the government departments in Apia because of his strong support for the HRPP. Understandably, he put all his effort into winning some of the Sāfa'ato'a votes to the HRPP candidate, even though the latter has a relatively low status in his own village and the subdistrict. From

Sāfa'atoa's point of view, their compatriot who 'defied' the village tradition and election instructions was a traitor of the first order. Luckily for them, however, the election result was reversed in Le Māmea's favour following the counting of special votes several days after the election night announcement of the provisional results. The 'traitor' was expelled from his village's council of *matai*.

A more serious threat to customs and traditions, however, was Tui Ātua Tupua Tamasese 'Efi's defeat by a relatively low-ranking *matai* of the same village in the 1991 general election.[2] Among the major political factors acting against Tupua Tamasese 'Efi were the affiliation of voters in his constituency with the two main political parties, HRPP and SNDP, and the addition of new voters following the introduction of universal suffrage. Two of the main villages comprising the constituency are Falefā and Lufilufi. Falefā is the village where members of Sa Fenunu'ivao live, while Lufilufi is the capital village of Ātua district, whose six high-ranking *tulafale* comprise the orator group which confers the Tui Ātua title. Among the *matai* comprising the traditional Sa Fenunu'ivao (whose *tama-a-'āiga* is Tupua) is Moe'ono.[3] One of the two holders of this title at the time was a senior member of the police force. Moe'ono has told the present author that he was among those responsible for trying to get the voters in his village to vote for Tupua. He had to do this, in accordance with the traditional status and relationship of his title and village to the Tupua title, he said. His job was not made any easier when his own brother, who had just arrived from New Zealand to participate in the election campaign, put all his energy into supporting Tupua's rival. Worse still, one of his own sons sided with his brother from New Zealand. Following the announcement of the results, which saw Tupua lost his seat, Falefā was split between the supporters of Tupua and his rival, Moananu.

A younger son of Moe'ono had stood by his father. On his way home from school by bus, this son fought with other members of his village who supported Moananu. The brawl had worsened by the time the bus arrived at Falefā. Some of Tupua's supporters started throwing stones at the house of one of Moananu's main supporters. The latter came out of his house with a gun and started shooting at the stone throwers, and one of them was seriously injured. As one of the senior *matai* of Falefā, Moe'ono summoned a village emergency meeting, in which he urged everyone to lay down their 'weapons' and keep the peace. Everyone obeyed. Moe'ono was frustrated, not just because Tupua had lost (a situation to which his brother and one of his sons had contributed) but because, as one of the senior *matai* of Falefā, he had to maintain law and order in the village. He told his brother that he did not want to see his face again, and that he was to pack his bags and leave his house immediately. It was a reaction not befitting of an older brother who had not yet had time to welcome his brother from overseas. Worse still, Moe'ono punched his son on the jaw so hard that the boy fell unconscious and, in the process, Moe'ono broke his own hand. His wife came to the boy's rescue.

Like Falefā, Lufilufi was also divided. Paralleling Moe'ono's role in Falefā village, a high-ranking *tulafale* of Lufilufi was also responsible for organizing the voters in his village to vote for Tupua. The high-ranking *tulafale* of Lufilufi comprise the six *tulafale* of the *faleono* (house of six), one of whose traditional responsibilities is to confer the Tui Ātua title. Thus, in accordance with traditions, they had to uphold the dignity, prestige and honour associated with the Tui Ātua title. In modern terms, this has meant making sure that any holder of the Tui Ātua title is victorious in all parliamentary elections. Better still, any holder of the Tui Ātua title should be elected unopposed. However, the Lufilufi *tulafale*, like his Falefā counterpart Moe'ono, encountered 'domestic' problems throughout the campaign. His own niece (sister's daughter) was among the vigorous campaigners for Moananu. As one of the leading *tulafale* of Lufilufi, he had to put his village and traditional obligations and responsibilities before immediate family relations; consequently, his niece and members of her immediate family were banished from the village.[4]

Tupua Tamasese 'Efi's defeat brought home to the traditionalist what they had always feared: giving the non-*matai* the right to vote undermined the *matai* system and all the values associated with it. Because the non-*matai* are not as well informed as the *matai* about customs and traditions, they do not see any value in adhering to them. Ignorance of customs and traditions can ultimately breed non-appreciation of the practices and values associated with them. Tupua regained his seat after two by-elections.[5] In his campaign before the first by-election on 9 August 1991, Tupua reminded some of the voters in the constituency, 'I am your *tama-a-'āiga*, something you cherish as dear to you'.[6] Likewise, Tupua's campaigners told other Anoāma'a East voters 'to vote for the *tama-a-'āiga*'.[7] In a different meeting with other Ānoāma'a East voters, Tupua told one of them,

'...I have a job in China but I have come back to carry my cross but I see that you are not helping to carry my cross'.[8] Tupua's comments implied the high regard with which the titles he holds are seen in Sāmoan eyes, and conversely, the humiliation of having the holders of the titles lose in a parliamentary election, and worse still, to a relatively low-ranking *matai* titleholder.[9]

Notes

1   For more information on the origin of Tuisāvailu'u and its socio-political status in Lefaga subdistrict and Ā'ana district, see Chapter 1.

2   Following the conferral of the Tui Ātua, Tupua and Tamasese titles on Lealofi IV in 1965, he was elected unopposed by Ānoāma'a East constituency as their MP in the 1970 general election. Being elected unopposed was befitting of the status of the titles he held; in accordance with traditions no one in his constituency should stand against him. He was again elected unopposed in the general election of 1973. However, with the increasing polarisation of parliament following the 1970 prime ministerial election, Tupua Tamasese L. IV had to fight for his seat in the 1976 general election. He won with 126 votes against his two rivals' combined votes of 51 (*WSG*, 6[40A], 5 March 1976). He was appointed to the council of deputies following Tupuola 'Efi's prime ministerial victory. Tupuola 'Efi succeeded to all the titles Lealofi IV held in 1987 following Lealofi IV's death on 9 July 1983. Having held all these titles, 'Efi switched constituency to Ānoāma'a East, Lealofi's old constituency, where he was elected unopposed in 1988. However, in 1991, he had to fight for his seat against a low-ranking *matai* from his own village of Falefā. More important in this context, though, was the manner in which support for him was being drummed up.

3   For the composition of Sa Fenunu'ivao and the respective responsibilities of the *tulafale* and *ali'i* comprising it, see Chapter 1.

4   Judgement of Chief Justice Ryan in *Fa'amatuāinu Tala Mailei and Suilaufetuani Feterika Manuō (Petitioners) vs Moananu Salale (Respondent)*, 12 June 1991; *Observer*, 10 April 1991.

5   Moananu Salale's election night win was later invalidated by the Supreme Court following evidence of treating. The court ordered a by-election which Tupua Tamasese won. Moananu Salale lodged an election petition claiming that Tupua Tamasese was guilty of treating. The petition was upheld by the court, which ordered another by-election. This by-election was again won by Tupua Tamasese. Moananu Salale decided not to file another election petition, thus allowing the speaker of parliament to confirm Tupua Tamasese's election in early 1992.

6   *The petition of Moananu Salale of Falefā*, Ānoāma'a East, a candidate for election, 20 August 1991, pp. 2–3.

7   *The petition of Moananu Salale of Falefā*, Ānoāma'a East, a candidate for election, 20 August 1991, p 8.

8   *The petition of Moananu Salale of Falefā*, Ānoāma'a East, a candidate for election, 20 August 1991, pp. 9–10.

9   It is a feeling experienced not only by any holder of the Tui Ātua, Tupua and Tamasese titles, but by all the families, *matai*, villages and districts associated with these titles. Throughout their whole political careers, the other two *tama-a-'āiga*, Matā'afa F. M. and Tupua Tamasese Lealofi IV, had never lost their parliamentary seats.

References

Abbreviations used in citations:

PIM	*Pacific Islands Monthly*
SB	*Sāmoa Bulletin*
SO	*Sāmoan Observer*
SR	*Sāmoa R*
ST	*Sāmoa Times*
CCD	*Constitutional Convention Debates*
SNL	*Sāmoa Newsline*
WCM	*Working Committee [on self-government] Minutes*
WSG	*Western Sāmoa Gazette*
WSH	*Western Sāmoa Hansard*

Ah Mu, A. 2007. 'Thousands march, say no to RHD', *Sāmoa Observer*, 18 December 2007.

_____ 2006a. 'Court warns Lano', *Sāmoa Observer*, 8 August 2008.

_____ 2006b. 'Court critical of Lano petition', *Sāmoa Observer*, 16 August 2008.

_____ 2006c. 'Su'a's back in Lano', *Sāmoa Observer*, 5 November 2006.

_____ 2006d. 'Lepou's banishment illegal and not customary, court says', *Sāmoa Observer*.

_____ 1993. 'A blow to free press', *Pacific Islands Monthly*, 63(4).

Ah Mu, A. and Semu, A.T. 2006a. 'Sua banned Mulitalo unaware', *Sāmoa Observer*, 19 July 2006.

_____ 2006b. 'Lotolano burned', *Sāmoa Observer*, 18 August 2006.

_____ 2006c. 'Lepea respects court letter, stops banning', *Sāmoa Observer*, 21 March 2006.

Aiāvao, U. 1993. 'Sāmoa's rulers search for sources', *Islands Business*, 19(3).

Ai'ono, F. 1992. 'The Sāmoan culture and government', *Culture and Democracy in the South Pacific*, Suva, Fiji: Institute of Pacific Studies, University of the South Pacific.

Ala'ilima, F. C. and Ala'ilima, V. J. 1966. 'Consensus and plurality in a Western Sāmoan election campaign', *Human Organization*, 25(3).

Ale, L. L. I. 1990. 'The development of political parties in Western Sāmoa', an unpublished essay in the author's possession.

Anon. n.d. *O 'Gafa' Eseese o Sāmoa ına ia Faitau i ai Tupulaga Tuufaasolo i le aga'i i luma.* (A4, photocopy, bound, no place of publication, copy in author's possession.)

Boyd, M. 1969. 'The decolonization of Western Sāmoa': *In* P. Munz (ed.) *The Feel of Truth: Essays in the New Zealand and Pacific History.* New Zealand: A. H. and A. W. Reed.

_____ 1968. 'The military administration of Western Sāmoa 1914–1919', *The New Zealand Journal of History*, 2(2):148–164

'British Consulate Apia (BCA) – Foreign Office to Consuls, 1851-1887': *In* Gilson Papers – Folder 101, Reading Room, Department of Pacific and Asian History, The Australian National University, Canberra.

'British Consulate Apia (BCA) – Foreign Office to Consuls, 1848-1887': *In* Gilson Papers – Folder 102, Reading Room, Department of Pacific and Asian History, The Australian National University, Canberra.

'British Consulate Apia (BCA) – Foreign Office to Consuls, 1848-1887': *In* Gilson Papers, Reading Room, Department of Pacific and Asian History, The Australian National University, Canberra.

Davidson, J. W. 1967. *Sāmoa Mo Sāmoa: The Emergence of the Independent State of Western Sāmoa.* Melbourne: Oxford University Press.

_____ 1966. 'Problems in Pacific history', *The Journal of Pacific History*, 1(5).

Davidson Papers, held at the National Library of Australia.

Duverger, M. 1954. *Political Parties: Their Organisation and Activity in the Modern State.* Translated by Barbara and Robert North with a Foreword by D. W. Brogan. Cambridge: University Printing House.

Ella, S. 1895. 'The ancient Sāmoan government', *Reports, Australasian Association for the Advancement of Science*, 6.

Eteuati, K. 1982. '*Evaevaga a Sāmoa*: Assertion of Sāmoan autonomy', unpublished PhD thesis, The Australian National University, Canberra.

Fa'afia, L. 2007. 'He's back in parliament', *Sāmoa Observer*, 21 April 2007.

Field, M. J. 1984. *MAU: Sāmoa's Struggle for Freedom.* Auckland: Polynesian Press.

Firth, S. (ed.) 2006. *Globalisation and Governance in the Pacific Islands.* Canberra: ANU EPress.

Geraghty, P. 1991. 'Proto Central Pacific, Pulotu, and the Polynesian homeland'. Paper presented at the Sixth International Conference on Austronesian Linguistics, Honolulu, May 1991.

Gilson, R P. 1970. *Sāmoa 1830 to 1900: The Politics of the Multi-cultural Community.* Melbourne: Oxford University Press.

Gilson Papers, held at Reading Room of Pacific and South-east Asian History Department – The Australian National University, and at the National Library of Australia, Canberra.

'Gurr Papers' *In*: Gilson Papers – Folder 86, Reading Room, Department of Pacific and Asian History, The Australian National University.

Henry, F. 1980. *SĀMOA: An early History*. Pago Pago: American Sāmoa Department of Education.

Holstine, J. 1971. 'American Diplomacy in Sāmoa 1884-1889', Ph D thesis, University of Indiana, Michigan, University Microfilms.

Howe, K. R. 1977. 'The fate of the 'savage' in Pacific historiography', *The New Zealand Journal of History* 11(2):137–154.

Jagmohan, M. (ed.) 1993. 'Growing Pains for the Media', *Pacific Islands Monthly*. 63(4):4.

Kelekolio, M. 2007. 'PM tells why RHD', *Sāmoa Observer*, 15 December 2007.

Kennedy, P. M. 1974. *The Sāmoan Tangle: A Study in Anglo-German-American Relations 1878-1900*. Dublin: Irish University Press.

Kramer, A. [1902] 1994. *The Sāmoa Islands*, Volume I. Translated by Dr. Theodore Verhaaren, Polynesian Press.

Lafai, S. F. S. A. 1988. *O le Mavaega i le Tai*. Apia: Malua Printing Press.

Leala'i'auloto, N. K. and Fuataga, L. T. 1985. *O le Faavae o Sāmoa Anamua*. Apia: Malua Printing and Publishing.

Lesā, K., 2006a. 'PM sleeps easy, HRPP sweeps back', *Sāmoa Observer*, 1 April 200.

_____ 2006b. 'Misa wins vote by 10', *Sāmoa Observer*, 12 April 2006.

_____ 2006c. 'HRPP rejects independents', *Sāmoa Observer*, 4 April 2006.

Le Tagaloa, P. 1991. *Ofa: Se Faalepo po o se Faalani*. Apia: Pacific Printers Company Limited.

Liua'ana, F. 2001. 'Sāmoa Tula'i: ecclesiastical and political face of Samoa's independence', PhD Thesis, The Australian National University, Canberra.

_____ 1993. '*Tali i le lagi sou malo*: Sāmoan Christians and Sāmoan politics, 1830-1899', unpublished Master of Theology thesis, Pacific Theological College, Fiji.

_____ 1991. 'Resurrecting *aitu* as a contemporary theological concept', unpublished Bachelor of Divinity thesis, Pacific Theological College, Fiji.

'London Missionary Society, South Sea Letters, 1836-1879', *In*: Gilson Papers – Folders Numbers 19, 20, 21, 22, 23 ,24, Reading Room, Department of Pacific and Asian History, The National University of Australia, Canberra.

Ma'ilo, S. P. 1972. *Tusi o le Vaega Lua lenei o le Aganuu Sāmoa "O Sāmoa o le atunu'u tofi: ae le o se atunu'u taliola ua faavae i tu faaaloalo ma upu faaaloalo": I le Tofa Loloto a Tamalii ma le Faautaga Mamao a Tulafale*. Apia: Western Sāmoa.

Meleiseā, M. 1995. 'To whom gods and men crowded: Chieftainship and hierarchy in ancient Sāmoa', *In*: J. Huntsman, ed., *Tongan and Sāmoa: Images of Gender and Polity*, Macmillan Brown Centre, University of Canterbury.

Meleiseā, M. 1987a. *The Making of Modern Sāmoa: Traditional authority and colonial administration in the history of Western Sāmoa*. Suva, Fiji: Institute of Pacific Studies, University of the South Pacific.

_____ 1987b. 'Ideology in Pacific Studies: A personal view', *In*: A Hooper, *et al.*, eds., *Class and Culture in the South Pacific*. Centre for Pacific Studies, University of Auckland, NZ and Institute of Pacific Studies, University of the South Pacific, Fiji.

Meleiseā, M. and Meleiseā, P. (eds). 1987. *Lagaga: A short history of Western Sāmoa*. Suva: Institute of Pacific Studies, University of the South Pacific, Fiji.

Methodist Conference Records, 1857-1913', *In*: Gilson Papers – Folder 26, Reading Room, Department of Pacific and Asian History, The National University of Australia, Canberra.

Morrell, W. P. 1960. *Britain in the Pacific Islands*. London: Oxford University Press.

Moses, J. A. 1972. 'The Solf regime in Western Sāmoa: ideal and reality', *The New Zealand Journal of History*, 6(1):42-56.

Neumann, S. 1956. *Modern Political Parties*. Chicago: University of Chicago Press.

Powles, C. G. 1979. 'The Persistence of Chiefly Power in Western Polynesia', unpublished Ph D. thesis, The Australian National University, Canberra.

_____ 1973. 'The status of customary law in Western Sāmoa', Master of Laws thesis, Victoria University of Wellington, NZ.

_____ 1970. 'Fundamental rights in the Constitution of Western Sāmoa', Research paper submitted to Victoria University of Wellington, NZ, September 1970.

Pratt, G. 1862. *Pratt's Grammar and Dictionary of the Sāmoan Language*. Apia: Malua Printing Press.

Rampell, E. 1988. 'Sāmoa's principle PM', *Pacific Islands Monthly*, 59(9):46-49.

Said, E. W. 1995. *Orientalism*. Penguin Books.

Schoeffel, P. 1999. 'Samoan exchange and fine mats: an historical reconsideration', *The Journal of Polynesian Society*, 108(2).

Sio, M., 2006. 'Sua fined, returns award', *Sāmoa Observer*, 29 September 2006.

So'o, A. 2005. 'Political parties in Samoa', *In*: R. Rich, ed., *Forthcoming*.

So'o, A. 2000. 'Civil and political liberty: the case of Sāmoa', *In*: E. Huffer and A. So'o, eds, *Governance in Sāmoa: Pulega i Sāmoa*, IPS Publications, The University of the South Pacific.

So'o, A. 1993. 'Universal suffrage in Western Sāmoa: the 1991 general elections',

Regime Change and Regime Maintenance in Asia and the Pacific, Discussion Paper Series, Number 10, Political and Social Change, Research School of Pacific and Asian Studies, The Australian National University, Canberra.

Stair, J. B. [1897] 1983. *Old SÅMOA or Flotsam and Jetsam from the Pacific Ocean.* Papakura: R Macmillan Publisher.

_____ 1895. 'Early Sāmoan voyages and settlement', *Reports, Australasian Association for the Advancement of Science,* 6(6)12–8.

Stathis S. W. 1982, 'Albert B. Steinberger: President Grant's man in Sāmoa', *The Hawaiian Journal of History,* 16:85–111.

Stevenson, R. L. 1892. *A Footnote to History: Eight Years of Trouble in Sāmoa.* New York: Charles Scribner's Sons.

'The Sāmoa Law Code, 1873', *In:* Folder 75, Gilson Papers, Reading Room, Department of Pacific and Asian History, The Australian National University, Canberra.

'The Steinberger Constitution [1875]', *In:* Folder 75, Gilsons Papers, Reading Room, Department of Pacific and Asian History, The Australian National University, Canberra.

Tupua, T. E. 1995. 'Tamafaiga – Shaman, King or Maniac?', *The Journal of the Pacific History,* 30(1):3–21.

_____ 1994. 'The riddle in Sāmoan history', *The Journal of the Pacific History,* 29(1):66–79.

_____ 1992. 'Who is the son of a bitch who drew this map', A paper presented at the IX Pacific History Association Conference, 2–5 December, University of Canterbury, Christchurch, New Zealand.

Turner, G. 1884. *SÅMOA: A hundred years ago and long before.* Reprinted by Institute of Pacific Studies, University of the South Pacific, Fiji, 1984.

Ulale, U.P. 1991. 'Proposed restructure and reorganization of the Human Rights Protection Party', unpublished document a copy of which is in the present author's possession.

Va'a, F. 1989. 'The emergence and significance of new political parties in Western Sāmoa', unpublished Paper presented at the Pacific Islands Political Science Association, 1989.

_____ 1977. 'The heads of tall poppies roll in Western Sāmoa', *Pacific Islands Monthly,* 48(3):11-12.

_____ 1976a. 'Home rules for Sāmoa Minister', *Pacific Islands Monthly,* 47(6):10-11.

_____ 1976b. 'Sāmoan indigestion on the way', *Pacific Islands Monthly,* 47(9):19.

_____ 1975. 'Is the dominance of royal sons ending in Sāmoa?', *Pacific Islands Monthly,* 46(6):15, 73.

_____ 1974a. 'Experience wins in Sāmoan fono fight', *Pacific Islands Monthly*, 45(2).

_____ 1974b. 'Economic hari-kari', *Pacific Islands Monthly*, 45(2).

_____ 1974c. 'Opposition leaders challenges the princes', *Pacific Islands Monthly*, 45(3).

Va'ai, S. 1999. *Samoa Fa'amatai and the Rule of Law*. Apia: National University of Sāmoa.

Wendt, A. 1965. 'Guardians and Wards', Unpublished M. A. thesis, Victoria University of Wellington, NZ.

Wilkes, C. 1845, Narrative of the United States Exploring Expedition, during the years 1838, 1839, 1840, 1841, 1842. Philadelphia: Lea and Blanchard.

Index